From Classrooms to Conflict in Rwanda

This book questions the conventional wisdom that education builds peace by exploring the ways in which ordinary schooling can contribute to intergroup conflict. Based on fieldwork and comparative historical analysis of Rwanda, it argues that from the colonial period to the genocide, schooling was a key instrument of the state in contributing to the construction, awareness, collectivization, and inequality of ethnic groups in Rwanda – all factors that underlay conflict. The book further argues that today's post-genocide schools are dangerously replicating past trends. This book is the first to offer an in-depth study of education in Rwanda and to analyze its role in the genesis of conflict. The book demonstrates that to build peace, we cannot simply prescribe *more* education, but must understand who has access to schools, how schools are set up, and what and how they teach.

Dr. Elisabeth King is a Fellow at the Balsillie School of International Affairs in Waterloo, Canada. She holds a PhD in Political Science from the University of Toronto (2008) and was a Postdoctoral Research Fellow at Columbia University (2008–2012). Dr. King works on issues at the intersection of conflict, peacebuilding, and development in Sub-Saharan Africa. She has published articles in *African Studies Review*, the *Journal of Genocide Studies and Prevention*, and the *Journal of Development Effectiveness*, and she has contributed chapters to several edited volumes. Dr. King has conducted fieldwork in Croatia, India, Kenya, Liberia, the Philippines, Rwanda, and Tanzania. She has worked with nongovernmental organizations on the global landmine crisis, world literacy, and community-driven development, and she is currently working on several development impact evaluations. She uses a variety of research methods to examine how development and peacebuilding efforts really work (or not) for people in the Global South.

To the children of Rwanda

From Classrooms to Conflict in Rwanda

ELISABETH KING

Balsillie School of International Affairs, Waterloo, Canada

CAMBRIDGE
UNIVERSITY PRESS

CAMBRIDGE
UNIVERSITY PRESS

32 Avenue of the Americas, New York NY 10013-2473, USA

Cambridge University Press is part of the University of Cambridge.

It furthers the University's mission by disseminating knowledge in the pursuit of education, learning and research at the highest international levels of excellence.

www.cambridge.org
Information on this title: www.cambridge.org/9781107557550

First published 2014
First paperback edition 2015

A catalogue record for this publication is available from the British Library

Library of Congress Cataloguing in Publication data
King, Elisabeth, 1978– author.
From classrooms to confl ict in Rwanda / Elisabeth King, Balsillie School of International Affairs, Waterloo, Canada.
    page   cm
Includes bibliographical references and index.
ISBN 978-1-107-03933-9 (hardback)
1. Education – Social aspects – Rwanda.   2. Ethnic confl ict – Rwanda.   3. Discrimination in education – Rwanda.   4. Rwanda – Ethnic relations.   I. Title.
LA2090.R95K56   2013
306.4320967571–dc23   2013013356

ISBN 978-1-107-03933-9 Hardback
ISBN 978-1-107-55755-0 Paperback

Contents

Figures

Preface and Acknowledgments

When I was a student in the French-language school system in Ontario, Canada, I learned history from a different perspective from my friends attending English-language schools. In my education, for example, the 1759 battle on the Plains of Abraham, after which French troops had to relinquish New France (Québec) to Great Britain, was presented as a pivotal moment in our country's history. Many friends studying in English-language schools could barely remember the Plains of Abraham. In pondering our country's conflict between Anglophones and Francophones, it struck me as important that I had a different understanding of where we had been as a country from the many Anglophones who became my university classmates. I wondered about similar situations in countries that suffer even more acute conflict, especially violent ethnic conflict. When I later had the opportunity to visit Bosnia-Herzegovina as part of my NGO work on the landmine issue, a local colleague pointed out two schools, at the end of a road, one for Croats and one for Bosniaks, in a place where there had been one before the war. I intuitively felt that this move was in the wrong direction. During graduate school, when I pursued my strong interest in post-conflict peacebuilding, I was surprised by how schooling was left out of most political science texts on the subject, and how, when it was included, it was often mentioned in passing as an important part of rebuilding a society after conflict, without details or questions. As I became interested in Rwanda, which was, then and now, undertaking significant educational reform, I realized that a study such as the one undertaken here could make an important contribution. When I present this book, people often approach me to discuss how it resonates with their personal experiences in places as different as Afghanistan, Israel, and the United States. I approach this book as a great believer in the power and promise of education.

Thank you, merci, and *murakoze*, to the many people who helped bring this book to fruition. This project would not have been possible without the generosity of the many Rwandans who agreed to share their experiences with me. I will always remember the warm welcome and long conversations with the Rwandans who opened their homes to me, introduced me to their families and friends, took me for my first goat brochette, and helped me make my way through the hills of Rwanda. Officials at the Rwandan Ministry of Education also helped make this study possible. Several Rwandan-Canadians were invaluable in helping me plan my research and fieldwork. I promised all of these participants anonymity and thus cannot thank them by name.

My research in Belgium was aided by the members of Mémoires du Congo who helped me track down missionaries and administrators who had served in Rwanda's colonial period. The conversations I had with these individuals, to whom I also promised anonymity, were fascinating and greatly enriched my analysis.

This book began in the Department of Political Science at the University of Toronto. I became intrigued by Africa and especially Rwanda thanks to Richard Sandbrook; committed to peacebuilding thanks to Robert O. Matthews; and dedicated to further exploring education thanks to Kathy Bickmore. The manuscript took shape at Columbia University, working under the mentorship of Macartan Humphreys, from whom I learned a great deal. The book was published while I was based at the Balsillie School of International Affairs, thanks in large part to support and guidance from David Welch. Each of these institutions, and the people based there, provided welcome and thought-provoking environments in which to forward this work. Throughout the research, writing, and publication process, Séverine Autesserre, Dana Burde, and Ian Spears provided especially careful reading, ideas, and friendship. I was also fortunate to benefit from conversations and advice from many other generous scholars and practitioners including Monisha Bajaj, Lili Cole, Peter Coleman, the late Alison Des Forges, Danielle de Lame, Tad Homer-Dixon, Jean-Damascène Gasanabo, Herb Hirsch, Mahmood Mamdani, Karen Mundy, Karen Murphy, John Mutter, Catharine Newbury, Filip Reyntjens, Alana Tiemessen, Katherine Reilly, Marc Howard Ross, Jack Snyder, Scott Straus, Susan Thomson, JennWallner, Peter Uvin, Sarah Warshauer Freedman, and Harvey Weinstein. Contributions from discussants, co-panelists, and audience members at numerous conferences and workshops also improved this book. In writing a book about education, I do not underestimate the impact of all these teachers on me and my work.

Noel Anderson, Travis Coulter, Katie Degendorfer, Aaron Kates-Rose, Max Margulies, Sarah Ngu, Henry Wells, and Aliénor Westphalen – most of whom were at some point my students, from whom I always learn a lot – provided various forms of research support and assistance. Stephanie Bouris, Maude Patry, Sarah Pilon, and Florence Ting helped with transcription. Jean-Pierre Rubibi provided excellent Kinyarwanda-French translation. René Lemarchand kindly allowed me to reprint a figure from his book *Rwanda and Burundi*. David Cox designed the map and Kevin Millham skillfully created the index.

Thanks to Lew Bateman, Shaun Vigil, and their colleagues at Cambridge University Press who turned my manuscript into a book. The excellent suggestions from two anonymous reviewers made this book much stronger, and I hope they recognize their inspiration in many passages. Of course, the remaining errors are my own.

Generous funding for this project came from the Social Sciences and Humanities Research Council of Canada (SSHRC), the Canadian Consortium on Human Security, the University of Toronto's Department of Graduate Studies and Trudeau Peace and Conflict Centre, and Columbia University's Earth Institute and Institute for Social and Economic Research and Policy (ISERP).

A long list of family and friends also helped make this book possible and I am grateful to them all. I especially acknowledge my parents and sister, Ann, Chris, and Jessica Farrell; my uncle and aunt, Ken and Danuta Kitay; my parents-in-law, Shannon and Lloyd Noseworthy; and my dear friend Tara Bedford. Thanks finally to my husband, David Noseworthy, who supported me in so many ways and who asked me on innumerable occasions "tell me more about Rwanda," and to our beautiful one-year-old daughter, Ella Josephine, who already loves books.

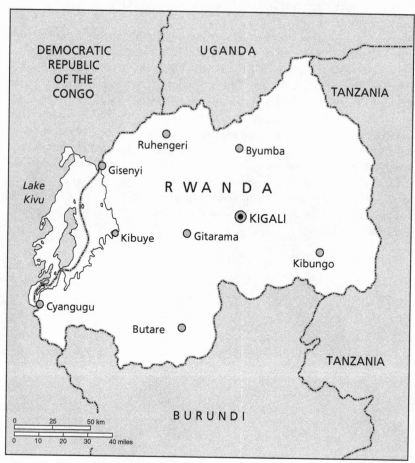

FIGURE O.I Map of Rwanda.

Introduction

In the aftermath of the 1994 genocide, which left approximately 800,000 people dead and a country devastated, Rwanda's young people are vested with great hope and responsibility. With nearly 43 percent of Rwanda's population under the age of fourteen, it is easy to see why this would be the case.[1] As a representative of Rwanda's National Unity and Reconciliation Commission (NURC) explained, "It's easier to transform youth than it may be to transform someone who is fifty years old."[2] Schooling plays a key role in the country's transformation. The Rwandan government is currently investing significantly in schools and placing tremendous faith in the power of education as a tool of unity and reconciliation. One young teacher at a girl's school in northern Rwanda told me, "We teach about reconciliation. We teach to never again take the same actions as in the past and to find ways to bring everyone together, to foster friendship, and to not dream of killing others."[3] The last panel on display at Rwanda's main genocide memorial sums up the beliefs of many: "Education has become our way forward."

Indeed, many Rwandans, the Rwandan government, and some scholars tend to explain intergroup conflict, and especially the genocide, by a lack of education. I heard repeatedly in my interviews that a lack of formal education resulted in societal ignorance.[4] Nearly 88 percent of Rwandans interviewed by the senate for its report, *Genocide Ideology*, thought that ignorance played

---

[1] CIA, 2012.

[2] Author's interview, National Unity and Reconciliation Commission, Kigali, March 29, 2006. Most interviews were conducted in French, and quotes are the author's translation. Quotes from other French-language sources have also been translated by the author.

[3] Author's interview, female of unknown ethnicity, northern Rwanda, March 21(A), 2006. The letters after the dates, such as A here, distinguish, wherever appropriate, multiple interviews that took place on the same date.

[4] See also Gourevitch 1998, p. 180; Njoroge 2007. On the prominence of this narrative, see Longman and Rutagengwa 2004; Zorbas 2009.

a "high" or "very high" role in the genocide.[5] These explanations reflect the
common view that education leads to better understanding between members
of different, often hostile, groups.

Yet, as this book shows, the education system in Rwanda has and continues to play a more harmful role in intergroup relations. I spoke with a Tutsi
teacher, who had lost most of her family in the genocide, about the relationship
between schooling and conflict. Having been a student in the 1970s and 1980s
under a Hutu-dominated government, whose hard-liners ultimately orchestrated the genocide, she reflected:

> I think that education contributed a lot [to violent conflict] because from primary
> school, from the youngest age, you had to differentiate the Hutu and the Tutsi.
> Every time Tutsi were the minority in relation to the Hutu. We were also taught
> in history that the Tutsi had in some way been exported, that they came from the
> north near the Nile river, that they met Twa and Hutu here [in Rwanda] and that
> they sort of colonized the country. They said all this and we learned it from a very
> young age. I think that it is normal that there be hatred between Hutu and Tutsi
> starting from this very young age.
>
> ... My little sister would tell me that at primary school, they asked you to stand
> up (because even in class they would ask "Hutu get up, Tutsi get up") and from
> a certain moment my little sister didn't want to get up because she found that
> they were just two [Tutsi] in class. Every time she would ask, "Why aren't I like
> everyone else?" She felt a bit marginalized. And then, you grew up with this as
> if you are born of an ethnicity that colonized the other. And then, as you grow
> up, you don't feel comfortable at school with the other students. And the Hutu
> were proud because they were the majority, and moreover that they were the
> indigenous, those that should be in the country. The others [Tutsi] shouldn't be
> in the country.
>
> Then, at the end of primary school, we did an exam that we call in Kinyarwanda,
> *iringaniza* [rough translation: social justice], to share the places in secondary
> school. You had to have, I don't remember quite well the percentage, I think it
> was something like 2 percent Tutsi, 98 percent Hutu, 1 percent Twa, something
> like that. And they taught us that. You had to have an ethnic equilibrium. You
> studied, even if you were first in your class, all the while knowing about *irin-
> ganiza*. Even if you had a lot higher grades than a Hutu, the Hutu had to pass
> first. And we had that in our heads, the Hutu's right to study. Tutsi felt [left out],
> even if at a certain moment we came to accept that. You told yourself that that
> was the way it was and that it could not be otherwise. As we are the minority,
> the majority had to go to school. The minority would come afterwards. And we
> thought this from a young age.
>
> ... Even from the youngest age you learned that ... [Tutsi] found Rwanda and
> thought it was a nice country, so they settled, and little by little they took the land
> of the Hutu who were there. Well, they taught us that in primary school. They
> taught us that in history. And you had to learn it by heart because you were asked

5 RoRa 2006, pp. 99 and 156.

it on an exam. Imagine what that does in the head of a child. Yes, I think [education] really contributed [to conflict].[6]

The post-genocide, Tutsi-led government has likewise blamed pre-genocide schooling for failing the nation.[7] Yet allegations of the links between education and conflict do not stem from Tutsi alone or from only the pre-genocide period.[8] I heard variants on the key themes that this teacher raised from Hutu and Tutsi who were educated in both the colonial period and since the genocide. Teasing out the various roles of schooling in peace and conflict is essential for moving forward with educational scholarship and practice. Moreover, insight into education's nuanced role is crucial for understanding the genesis of ethnic conflicts in Rwanda's past and for thinking carefully about the country's future.[9]

Key Questions

We are faced with conflicting narratives about the effects of education on conflict. Some praise schooling for its role in conflict prevention and peacebuilding, while others blame schools for fomenting violent conflict. How can these accounts be reconciled? To address this dilemma, I pose several questions in the context of Rwanda: How has formal education in Rwanda contributed to intergroup conflict and/or its mitigation? Through what channels? What does Rwanda's experience teach us about the role of education in conflict and peacebuilding more generally?

A Conversation between Education and Peace and Conflict Scholars

Answering these questions involves much needed cross-disciplinary dialogue between scholars and practitioners of education and those who work on peace and conflict. The education literature is stronger in its understanding of the importance of education and its potential for peace, but weaker in explaining how education contributes to violent intergroup conflict, especially at a societal level. In contrast, the peace and conflict literature has stronger theories on violent intergroup conflict (which I shorthand as "conflict" throughout, recognizing more generally, of course, that not all conflict is violent), but is weak in terms of appreciating the importance of education, as well as how a

---

[6] Author's interview, female Tutsi, Kigali, February 8(G), 2006.

[7] RoR 2002b p. 5; RoR 1995 pp. 5, 16, 25, 44, 56.

[8] Following the practice of numerous scholars, I do not pluralize the nouns Hutu, Tutsi, and Twa by adding an "s". Some have alleged that this practice collectivizes Hutu, Tutsi, and Twa individuals. In contrast, I found that it most often reflects Rwandans' own usage of these terms in English and French.

[9] While I recognize, in this book, some common roots of different forms of violent conflict and genocide, I am not contending that they have all of the same underlying causes, or proximate causes, or that they manifest themselves in the same way.

nuanced understanding of education illuminates conflict and the potential for peace. The dialogue in this book addresses these weaknesses and thus advances both fields.

First, the same educational trends that I heard in Rwanda are common the world over, particularly in mainstream educational conversations. The dominant view is that education contributes to building peace. When wars end, the international community rallies to get children back into schools. After the fall of the Taliban in Afghanistan, for example, reopening schools was a top priority for the foreign forces, and the world cheered the return of three million children, including girls, to classrooms. As the Director General of the United Nations Educational, Scientific and Cultural Organization (UNESCO) stated, "Education ... will enable us to move from a culture of war, which we unhappily know only too well, to a culture of peace."[10] The UN's *Education for All* action reports also present education as one of the best means of averting conflict and overcoming violence.[11] Similarly, at a special session of the UN General Assembly on education in conflict-affected contexts, the representative from Iraq commented that "[l]ack of education is a more deadly weapon than the most destructive arms."[12] In the past fifteen years, a significant subfield of "education in emergencies" has developed, centered on short-term educational responses to conflict and the importance of educational service provision as part of humanitarian action.[13]

Others focus on the relationship between education and violent conflict. Usually, when we hear about education and conflict, the causal arrow points from conflict to education, examining how conflict disrupts the provision of education. Graça Machel emphasizes the interruption of schooling in her well-known report, *The Impact of Armed Conflict on Children*, and the 2011 *Education for All Global Monitoring Report* identifies the impact of armed conflict on education as a "hidden crisis."[14] Indeed, conflict is likely to hinder the achievement of universal education targets significantly; while conflict-affected and fragile states are home to 18 percent of the world's children of primary school age, they account for 42 percent of the world's out-of-school children in this age group.[15] Among educators, there is also acknowledgment that schools themselves become sites of violence. Recent reports note widespread attacks and threats against students, teachers, and schools around the world.[16]

[10] Quoted in Harber 1996, p. 151.
[11] Education For All Global Monitoring Report team 2004.
[12] Author's notes upon attending.
[13] See, for example, Aguilar and Retama 1998; Inter-Agency Network for Education in Emergencies & UNESCO 2004; Nicolai and Tripplehorn 2003; Pigozzi 1999.
[14] Education For All Global Monitoring Report team 2011; Machel 2001.
[15] Education For All Global Monitoring Report team 2011, pp. 2 and 15.
[16] O'Malley 2010; UN General Assembly 2011; UNESCO 2010b.

In contrast, scholars have only infrequently reversed the arrow of causation to investigate the link from education to violent conflict – an imbalance this book seeks to address. This reversal, which considers the potentially fraught relationship between education and conflict, can be placed alongside the broader move in development practice, initiated largely after the Rwandan genocide, to reassess initiatives previously assumed socially neutral or positive. Thus, scholars and practitioners began to question the role of "ordinary," everyday education and to acknowledge that education's role in conflict has "two faces" – one positive, one negative.[17] Alongside the more common "positive face," the "negative face" of education recognizes the harmful effects of inequitable distribution of schooling, cultural repression through schooling, and propagandistic textbooks that promote intolerance.[18] Yet, despite recent interest in "education and fragility" and more widespread, if still limited, acknowledgment of the "two faces" of education in conflict, our understanding of how, and to what extent, education may contribute to conflict remains limited. Education specialists know more about "education politics" – that is, issues internal to education systems – than about "the politics of education," which asks how schooling interacts with broader societal systems.[19] In other words, we still know relatively little about how and what types of formal schooling conduce to violent intergroup conflict at the societal level.[20] More than a decade after the idea of "two faces" was introduced, calls for better frameworks and stronger empirical research remain widespread.[21]

Meanwhile, in both peace and conflict studies and international studies – disciplines that specifically study the causes of violent intergroup conflict – education is relegated to the margins. To illustrate, I conducted a quantitative analysis of articles published in the two top peace and conflict journals (*Journal of Peace Research*, JPR; *Journal of Conflict Resolution*, JCR).[22] I also analyzed the five journals published by the International Studies Association (*International Studies Quarterly*, *International Studies Review*, *International Studies Perspectives*, *Foreign Policy Analysis*, and *International Political Sociology*). Covering all articles from 1994, the year of the Rwandan genocide, to 2010, I did a broad search for the terms "schools" and/or "educat*" (thus including educate, education, educators, etc.) in the title, keywords, and/

[17] These include Bush and Saltarelli 2000; Davies 2004; Inter-Agency Network for Education in Emergencies Undated; Salmi 2000; Smith and Vaux 2003; Tawil and Harley 2004; Williams 2004; Williams and McGill 2004. See also Paulson 2008.
[18] Bush and Saltarelli 2000.
[19] Bird 2009 p. 4; Novelli and Cardozo 2008.
[20] Davies 2004, p. 5; Kuppermitz and Salomon 2005; Salomon 2002.
[21] Bird 2009; Burde et al. 2010; Davies 2005; Inter-Agency Network for Education in Emergencies Undated, p.10.
[22] These are the top journals focusing on peace and conflict in the *Social Sciences Citation Index* (Thomson Reuters) *Journal Citation Reports*. By impact factor, they rank fifth and fifteenth, respectively, in the more general "political science" category. Thanks to Clark-Kazak 2011 for the inspiration.

or abstract.[23] Only 1.5 percent of the articles published in the peace and conflict journals (or 37 of 2,341 articles), and just 3 percent of articles published in the International Studies Association journals (or 76 of 2,500 articles) emerged from this search. Taken together, only slightly more than 2 percent of articles published in these seven journals referred to schools or education. When I dropped articles on curricula and pedagogical techniques targeted at universities in North America and Europe, as well as hits from terms like "schools of thought," education is even more clearly at the periphery. Only 1 percent of articles in JPR and JCR and only 0.5 percent of articles in the five International Studies Association journals address education substantively, or as a variable of interest, even if one among many.

My qualitative examination of these articles shows that when education is studied in relation to conflict, it is addressed in particular ways. Education is most frequently considered in the context of peacebuilding, usually meaning nonformal education. Articles include studies of the impact of peace education programs on perceptions of peace, the importance of grassroots education in overcoming weaknesses in peace agreements, the role of public education in addressing the emotional and symbolic roots of conflict, and education's impact on one's propensity to forgive.[24]

When, in fairly rare cases, education is considered in the context of *conflict*, conflict is often studied as the independent variable with education as the dependent variable. Lai and Thyne, for example, find that civil war decreases education expenditures and enrollment and is "devastating" for education systems.[25]

When education is studied as the independent variable with conflict as the dependent variable, most studies examine the impact of net societal education rates on the likelihood of conflict or on individuals joining a rebellion. In a cross-national study of regions in Sub-Saharan Africa, Gudrun Østby and colleagues find that lower education levels increase the risk that a region will experience conflict onset – a finding that is statistically significant and strong. They posit that education likely represents the recruitment costs of conflict. An oft-cited study by Paul Collier and Anke Hoeffler also shows a positive correlation between low levels of education and the probability of conflict, focusing on male secondary education as a proxy for opportunity for rebel recruitment. Some case studies relying on individual-level surveys make similar claims. In examining the case of Nigeria, Aderoju Oyefusi finds that low educational attainment increases the probability that one joins a rebel group and suggests low opportunity cost for recruitment as the key mechanism. He discovers that moving from no education to completion of primary school, from completion

[23] Three of the journals (*International Studies Perspectives, Foreign Policy Analysis,* and *International Political Sociology*) were searched back to their inaugural volumes in 2000, 2005, and 2007, respectively.
[24] Azar, Mullet, and Vinsonneau 1999; Biton and Salomon 2006; Kaufman 2006; Maney et al. 2006.
[25] Lai and Thyne 2007.

of primary school to completion of secondary school, or from completion of secondary school to completion of tertiary education reduces the odds of a person's willingness to join a rebel group by 36 percent. Macartan Humphreys and Jeremy Weinstein similarly found that in Sierra Leone, uneducated youth were nine times more likely to become rebels than people who had completed post-primary schooling.[26] Overall, in this rebel recruitment literature, lack of education is highlighted as a contributor to conflict, but is measured by its quantity. Schooling is treated as a simple binary variable without examination of its quality or heterogeneous effects.

Other scholars build and elaborate on the rebel recruitment thesis.[27] Clayton Thyne shows strong pacifying effects of both primary enrollment and secondary male enrollment on likelihood of conflict onset, and also suggests two additional mechanisms, aside from opportunity costs, by which education may reduce conflict likelihood. First, educational investment is a signal to citizens that their government is committed to improving their lives, thereby lowering grievances. Second, education provides people with the tools to resolve conflicts peacefully. This model thus includes the quality and content of education. Problematically, however, it virtually equates quantity with quality, making untenable assumptions about the content of education. Only a few articles that emerged in my search otherwise examine the impact of quality and content of education on conflict and violence.[28] These articles are preoccupied with Islamic madrassas and fundamentalist teaching, a focus that has also become popular in the press in the aftermath of September 11.[29]

In sum, education is marginalized in peace and conflict studies and international studies. When this literature considers education's role in conflict, it usually concentrates on a lack of schooling, not on how schooling itself can contribute to conflict. Schooling is generally treated as a black box without examination of who has access or of the educational and psychocultural processes going on in schools. In contrast, I argue that schooling itself can contribute to underlying conflict, and that unpacking the structure of schools, as well as the content of education, matters in this process. Understanding the role that schools play in conflict fills in important parts of an overall picture of intergroup conflict.

Arguments: Education as a Key Piece of the Puzzle

The concept of education is the linchpin of this book. By education I mean formal state-led schooling and use the terms "schooling," "formal schooling," and "education" interchangeably. I examine how ordinary, mass education at

---

[26] Collier and Hoeffler 2004; Humphreys and Weinstein 2008, p. 447; Østby, Nordås, and Rød 2009, p. 315; Oyefusi 2008.

[27] Thyne 2006.

[28] Some of these are Bar-Tal 1998; Borchgrevink 2008; Sullivan 2007.

[29] Borchgrevink 2008; Sullivan 2007.

primary and secondary levels contributes to wider conflict and peacebuilding processes. My focus is not on special activities or classes about peace and conflict resolution, nor is my focus on informal education, although this is complementary to formal schooling.

Schooling is widely believed to be a key element of socialization and, along with most work in the field of education, this book begins with the premise that schooling can shape understandings, attitudes, values, and the behavior of individuals. Education is regarded as an important agent of socialization and influence on social citizenship.[30] Nelson Mandela has called education "the most powerful weapon to change the world," and Barack Obama has referred to education as "the currency of the 21st century."[31]

International and domestic policies also reflect a faith in education's socializing ability. Prior to armed intervention in Iraq, the U.S. government sent out a tender to "de-Baathify" Iraq's schools.[32] During the Cold War, the United States considered formal education to be one of the most important methods to spread anticommunist ideology in Afghanistan.[33] After the Second World War, Germany and England embarked on textbook exchanges to minimize the most offensive images on both sides and to improve relations.[34] Examples abound supporting Ernest Gellner's quip that "[t]he monopoly of legitimate education is now more important, more central than is the monopoly of legitimate violence."[35]

Primary school is particularly important because it is the only level of education to which most young people have access in the Global South. Net primary enrollment rates in what the United Nations Childrens' Fund (UNICEF) calls the least developed countries are 76 percent for girls and 81 percent for boys, whereas net secondary enrollment rates are just 27 percent and 31 percent, respectively.[36] Furthermore, primary education is important for the questions of this book, because ethnic attitudes are formed early and, once formed, tend to increase in intensity with time.[37] According to theories of cognitive development, children develop perceptions of others and develop race and social class attitudes between ages seven and nine.[38] Secondary school is also important, because both early childhood and adolescence are critical periods in which significant events can have a greater impact on our understanding of history

---

[30] Anderson 2003; Gellner 1983; Green, Preston, and Janmaat 2006; Marshall 1965.

[31] Howe and Lewis 1990; Obama's comments at the University of Cairo quoted in Barbara Zasloff 2009.

[32] USAID, "Request for Proposals M/Op-03-Edu2 Revitalization of Iraqi Schools and Stabilization Education (Rise)," http://www.usaid.gov/iraq/pdf/web_education.pdf; Wurmser 2003.

[33] Spink 2005.

[34] Dance 1960.

[35] Gellner 1983, p. 34.

[36] UNICEF 2009, p. 26, statistical tables.

[37] Allport 1958; Padilla, Ruiz and Brand 1974 in Bush and Saltarelli 2000, p. 3.

[38] Oesterreich 1995, pp. 196–197.

than later on.[39] In addition, secondary education is correlated with access to employment and economic growth, especially in the Global South, making it highly sought after.

Moreover, schooling is particularly influential in the Rwandan case. European-style education is highly valued in Rwanda, and expectations for social advancement have, from the colonial period to today, followed directly. Many Rwandan students with whom I spoke were confident that schooling could help them improve their lives. Some children talked about their dreams of becoming doctors, pharmacists, and accountants, and of the important role of schooling in reaching their goals. One representative from an NGO explained to me that even the street children with whom she works feel excluded if they do not go to school. "Kids know that the possibility is there" for schools to help them achieve a better life.[40] Historically, too, Rwandans have been committed to education; successive Rwandan governments have spent more on primary schooling than their neighbors. School's messages may also have particular salience given the paucity of alternatives; for instance, Longman argues that during the colonial period at least, there were no published substitutes to the history that students were taught in schools.[41] Given Rwandans' great respect for formal education, they may be pre-socialized to be socialized by schooling. In this strong educational context, we might well expect schooling to yield the positive social cohesion and peacebuilding outcomes with which educational institutions have often been associated.

Yet I argue that in Rwanda, ordinary, everyday schooling achieved the opposite result. Additionally, I argue that social-structural and psychocultural processes that transpired in schools help make sense of currently under-explained dimensions in the literature on conflict in Rwanda. Specifically, many leading accounts of violent conflict in Rwanda rely on a foundation of intergroup inequalities and psychocultural/identity processes (categorizing, collectivizing, and stigmatizing ethnic groups) as underlying factors explaining conflict at different times. These explanations, however, beg questions about *how* these underlying processes develop. I show that from the perspective of those inside the system, Rwanda's schools produced and reinforced horizontal inequalities and psychocultural processes, providing a fertile foundation for violent intergroup conflict. Schools were a key institution of the state and the church that ultimately helped foster interethnic conflict in both the colonial period and in independent Rwanda.

At the same time, I argue that schooling in Rwanda can and has contributed in some ways to peacebuilding, although these processes are a less dominant part of the story. I further argue that while positive strides are being taken today, schools are still dangerously replicating past trends. By highlighting and

---

[39] Devine-Wright 2003, p. 13.
[40] Author's interview, NGO representative, eastern Rwanda, March 9, 2006.
[41] Longman 2010, pp. 65–66.

explaining the ways in which Rwandan schools became implicated in violent intergroup conflict, I also hope to forward an understanding of the ways in which schools can alternatively oppose conflict and build peace.

Opportunities and Challenges of Research in Post-Genocide Rwanda[42]

I develop my arguments through comparative historical analysis over three periods: colonial Rwanda (1919–1962), the Rwandan Republics (1962–1994), and post-genocide Rwanda (1994–present). Each of these periods is complex in distinct ways because different groups were in power. The first two periods ended in extreme violence along ethnic lines.

The argument presented in this book stems principally from seventy semi-structured, one on one interviews that I conducted in 2006 with Rwandans who attended or taught primary school in Rwanda from the colonial period to 2006, as well as five interviews with Belgian colonial administrators and missionaries. At the time of the interviews, some interviewees were still students or teachers while a number had moved on to become farmers, some worked with NGOs or were civil servants, several were unemployed, a couple were pastors, and a few were prisoners. Further information on the contributions and demographics of interviewees is detailed in the Appendix.

While I am confident that I gathered a good cross-section of opinions, it was a challenge to assemble a demographically diverse group of interview participants. While I was generally aware in advance of numerous identifying factors about a potential interviewee (gender, place of origin, current residence), I rarely knew his/her ethnicity, rendering balance on this feature very difficult to achieve. As I discuss in Chapter 4, public ethnic identification is barred in post-genocide Rwanda, and researchers cannot ask for this information. Neither can it be readily discerned from name or mere appearance. Nonetheless, I deemed it essential that I speak with people from different groups in order to fairly answer the research questions. In the end, many interviewees privately told me their ethnicity during the interview, while others often offered strong clues to allow me to identify them ethnically.[43] It is possible that I have made a few mistakes in attributing ethnicity either through personal error or through "ethnic faking," discussed more in Chapter 2, but I am also assured that I gathered a diverse range of perspectives.

Conditions in Rwanda also gave rise to a number of biases in my sample. For example, after encountering nearly exclusively Tutsi in Kigali, I turned to the predominantly Hutu north to seek opinions from what I presumed would be mostly Hutu Rwandans. Moving north did broaden the range of my

---

[42] This section builds on King 2009 in which the challenges and opportunities of this research are described in further detail. I gratefully acknowledge the editors of *African Studies Review* for permission to reprint sections of that article.

[43] See Samuelson and Freedman 2010 for details on such clues.

interviewees, although my informant base was still skewed because ethnicity was confounded by region. Another bias is that no interview participants identified themselves as Twa. Twa are the third group in Rwanda, comprising about 1 percent of the Rwandan population. They are generally excluded from politics and looked down upon by Hutu and Tutsi alike. I do not discuss them in any depth in this book because of their small numerical presence in the population and the fact that they have not played a major role in intergroup conflict. Finally, because I conducted a few interviews in English and the rest in French without an interpreter, my subject pool was also biased toward people with more-than-average education and a related socioeconomic status.[44] This was an important trade-off: I forewent a translator and sacrificed the knowledge that Kinyarwanda-only speakers would have added so that I could speak with interviewees one on one. As I elaborate later in the book, in the context of post-genocide Rwanda, this likely gave people the opportunity to be more open than they would have been with a third party and, indeed, this was my experience when I later worked with a translator on another research project. I also reasoned that teachers and students are overrepresented in the group of Rwandans that speak French and/or English, and therefore that this group would be able to provide me with pertinent information.

In addition to these more formal, semi-structured interviews, I took advantage of the constant flux of guests who stayed or dined at the *centre d'accueil* in Kigali, where I was based, to talk less formally with Rwandans about their experiences. I also carried out a brief update visit to Rwanda in 2009 and remain in touch with a number of contacts to this day.

I conducted interviews with nearly thirty experts as well: officials from the Rwandan Ministry of Education, professors from the National University of Rwanda, and others involved in educational reform. Most chose to speak as private citizens, as well as in their official capacities, thereby also sharing personal educational experiences.

In analyzing the findings from my interviews, I had to remain aware of Rwanda's political reality, which I discuss in Chapter 4, of an authoritarian post-genocide state whose history is highly contested and where freedom of speech is limited. In this environment, it is likely that interviewees engaged in what I call "selective reporting," which entails self-censorship or self-serving bias. Sometimes, for example, interviewees may have lied to say what they believed I wanted to hear or to present themselves in a positive light. More systematically, people must often toe the line by voicing politically sanctioned narratives – what James Scott calls "public transcripts" – rather than sharing "private transcripts."[45] Scott argues that in most cases subordinate groups come to associate their own well-being with the reproduction of the public

---

[44] The 2002 Rwandan census reported that only approximately 5.5% of Rwandans speak English or French (RoR 2002e). This number has since risen.

[45] Scott 1990.

transcript or narrative, thus perpetuating a discourse systematically skewed toward the dominant elite. In Rwanda, citizens can be charged and jailed for a vague offense called "divisionism," which, while meant to eradicate "genocide ideology," increasingly seems to mean simply disagreeing with the government.[46] As one Rwandan woman told me, "Rwandans have become liars. We can't say anything because they'll imprison us or kill us."[47]

Interviewees may also selectively reproduce group narratives. While I wish to be cautious about overgeneralizing and essentializing Hutu and Tutsi categories, there are different Hutu and Tutsi versions of a range of historical events and the causal factors behind those events. As one interviewee warned me, "Maybe I will tell you this and another [from the other ethnic group] will tell you another story. That is the problem of Rwanda."[48] While I keep interviewees anonymous to protect their safety, when I use direct quotes I provide the interviewee's gender and ethnicity, wherever possible, in addition to the location of the interview, in order to give readers the chance to situate the speaker.

A second potential challenge when drawing conclusions from interview data involves the fallibility of historical memory. I often asked my interviewees to reflect on experiences that had taken place many years in the past. Inevitably, their answers were filtered through memories of economic hardship, ethnic and regional politics, their gender, exile, violence, civil war, and genocide. Some interviewees also tended to mythologize the past.

While historical memory and mythologizing can be seen as inherent problems in interpreting firsthand accounts, we can also view them as "sources of understanding." In relation to her study of riots in Bangladesh, wherein villagers' memories often contradicted each other and official accounts, Beth Roy argues that "[w]hat sticks in people's memories, what they choose to say and when they choose to remain silent, how they distort what they know to be their experience, and overarching all, what I notice and what I overlook are all intensely informative."[49] Similarly, in some instances, interviewees remarked on circumstances that they had not directly experienced. These memories, transmitted to them by their parents or other members of their community, nonetheless tell a story and take on a meaning of their own. Anthropologist Lisa Malkki terms memories that are neither history nor myth "mythico-history": "not only a description of the past, not even merely an evaluation of the past, but a subversive recasting and reinterpretation of it in fundamentally moral terms."[50] These accounts influence the perceptions and sentiments of those recalling them, and so they too are worth repeating here. I follow

---

[46] International Crisis Group 2002; Reyntjens 2004; Reyntjens 2006; RoR 2006a.
[47] Author's interview, female Hutu, northern Rwanda, March 22(A), 2006.
[48] Author's interview, male Tutsi, Kigali, March 11, 2006.
[49] Roy 1994, p. 142.
[50] Malkki 1995, p. 54.

both Malkki's and Roy's leads in interpreting and taking seriously silences, distortions, omissions, and mythico-histories.

Conducting interviews one on one, with guarantees of anonymity, gave people the opportunity to be more open than they might otherwise have been. When we met in her home in northern Rwanda, an elderly Rwandan woman said, "If foreigners arrive on our hill, the government gives them someone to show them the path that they will follow. On this path, they have put things, educated people, what they need to say, what they need to show, what they need not to show, what they need not say." She continued: "When whites come, they [the government] do not show the people. They have traced, I would say, a tourism itinerary.... So, if you were to arrive here where I or another person could tell you something, they [instead] make the itinerary to show you who you must find, with whom you must speak. And all of the people who come from the outside pass like this. And they leave with an image of I don't know what." Her point was that "if they dared, like you, to enter into the country-side, a little, a little, a little," that they would find something different. Indeed, that people were repeatedly willing to deviate from public transcripts to share private ones increased my confidence in my findings.[51] While challenges and biases certainly remain, my interviews provided me with rich insight into the educational system in Rwanda and its role in conflict and peacebuilding. They also afforded me an opportunity to learn from the perspectives of those within the system.

To complement interview data, I analyzed history curriculum and educational policy documents. This included primary school documentation, which I had translated from Kinyarwanda, as well as secondary school documentation, which I was able to read directly, as it is mostly in French. In many of the poorest parts of the world where, as in Rwanda, schools lack resources and teacher training is inadequate, such documents are carefully followed.[52] While written documentation gave me the opportunity to cross-check the findings I gathered through interviews, the matter of selective reporting also pertains to written sources and, as I show in subsequent chapters, historical and political literature on Rwanda is often similarly polarized.

Contribution

The findings of this book will be of interest to several audiences. For specialists on Rwanda, this book is the first to provide an in-depth longitudinal study of education – a key political issue in Rwanda – and to analyze its role in conflict and peacebuilding. The relevance of this book also extends beyond Rwanda: despite the fact that education is a profoundly political issue, the disciplines of

---

[51] Author's interview, female Hutu, northern Rwanda, March 21(C), 2006. For a similar experience, see Fujii 2009, pp. 181–182.

[52] Milligan 2003; Scrase 1993.

political science and education interact relatively infrequently. For those interested in ethnic conflict and peacebuilding, this book draws attention to schools as an important, yet understudied, factor in developing identity and views of the other. For education specialists, this book provides a framework to analyze multiple dimensions of education, often considered in isolation, and draws attention to the impact of schooling on group and societal-level political processes, linking micro- and macro-levels of analysis. Most importantly, I hope that this book is of interest to those endeavoring to make a practical contribution to the prevention of conflict and the building of sustainable peace in Rwanda and other parts of the world. Rather than simply prescribing *more* education, we need to understand what *kinds* of education contribute to conflict, and what *kinds* foster peace.

Because this book crosses disciplinary boundaries, the theories and concepts it presents will be occasionally familiar to readers in one field, but not to others. For example, ethnic conflict specialists will know the theories of primordialism and constructivism, while education specialists will be familiar with concepts like hidden curriculum and the contact hypothesis. Rwanda and Great Lakes experts will be most familiar with the history of Rwanda presented here. One of this book's goals is to bridge disciplines, and I kindly ask readers to be patient with the sections they know best.

While there are many ways to read this book, there are two ways in which I do not intend it to be read. First, when Kenneth Bush and Diana Saltarelli published *The Two Faces of Education in Ethnic Conflict*, perhaps the first widely read piece on the conflict-conducive facets of education, some reported that donor governments became reluctant to fund education in emergencies.[53] That education can conduce to violent conflict does not mean that no education builds peace. I do not intend to divert attention or funding from schooling. Access to education is an essential human right articulated in numerous international documents. To the contrary, I aim to increase awareness of the importance of education in Rwanda and beyond. Second, this book's main goal is to understand the subtle influences of education, not to present it as *the* decisive factor in peace or conflict. No simple causal relationship exists between education and conflict, or education and peacebuilding. Families, communities, peers, churches, and political parties, among others, are important vectors of socialization and interact with schooling but are not the focus of this book. While education is neither a smoking gun nor a panacea, the relationships between education, peace, and conflict deserve far more attention. Insofar as violent conflict has such immense social costs and peacebuilding is so obviously important, we need to know more about this important influence on both processes.

Chapter 1 offers an overview of the causes of intergroup conflicts in Rwanda and develops a framework for locating education in their genesis. Chapters 2 to 4 comparatively analyze three periods in Rwandan history: the Belgian

---

[53] Tomlinson and Benefield 2005, p. 12.

colonial period, the two Republics, and post-genocide. Each of these chapters sketches the sociopolitical history of the period and outlines the development of schooling before turning to my findings and arguments. Chapter 5 considers Rwanda in comparative context. Rwanda's experience with schooling and conflict has much to teach us regarding the harnessing of education for peace-building. The conclusion revisits key arguments and explores the theoretical and policy implications of the links between classrooms and conflict.

I

Moving Education from the Margins to the Mainstream

During the Rwandan genocide, *The Guardian* reported that "people were driven by atavistic fury that goes back to the times when human beings moved in packs and ate raw meat."[1] Likewise, *The New York Times* wrote about the "age-old animosity between the Tutsi and Hutu ethnic groups."[2] It described earlier violence, in the 1960s, as "savagery mark[ing] Rwandan tribal warfare."[3] These popular accounts cast violent conflict as primordial, natural, and flowing directly from objective differences, thus requiring no further explanation. Primordialism, or pathologies inherent in ethnically plural societies, has been blamed for conflicts from Liberia and Somalia to the Balkans.[4] Many academic analyses also place a high explanatory value on the group attributes of ethnic identity and hatred in the case of Rwanda.[5]

Although current explanations present a more complex view of the causes of intergroup conflict at various times in Rwanda, even leading accounts leave much under-explained: in particular, how the underlying roots of violent conflict developed and the role of education in this process. This chapter discusses current explanations of Rwandan intergroup conflict. It then presents several pathways through which education is linked to conflict and to peacebuilding.

[1] Cited in Allen and Eade 2000.
[2] James C. McKinley Jr., "Fighting Outlasts Defeat of Mobutu," *The New York Times*, October 13, 1997.
[3] Robert Conleys, "Savagery Marks Tribal Warfare in Rwanda; Watusi, Once Feudal Lords, Flee to Neighboring Lands – Bahutu Kill Thousands Regime Said to Permit Raids as Reprisals for Terrorism by Monarchist Guerrillas," *The New York Times*, February 9, 1964.
[4] Anonymous, "7 Said to Be Killed in Monrovia During Shell Attack on Church," *The New York Times*, July 27, 2003; Horowitz 1985; Lake 1993; Kenneth B. Noble, "Democracy Brings Turmoil in Congo," *The New York Times*, January 31, 1994.
[5] See, for example, Mamdani 2001; Prunier 1997.

It suggests a framework, to be applied throughout the rest of the book, for bringing education from the margins to the mainstream.

Explaining Intergroup Conflict in Rwanda

Rather than characterizing the 1994 genocide as spontaneous violence, current explanations are complex and multicausal. They include proximate causes that directly affected the outbreak of war, as well as underlying causes (also known as permissive, remote, or root causes) that were required for the activation of proximate causes, but which on their own were insufficient to have caused violent conflict.

Leading scholars generally concur that underlying causes of the Rwandan genocide include deteriorating economic conditions, political power struggles, a historical foundation of ethnic manipulation and inequality, an ingrained fear of authority among Rwandans, and environmental pressures. Proximate causes include heightened domestic pressure for political reform, the unwillingness of a core group of elites to give up the benefits of power, and mobilization and coercion by political entrepreneurs. In addition, external triggers such as aggression from neighboring Uganda from the Tutsi-dominated Rwandan Patriotic Front (RPF), widespread Hutu-targeted violence in Burundi, and international pressure for political reform served as sparks for the conflict.[6] As I show in the next chapter, the same kind of multicausal explanation, with underlying and proximate, domestic, and external factors, accounts for earlier violence surrounding independence.

Within these leading accounts, a number of conditions are inadequately explained. The role of ethnicity in explaining conflict remains a particularly important debate. In accounts of individual motivations for genocide, the pendulum has swung from a nearly exclusive focus on the motivating role of primordial "tribalism" to a minimization of ethnicity in explaining intergroup conflict. Lee Ann Fujii, for instance, argues that neither ethnic hatred nor ethnic fear explains why individuals became involved in genocide, that there were other equally important cleavages in Rwanda, and that personal ties and geographic proximity to extremists were the key factors in mobilization.[7] Scott Straus's account of his interviews with *génocidaires* also downplays the role of ethnic prejudice and antipathy, although he acknowledges that these motivations were of importance to some Rwandans and makes clear that, overall, "the categories matter."[8]

In this book, I work from the perspective that ethnicity, socially constructed over a long period of time, is integral to understanding violent intergroup conflict in Rwanda. I define ethnicity broadly as an identity, a feeling of belonging,

---

[6] Des Forges 1999; Longman 2010; Straus 2006.

[7] Fujii 2009.

[8] Straus 2006, p. 8.

"a greatly extended form of kinship,"[9] or an "imagined community."[10] Ethnicity may be based on racial, geographic, linguistic, religious, or other differences, the emphasized referents may shift with time, and subjective perceptions are central. As I discuss in relation to Rwanda, the meaning and importance of ethnicity has changed with time. Indeed, different forms of identity emerge and change in distinct institutional settings around the world.[11] Some in Rwanda today claim that differences between Hutu, Tutsi, and Twa groups are not definitionally or anthropologically "ethnic." Yet whether ethnicity exists objectively is beside the point; what really matters is the meaning and value that people attribute to these differences and that, alongside class and regional provenance, ethnicity has been and remains a meaningful identity and source of cleavage in Rwanda.

Specifically, categorization, collectivization, and stigmatization by ethnic group were important underlying factors that made violent intergroup conflict possible at different times in Rwanda. Of course, the mere categorization, or existence, of distinct ethnic groups need not be problematic. However, as I elaborate in the coming chapters, exclusive categorization (being a member of only x or y primary group), combined with a second factor, collectivization or essentialization (thinking about all individuals within a group as being the same, or of the same essence), are parts of the explanation for conflict. According to genocide scholars, classification is a first step in a multicausal process toward mass violence along ethnic lines.[12] As Straus notes, "the logic of extermination in Rwanda depended on the idea that Tutsis are fundamentally alike."[13]

The third component of ethnic construction that leads to intergroup conflict is stigmatization. Stigmatizing a group involves attributing disapproval or reproach and can be part of the process of the social construction and interaction of identity groups. Violence surrounding Rwandan independence transpired along ethnic lines in part because of an effective campaign by prominent Hutu leaders of stigmatizing and scapegoating Tutsi. Likewise, many political and regional grievances were channeled into ethnic grievances before the genocide. Stigmatization can also provoke fear, another important contributor to conflict in Rwanda and beyond.[14] Some interviewees shared similar explanations for intergroup conflict: "We learned this everywhere. 'Be careful of those snakes. You can't marry other ethnicities.' ... This is what incited the youth, even the older who knew how to write. It was this [stigmatization] that was very bad."[15]

[9] Horowitz 1985.
[10] Anderson 2003.
[11] Eller 1999; Malkki 1995; Posner 2004.
[12] Stanton 1998.
[13] Straus 2006, p. 8.
[14] Lake and Rothchild 1998; Straus 2006.
[15] Author's interview, female Tutsi, Kigali, January 27, 2006.

Borrowing from Marc Howard Ross, I call these three factors – categorization, collectivization and stigmatization – rooted in identities, images, and metaphors, *psychocultural* (others have called them subjective or intangible) causes. Psychocultural factors "emphasize the role of culturally shared, profound 'we-they' oppositions, the conceptualization of enemies and allies, and deep-seated dispositions about human action stemming from earliest development."[16] While often ignored, psychocultural factors are essential to understanding intergroup conflict. For example, emotion and response to symbols are central to explaining violent conflict in the former Soviet Union and the former Yugoslavia.[17]

Inequalities between ethnic groups also underlay conflict in Rwanda. Inequalities are a *social-structural* factor (sometimes called objective or tangible causes), which are based in divergent interests, the social, economic, and political organization of society, and the quality and intensity of ties within and between communities.[18] In analyses of intergroup conflict in Rwanda, "horizontal" inequalities between groups are sometimes neglected in favor of concentrating on "vertical inequalities" between a small elite and the rest of the population.[19] I contend that both matter and that horizontal inequalities, in particular, played important social-structural as well as psychocultural roles in underlying conflict.

We do not know enough about how exactly these underlying intergroup, societal-level conditions developed. Some of the answers can be found in existing literature. Peter Uvin, for instance, considers the role of the development aid community in intensifying inequalities and exclusion and in failing to recognize state-sponsored racism.[20] Timothy Longman explores the role of churches in shaping ethnic and political relations and in developing profound respect of authority.[21] Other key institutions, however, are under-examined. In particular, schools are an important factor in constructing group identities, shaping attitudes toward the other, and structuring relations between groups. While other analyses of the Rwandan genocide have mentioned education among the many factors that made the violence possible,[22] this book offers the first systematic examination of how education fostered an atmosphere permissive to conflict in Rwanda.

Ultimately, an extensive set of arguments exist for why intergroup violent conflict occurred at various times in Rwanda. Nonetheless, these explanations often presume the existence of a set of underlying conditions without fully explaining how they developed. Furthermore, they inadequately account for the role of schooling. As the remainder of this chapter demonstrates, the education

---

[16] Ross 1993 p. 15; see also pp. 17–34.
[17] Kaufman 2001.
[18] Ross 1993, pp. 17–34.
[19] Horowitz 1985; Stewart 2000; Uvin 1998.
[20] Uvin 1998.
[21] Longman 2010.
[22] A few are Chrétien 2003, p. 285; Gourevitch 1998, pp. 57–58; Lemarchand 1970.

system must be considered an important factor in shaping these psychocultural and social-structural conditions. The forthcoming chapters provide a more thorough understanding of the complex role of education and show that factoring education into our explanations of violent conflict in Rwanda moves forward our overall understanding of these tragic events.

What Education Can Tell Us about Violent Intergroup Conflict

This book is concerned with how the content and structure of ordinary primary and secondary schooling contribute to conflict and peacebuilding. The *content of schooling* has two key parts. First, it encompasses curriculum and curriculum policy. Curriculum inculcates "'desired' knowledge, skills, and attitudes" and emphasizes "the crucial issue of the authority to define and select legitimate knowledge."[23] Curricula play a role in the formation and transmission of collective identity, memory, sense of citizenship, and shared destiny.

Different subjects such as history, civics, geography, literature, and even mathematics contribute to these processes and hold implications for conflict and peacebuilding. In late 1980s and early 1990s Afghanistan, for instance, grade four math students were asked: "The speed of a Kalashnikov bullet is 800 meters per second. If a Russian is at a distance of 3200 meters from a mujahid, and that mujahid aims at the Russian's head, calculate how many seconds it will take for the bullet to strike the Russian in the forehead."[24] I concentrate here on history, however, because it is the discipline most often implicated in identity formation and ethnic stereotyping and is, in Rwanda and beyond, highly contentious.

Second, I look at pedagogical practices that transmit a hidden curriculum. By this, I mean "the tacit teaching ... of norms, values, and dispositions that goes on simply by [students] living in and coping with the institutional expectations and routines of schools day in and day out for a number of years."[25] Even small changes in behavior may have more of an impact on students' values and learning than trying to directly teach values and attitudes.[26] Indeed, some say that approaches to teaching are as important, or even more important, than curriculum, but receive far less attention.[27] I refer to history content and pedagogy collectively as the *content of schooling*.

The structure and processes of educational access and governance – what I refer to as the *structure of schooling* – constitute the second key dimension of educational inputs. Structure includes who has access to schooling, de jure or de facto. Besides procedures to grant or deny access directly, linguistic and symbolic processes also matter indirectly. For example, in Bosnia-Herzegovina,

---

[23] Apple 1979, p. 1.
[24] Mamdani 2004, p. 137.
[25] Apple 1979, p. 14.
[26] McCauley 2002.
[27] Cole and Barsalou 2006.

symbols like a crucifix, an Islamic banner, or a Serbian flag make some children uncomfortable to attend school.[28] How schools are set up – for instance, whether classes are segregated by group as in apartheid South Africa – is another main part of the structure of education in conflict and peacebuilding.

Content and structure of schooling are both important, and I examine each equally in the case studies that follow. Scholars debate whether a "head-first" approach (which aims to change beliefs in order to then change behavior), as might occur through a history lesson, or a "feet-first" approach (which aims to change behavior in order to then change beliefs), as might occur via educational structure or pedagogical practices, has more of an effect on intergroup relations.[29] Yet, head-first and feet-first approaches are often intertwined and interact. Case study research in Northern Ireland and Israel suggests that desegregation – a reform in school structure – is insufficient for peacebuilding without significant changes in curriculum and pedagogy.[30] On the other hand, reform in one area may eventually lead to progress in other areas. In this book, I consider how both the content and structure of schooling contribute to violent interethnic conflict and/or sustainable peace.

Despite this book's attention to formal education, other forms of socialization proceed in tandem, offering alternative, complementary, or sometimes radically divergent perspectives to that of formal teaching. It is impossible to untangle the relative weights of, for example, family-based education, community socialization, peers, and formal schooling in terms of influence on a child. Moreover, the relative influence of education may vary over time and from individual to individual. Nonetheless, there are a number of processes through which education consistently contributes to conflict and/or sustainable peace.

First, schooling is often a *reflector* of existing social conditions. In this way, schooling can be a microcosm of society. Examining who makes it through the educational funnel tells us about social hierarchy and political structures. When an educational policy is altered, it often reflects a change that has already been undertaken within government. Similarly, when a historical narrative is published in a textbook, it illustrates the "commonplaces of historical thinking of a certain place and time" and tells us how those in power understand their positions.[31] For example, in Indian and Pakistani textbooks, major events like independence and partition, as well as key historical characters such as Gandhi and Jinnah, are very differently portrayed.[32] The forthcoming chapters similarly show how in Rwanda, various governments recount key historical narratives differently.

---

[28] Perry 2003.
[29] McCauley 2002.
[30] Hughes and Donnelly 2007.
[31] Dance 1960, p. 54; Ross 2007.
[32] Kumar 2001.

However, schools are not merely passive reflectors; they also actively shape politics and intergroup relations. Schooling serves as an *amplifier* of social categories and messages. Uneven distribution of education may not only reflect and reproduce, but also enhance and multiply economic and social divisions.[33] For example, while access to schooling may be based on ethnic identity, suggesting that schooling reflects categories that already exist in society, schooling also amplifies and reinforces these categories by legitimating them. In apartheid South Africa, the unequal school system is said to have not only imitated, but increased the cleavage between white and black South Africans.[34] Education also amplifies by fostering cognitive consistency – the tendency for people to assimilate new information into old.[35] What we learn delineates our bounds of thinking such that inconsistent information is often interpreted as invalid.[36] When students learn a historical narrative at school, this narrative may foster cognitive consistency, amplifying schools' messages, as students interpret new events and information as consistent with school lessons. In Cambodia, for example, the Khmer Rouge effectively used existing and emotionally salient local knowledge that had "ontological resonance" to draw in perpetrators.[37] Schooling can also play an amplificatory role by reaching beyond the classroom to influence friends, families, and communities. In Nazi Germany, even the youngest students had to report back to schools on what was said at home. In this way, schools magnified the messages they aimed to inculcate and shaped conversations and practices at home.[38]

Relatedly, schooling can be a *signal*, such as in the colonial and postcolonial periods, when widening schooling was meant to signal modernity to citizens across the developing world.[39] Post-conflict governments may also try to use schooling to signal that they are making progress and investing in their citizens.[40] In this way, schooling can be a highly visible peace dividend.

Schooling is also a *causal contributor*, motivating or empowering agents. Taught specific content, and socialized in certain ways, students become agents themselves. They use the tools and experiences from their schooling to respond to and actively influence their societies in both positive and negative ways. For example, Western university education during the colonial period empowered Africans such as Jomo Kenyatta and Kwame Nkrumah to be at the forefront of the anti-colonial movement and among the first leaders of independent African states.

---

[33] Bowles and Gintis 1976; Davies 2004, pp. 41–56.
[34] Nkomo, McKinney, and Chisholm 2004.
[35] Jervis 1977, p. 117.
[36] See Kuhn 1970.
[37] Hinton 2005, pp. 287–288.
[38] Mann 1938.
[39] Fuller 1990.
[40] Education For All Global Monitoring Report team 2011, pp. 14, 20; Inter-Agency Network for Education in Emergencies, "Understanding Education's Role in Fragility," (Undated), p. 10; Thyne 2006.

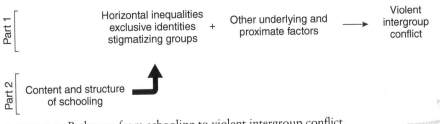

FIGURE I.I Pathways from schooling to violent intergroup conflict.

In sum, this book studies the content of education, including history teaching, pedagogy and hidden curriculum, as well as the structure of education, meaning who has access to schools and how classrooms are set up. These facets of education play a number of roles on the path toward conflict and/or in building sustainable peace. Education can reflect dominant government and society, amplify categories and lessons, send signals to citizens, and even contribute to specific actions among (former) students. Intentionally or unintentionally, these school-based processes play a role in conflict and peacebuilding.

Pathways from Education to Conflict

There are a number of pathways leading from the structure and content of schooling to violent conflict. They link micro-level educational factors with macro-level intergroup processes. Indeed, many of the pathways already recognized by scholars and practitioners as underlying conflict, both psychocultural and social-structural, can be produced by the educational system. The sections that follow review how a given pathway contributes to underlying conflict (Figure 1.1, part 1). Each discussion of a pathway is followed by an examination, based on the education literature, of how it transpires in schools (Figure 1.1, part 2). The pathways principally represent group-based processes, because individuals in interethnic conflict usually act and are received as members of a group.[41] These types of underlying factors can be termed "priming"; they are the foundation on which proximate causes, discussed in forthcoming chapters, build up to acute conflict.[42] Subsequent chapters argue that these conflict-conducive pathways not only *can* but, in the case of Rwanda, *have* manifested through schools. I then repeat a similar analysis to show the pathways through which schools can contribute to peacebuilding.

Horizontal Inequalities

Horizontal inequalities are severe social, political, and/or economic inequalities between groups that can underlie conflict. The concept builds on Ted Gurr's work on relative deprivation, which demonstrates that perceptions of

[41] Brown 1986, p. 533.
[42] Hinton 2005, pp. 282–288.

deprivation are based on comparisons to out-groups (meaning social groups with which one does not identify) rather than on the stand-alone position of an in-group (the group with which one identifies).[43] Group members themselves determine the relevance of a given inequality. In Kenya, for example, land is at issue, whereas housing, education, and jobs are more central in Northern Ireland. As I show, in Rwanda, education is of central importance to groups' perceptions of their relative standing. Horizontal inequalities are important substantively and instrumentally. For example, education is important in itself and also because it is often the strongest determinant of occupational status and life chances.

Whereas prominent studies show that the impact of individual inequality ("vertical inequality") does not have a significant impact on propensity for conflict,[44] recent quantitative studies provide evidence that intergroup conflict is more likely in societies with significant political, economic or social inequalities *between groups*.[45] They find that ethnic inequalities are particularly important, especially in Sub-Saharan Africa, and are a better predictor of conflict risk than both regionally and religiously based inequalities.[46] Many case studies also attest to the importance of horizontal inequalities in explaining intergroup conflict.[47] Two key mechanisms are identified. First, social-structurally, shared group grievances can promote discontent and intergroup competition over conflicting interests. Second, psychoculturally, given that in the constructivist approach to ethnicity adopted here ethnic groups are fluid, inequalities can also contribute to shaping and hardening identities themselves. In either case, perceptions of inequalities can matter, even in the absence of observable evidence.[48] Moreover, both the relatively deprived and relatively privileged may have incentives to initiate conflict.

Social-structurally, unequal access to education has been raised as an important inequality – and a major grievance – in many violent conflicts, such as in Angola, Burundi, Kosovo, and East Timor.[49] Exclusive use of language can further produce horizontal inequalities and can hinder access and outcomes of education. In pre-independence South Sudan, the Khartoum government's efforts to impose Arabic as the sole language of instruction led to resentment and the feeling that schools were sites of "subjugation and division."[50] Psychoculturally, because society's institutions shape its social climate, exclusive schools send the

---

[43] Gurr 1970.

[44] Collier and Hoeffler 2004; Fearon and Laitin 2003.

[45] Cederman, Weidmann, and Gleditsch 2010; Østby 2008; Østby, Nordås, and Rød 2009; Wimmer, Cederman, and Min 2009.

[46] Østby and Strand 2010, cited in Education For All Global Monitoring Report team 2011, p. 166.

[47] Fukuda-Parr et al. 2008; Stewart 2002; Stewart 2007; Stewart and Brown 2007.

[48] Brown and Langer 2010.

[49] World Bank 2005.

[50] Sommers 2005.

message that it is appropriate to divide society in certain ways and to entitle some to more than others, via the pathways discussed later in the chapter. Showing that some are less deserving than others may increase the likelihood of a group's mistreatment in other ways.[51]

Exclusive Identities

Exclusive and collectivized identity categories also frequently underlie conflict. Using categories to simplify complex society and situations is a basic and natural activity. Group categories, in particular, are a product of the need for social identity: "that part of an individual's self concept which derives from his knowledge of his membership in a social group (or groups) together with the value and emotional significance attached to that membership."[52] Social psychologists have helped explain how and why people satisfy their needs for positive identity through membership in a group and differentiation from other groups (out-groups). Simply being assigned to a group is enough to produce a feeling of groupness, and in-group members routinely favor other in-group members over members of an out-group, even without material bases.[53]

Once groups are categorized, they are often assigned a corporate, or essentialized, identity.[54] In other words, members of a given category are perceived as possessing various common attributes and as being more similar to each other than to members of another group. Through binary, non-overlapping identities, "they" are seen collectively as all the same and entirely different than "we." People are perceived as prototypical representatives of a group, rather than as individuals. In Nazi Germany, for example, all individuals with at least three Jewish grandparents were labeled Jewish, regardless of religious affiliation, level of assimilation, or self-identification, and were treated collectively as prototypical Jews. Thus, both the self and others are depersonalized in this process that produces group behavior.[55]

Social categorization is linked to intergroup conflict in a number of ways. As Henri Tajfel writes, "the erosion, preservation or creation of differentials [distinctions between various groups on important characteristics] has been ... one of the fundamental features of some of the most acute social and industrial conflicts."[56] In-group favoritism will more likely and easily lead to out-group antagonism when society is differentiated along a single primary category, as in Northern Ireland or Rwanda, because group relationships become zero-sum.[57] Essentializing, suggesting that groups "have essences that

[51] Staub 1989; Staub 2003.
[52] Tajfel 1982, p. 22.
[53] Tajfel et al. 1971; Turner 1975.
[54] See Brown 2000.
[55] Turner 1999, p. 14.
[56] Tajfel 1981, p. 223.
[57] Brewer 1999, p. 439.

differentiate them from other groups," is considered "an especially pernicious" and conflict-conducive form of categorization.[58]

School content can produce exclusive identities through categorization and collectivization. Perhaps one of the clearest cases is Germany in the lead-up to World War II and the Holocaust.[59] When the National Socialist German Workers (Nazi) Party took power in January 1933, remodeling education was a top priority. The propaganda minister likened education to a "kneading machine" turning humans into a "coherent mass" that could be "utilized and manipulated for the political aims of the state."[60] Based on his writings in *Mein Kempf*, Hitler's educational goal was to "burn the racial sense and racial feeling into the instinct and the intellect, the heart and the brain of youth."[61] Drawing on a foundation of economic and religious anti-Semitism already present in society and schools, the government revised curricula to make race the common thread across all subjects.[62] Students were taught to categorize the population into Jews and Aryans and to essentialize and collectivize Jews.

Studies of Northern Ireland also find that school content – in this case, teaching the two groups different religions and histories – "shap[ed] the ethno religious identities of Protestant and Catholic children" into polarized groups.[63] As Bernadette Hayes, Ian McAllister, and Lizanne Dowds write:

> For decades Catholic children were taught Irish history, often with overtly political overtones. In many history books there was an obsession with the Anglo-Irish conflict.... By contrast, Protestant children were rarely taught about Irish history, except when it related to British history.... [I]t still remains the case that a Catholic is likely to study more Irish history than a Protestant, and a Protestant will study more British history than a Catholic.[64]

Thus, schooling both reflected and amplified corporate group identities.

School structure can also contribute to categorizing and collectivizing. Naureen Talha argues that inequalities in education were a principal factor in the construction of Muslim nationalism in what became Pakistan.[65] In the case of Northern Ireland, a number of studies find that the segregated structure of the school system contributed to categorizing and collectivizing children into two distinct, essentialized, and polarized groups. Based on a pooled dataset from 1989 to 2003, Hayes, McAllister, and Dowds found that students that attended segregated schools were more likely to accept "traditional" strict Catholic/Protestant identities than those who attended informally or formally

---

[58] Hewstone et al. 2006, p. 272.
[59] See Hirsch 1995; Mann 1938; Wegner 2002; Ziemer 1972.
[60] Quoted in Blackburn 1985, preface.
[61] Quoted in Wegner 2002, p. 16.
[62] Blackburn 1985; Wegner 2002.
[63] Byrne 2000, p. 96.
[64] Hayes, McAllister, and Dowds 2007, p. 457.
[65] Cited in Brown and Langer 2010, p. 51.

integrated schools. They also found that students in segregated schools held more polarized positions vis-à-vis political identities and constitutional preferences than those who attended integrated schools.[66] Recent surveys in Lebanon and Malaysia also show that people educated in ethnically or religiously segregated schools have, on average, more negative perceptions of the other group than those who attended integrated schools.[67]

Stigmatizing Groups

Stigmatizing – a term I use broadly for different forms of societal disapproval – builds on categorizing and collectivizing groups as an additional factor underlying conflict. Stigmatization involves some or all of the following: ideologies of moral superiority of the in-group; negative stereotypes, devaluation, or even dehumanization of the out-group; scapegoating; and emotional detachment from the out-group, possibly to the point of excluding the out-group from the "sanctified universe of obligation."[68] Each of these manifestations could also be investigated as a separate pathway. While I group them together for simplicity here, I often try to parse them individually in the coming chapters. Nonetheless, various forms of stigmatization can contribute to conflict.[69] Stigmatization was an important facilitator of violence during the Holocaust, and in the former Yugoslavia, ethnic scapegoating, myths, and fears (as well as the opportunity to act on them) were necessary preconditions for war.[70]

School policies that value one group over another can cultivate stigmatization. As the Supreme Court justices in *Brown vs. Board of Education* (1954) wrote in the context of racial segregation of schools in the United States: "To separate Negro school children from others of similar age and qualifications solely because of their race generates a feeling of inferiority as to their status in the community and that may affect their hearts and minds in a way unlikely ever to be undone."[71] Research in Northern Ireland has likewise found that students in segregated schools tend to stereotype and stigmatize the other group. Based on interviews with twenty-four children, Sean Byrne found that the separation and lack of contact between Protestant and Catholic groups in Northern Ireland creates and perpetuates "extraordinary stereotypes," and that school segregation increased "mutual suspicion and ignorance."[72]

Stigmatization may alternatively transpire in school content through what Stephen Van Evera calls "chauvinistic mythmaking." Chauvinistic

---

[66] Hayes, McAllister, and Dowds 2006. See also Byrne 2000. Note, however, that because educational integration in Northern Ireland is the parents' choice rather than randomly distributed, several factors potentially confound findings on segregation.

[67] Education For All Global Monitoring Report team 2011, p. 170.

[68] Fein 1993, pp. 4–5; Hiebert 2008, pp. 328–332.

[69] Brewer 1999, p. 435; Paluck and Green 2009; Staub 1989, p. 60.

[70] Kaufman 2001; Musolff 2007.

[71] Quoted in Stephan 1999, p. 50.

[72] Barton and McCully 2003.

mythmaking proceeds by glorifying the in-group, whitewashing its faults, and portraying its victimization; it also occurs by devaluing the out-group, perhaps by rendering it a scapegoat for past crimes and tragedies or charging it with (possibly false) claims of harmful intentions.[73] For instance, in history texts during Germany's Third Reich, Jews were stigmatized as a historic and contemporary threat to Germany and were dehumanized as "parasites." This stigmatization contributed to "the ideological justification" for the Holocaust.[74]

Pathways from Education to Peace

Conversely, education may contribute to peace. Although evidence exists to support some pathways from education to peacebuilding, strong evaluations of the effectiveness of most types of peace education are in short supply.[75] The field of peacebuilding, more generally, is also marked by a dearth of evaluations and rigorous empirical studies to support key hypotheses.[76] This section thus proposes four ways that education may contribute to peacebuilding, with further discussion on success and feasibility to come in subsequent chapters, especially Chapter 5.

Horizontal Equity

Horizontal equity may contribute to building peace. The positive corollary of the horizontal inequality argument presented earlier is that intergroup conflict is less likely where groups have fewer significant political, economic, or social inequalities. While inequalities are very unlikely to be completely erased, horizontal equity exists when key groups accept a given level of horizontal inequality, making these inequalities unlikely to underlie conflict.[77]

Specific school structures may contribute to horizontal equity. For instance, equalizing educational opportunity can reduce group-based grievances over access to schools and possibly to subsequent jobs. In Malaysia, systematic affirmative action, including educational quotas and targets, is credited with improving the position of the Bumiputera vis-à-vis ethnic Chinese and helping dispel tensions between groups.[78] In Nigeria, although horizontal inequalities in education persist, initiatives to improve the positions of various ethnoregional groups in education and in the public sector are argued to have helped avert conflict.[79]

---

[73] Brown 1996, p. 587; Van Evera 1994, p. 27.
[74] Wegner 2002, p. 4.
[75] Bird 2003; Nevo and Brem 2002; Savedoff, Levine, and Birdsall 2006; Tomlinson and Benefield 2005.
[76] Blum 2010; Kawano-Chiu 2011; Lund 2003; Paluck and Green 2009b.
[77] Stewart and Brown 2007, p. 230.
[78] Stewart 2002, p. 20.
[79] Ukiwo 2007.

In some cases, educational design may also promote horizontal equity. Schools that foster a sense of equality and belonging for all are more likely to avoid laying the psychocultural roots of conflict. The contact hypothesis is rooted in the conviction that certain kinds of facilitated interaction between individuals of different groups can reduce ethnic prejudice and intergroup tension.[80] For example, students who attend integrated schools in Northern Ireland have more positive attitudes toward the other group than those attending segregated schools.[81] However, contact is not enough; a supportive institutional environment and equal status between groups are preconditions for producing these positive results.[82]

Inclusive Identities That Do Not Collectivize and Stigmatize Groups

It is widely believed that inclusive identities contribute to peacebuilding.[83] By inclusive identities I mean reconstructed identities of previously conflict-conducive, binary, collectivized, and stigmatized groups to inclusive or encompassing identities that emphasize similarities between individuals and/or are more accepting of their differences. Social psychologists, in particular, have focused on a number of different strategies for achieving more inclusive identities. They differ in terms of the psychological mechanisms hypothesized to foster improved relationships, as well as their approaches to dealing with existing groups. Several different strategies for creating inclusive identities have supporting laboratory evidence, although contrary evidence often exists and different strategies may help improve intergroup relations under different conditions.[84]

At one end of the continuum, the various strategies to *construct new identities* are consistent with the key understanding of constructivism that categories, especially identities, can be transformed and reconstructed. For example, the *decategorization* or *interpersonal* model urges individuation, moving people to view themselves and others as individuals rather than as "prototypical representatives" of an in-group or out-group. In Rwanda, for instance, this would mean considering Jean-de-Dieu, Joyeuse, and Marie individuals rather than members of Hutu or Tutsi groups. By shifting attention to the individual, it is possible to reduce the power of group distinctions and help lead to social cohesion. Psychologically, bias between groups should diminish because the social distance between one's self and former in-group members increases, while the social distance between one's self and former out-group members decreases.[85] In contrast to collectivizing or essentializing groups, decategorization aims to

---

[80] Allport 1958.
[81] Hayes, McAllister, and Dowds 2007.
[82] Allport 1958; Pettigrew 1998; Tal-Or, Boninger, and Gleicher 2002.
[83] Ali and Matthews 2004; Kelman 1999; Ross 2007.
[84] Capozza and Brown 2000; Crisp and Hewstone 2006.
[85] Gaertner et al. 1989, p. 240.

differentiate and heterogenize the out-group, so that it is come to be seen as comprising a variety of individuals and subgroups with different views and ideologies.[86]

A second approach to create inclusive identities is the *recategorization* model, also known as the *superordinate* perspective, which promotes the creation of a group identity at a higher level than existing groups, allowing members of former groups to think of themselves as one unit and thereby eliminating potentially dangerous social cleavages. In Rwanda, for example, this would mean focusing on a Rwandan identity rather than Hutu and Tutsi groups. At the psychological level, this model reduces the distance between members of each former group and should thus reduce bias. The cognitive processes that originally bound the in-group members may be refocused on establishing more positive relationships with former out-group members. Because people are still members of a group, albeit a new one at a higher level, their identity needs may still be met.[87]

In the laboratory setting, both decategorization and recategorization strategies reduced bias compared with a control group that maintained the original intergroup boundaries, but recategorization had a stronger impact on positive relations. Participants that experienced recategorization displayed more friendly, cooperative, trusting, and close interaction than those that participated in decategorization.[88] Yet, group identity has high psychological value and often becomes further entrenched with violence, meaning that recategorization is unlikely to be an achievable or sustainable solution.[89]

Moreover, findings from the laboratory do not always correctly predict outcomes in the real world.[90] In the real world, some attempts at recategorization have been quite successful. These have involved largely giving up original subgroup identities, either by assimilation, such as in the melting-pot image of early immigration to the United States, or by creating a new shared identity, such as between African and Arab Zanzibaris.[91] Nonetheless, a number of cases suggest that a homogeneity model, such as that implied by a pure recategorization strategy, is unlikely to build peace in many cases. Zsuzsa Matrai finds that the "national homogeneity equals cohesion" strategy, employed in Greece, Hungary, and Hong Kong, will not necessarily resolve societal conflict, and Nat Colletta, Teck Ghee Lim, and Anita Kelles-Viitanen reason that given the importance of ethnic identity to many people, the European model of a homogeneous nation is not feasible for much of the world.[92] Others point to the case of the former Yugoslavia, where Tito's attempt at recategorizing Serb, Croat, Macedonian,

---

[86] Bar-Tal and Rosen 2009.

[87] Gaertner et al. 1989, p. 240.

[88] Ibid., p. 82.

[89] Hewstone et al. 2006, p. 283.

[90] Paluck and Green 2009b.

[91] On the latter, see Mamdani 2001, p. 265, although, at the time of this writing, some actors were pushing for Zanzibari secession from mainland Tanzania to establish an Islamic state.

[92] Colletta, Ghee Lim, and Kelles-Viitanen 2001; Deutscher 2002; Matrai 2002.

Albanian, and Muslim groups into a Yugoslav identity was short-lived and ultimately unsuccessful, to suggest that recategorization is unfeasible.[93]

At the other end of the continuum from strategies to construct new identities are identity approaches that propose the *positive valuation of group distinctiveness* as a way to build inclusive identities. In this approach, the existing groups can continue to exist as primary identities, acknowledging the meaning vested in social groups. One example is the *mutual intergroup differentiation model*, which some might call multiculturalism or pluralism. The idea is that introducing a cooperative relationship between the groups can improve intergroup attitudes and relationships and induce group members to think of each group as "different but equal."[94] A related possibility is called *cross-categorization*, wherein individuals are simultaneously categorized as in-group and out-group members on multiple dimensions, such as ethnicity, gender, and region. Cross-categorization is thought to reduce bias by making social categorization more complex, decreasing the importance of the prime in-group/out-group distinctions, raising awareness of multiple subgroups within the out-group, increasing multiple classifications, and increasing trust and interpersonal interaction across boundaries.[95]

Most education scholars today place a high value on diversity and thus favor some form of this latter pluralism model.[96] Ross's recent work, based on research in Israel and Palestine, Northern Ireland, and South Africa, concludes that finding common ground paradoxically requires not ignoring differences, but acknowledging and working with them. He argues that pluralism is likely to be more successful at peacebuilding than other identity strategies because people are rarely willing to give up their group-based identities.[97] Psychologically, positive interaction at the group level may change attitudes faster than personalization because the whole group, rather than individuals, is involved.[98]

This type of diversity is also embraced by international organizations,[99] and a growing number of countries that originally emphasized ethnic assimilation, including Mexico and Guatemala, now formally (if not fully in practice) recognize cultural diversity along with nationalism. Yet, multiculturalism that promotes diversity may essentialize group differences, as some argue has been the case in Bosnia, Kosovo, Afghanistan, and Iraq.[100] Critical education

---

[93] Hewstone et al. 2006, p. 283.
[94] Hewstone and Brown 1986.
[95] Crisp and Hewstone 2000; Dovidio et al. 2006.
[96] Bickmore 2005; Harber 2004; Roberts-Schweitzer et al. 2006; Tawil and Harley 2004.
[97] Ross 2007, pp. 47, 319.
[98] Tal-Or, Boninger, and Gleicher 2002.
[99] UNESCO 2003b. See also Article 13 of the "International Covenant on Economic, Social and Cultural Rights" 1966; Education For All Global Monitoring Report team 2004, p. 23; Inter-Agency Network for Education in Emergencies, "Understanding Education's Role in Fragility" (undated).
[100] Simonsen 2005; Suchenski 2001.

theorists also contend that valuing diversity without an equal concern for social inequality is likely to be counterproductive, signaling the interconnectedness of different peacebuilding strategies like building inclusive identities and fostering horizontal equity.[101]

In between these two sets of approaches to building inclusive identities – which involve abandoning existing groups at one end and keeping existing groups but revaluing them at the other – is a subset of the recategorization model that some term the *dual identity model*, a combination of both approaches. This model involves preserving existing group identities within a common higher group identity. It requires "the acknowledgement of ambiguity, complexity, and hybridity within an individual self."[102] Indeed, Amartya Sen writes about the importance of defending our multiple identities and "the freedom to determine our loyalties and priorities between the different groups to all of which we may belong."[103] Psychological research has "found that a dual identity led to more positive out-group attitudes than did a superordinate identity alone."[104] Elizabeth Levy Paluck and Donald Green note in their review of prejudice reduction interventions that "the integrative [or dual identity] models ... claim the most empirical and normative support."[105]

Again, each of these strategies commands support and may help build peace under different conditions. A post-conflict identity strategy might alternatively employ the models complementarily or sequentially. For example, decategorization might be a first step to set the stage for recategorization or positive valuation of group differences.[106]

Schools may help set the conditions for inclusive identities that do not collectivize or stigmatize groups in a number of ways. Most of the social psychological literature examines the aforementioned strategies through school structure, and especially intergroup contact that brings students together on equitable footing. School content and pedagogy may also contribute to building more inclusive identities. For example, teachers may teach about regrouping.[107] Reframing mutually incompatible narratives, such as those taught in history class, might also contribute to more inclusive identities.[108]

Reconciliation

Reconciliation is widely considered a key element of building peace. It is a difficult-to-define term that highlights the importance of relationships and psychological changes on the part of disputants. According to John Paul Lederach,

[101] McGlynn 2009, p. 11.
[102] Davies 2004, p. 82.
[103] Sen 2006, p. 5.
[104] Hewstone et al. 2006, p. 284.
[105] Paluck and Green 2009b, p. 347.
[106] Hewstone et al. 2006, p. 285; Tal-Or, Boninger, and Gleicher 2002.
[107] Houlette et al. 2004.
[108] Ross 2002; Ross 2007.

relationships are both a basis of conflict and its long-term solution.[109] In Kinyarwanda, the native language of Rwanda, the word for "reconciliation" comes from the same root as "setting broken bones," reflecting the idea that reconciliation brings together relationships that were ruptured.[110] The literature suggests that there are many contributors to reconciliation – varying from acknowledgment, contrition, and forgiveness to trust, reciprocity, and interdependence – that may differ significantly depending on context. By including too many of these criteria, or by considering reconciliation as something that can be achieved rather than as a process without end, one may be setting the bar too high.[111] On the other hand, most peacebuilding scholars and practitioners agree that working to improve relationships is a worthwhile, if slow and difficult, endeavor and consider reconciliation to be one of the "pillars" of peacebuilding.[112]

Education contributes, through both school structure and content, to processes of reconciliation. For example, schooling can help *build a sense of reciprocity* across members of different ethnic groups and a *sense of a shared future*. Schools can also play a role in reconciliation through fostering *acknowledgment*.[113] In the latter cases, educational content and pedagogy may center on attempts to change perceptions of the other group through legitimating the other's collective narrative and engaging in "perspective-taking" (exercises to understand the thoughts, feelings, and motivations of other individuals or groups), as well as critically examining both sides' contributions to the conflict, as relevant, to break down limiting cognitive consistency.[114] Emphasizing the importance of multiple, nuanced narratives can often play a positive role in reconciliation.[115] Two other strategies that have led to improved attitudes toward other groups include studying a distant conflict and reading stories about groups against which prejudice exists.[116] Reconciliation and the strategies to work toward it are very much related to developing horizontal equity and inclusive identities; these different pathways toward peacebuilding are mutually reinforcing.

Critical Thinking Skills

Building critical thinking skills is another pathway to peacebuilding in which schooling can play a central role. Openness to diverse perspectives and developing purposeful and reflective judgment – rather than closed-mindedness and conformity – can help individuals question unequal institutions, framings,

---

[109] Lederach 1997, p. 26.
[110] Longman and Rutagengwa 2004, p. 172.
[111] Weinstein 2011.
[112] See for example Ali and Matthews 2004.
[113] For more, see Cole 2007; King 2010.
[114] Salomon 2002, p. 9.
[115] Barr 2010; Ross 2002, pp. 315, 320.
[116] See, respectively, Kuppermitz and Salomon 2005, p. 296; Paluck and Green 2009a.

narratives, myths, and images of the other. Critical thinking skills assist people in discovering conflict-management options.[117] These skills can also open people to the processes of cognitive dissonance – thinking away from the norm – that are required for peacebuilding.[118] Critical thinking skills may make individuals more resistant to leaders' efforts to scapegoat and motivate people to violence.[119] In contrast, institutions that promote conformity often emphasize automatic obedience, allowing individuals who commit violence to claim to have been merely following orders.[120]

In schools, while it may seem logical to avoid conflicts raised by multiple or opposing narratives, a growing number of studies argue that, paradoxically, children must be confronted with conflict and have practice with understanding it in order to be able to manage conflicts peacefully in their own lives. Scholars and practitioners encourage democratic classrooms with space for questions, multiple points of view, and "inclusive cooperation and open conversation about meaningful issues."[121] For classroom conflict to be productive, however, the classroom must be a safe and cooperative environment. A number of studies show that controversy in safe classrooms promotes "greater liking, social support and self-esteem among participants" than seeking concurrence does.[122] A study of civic education "found that students who participated in classroom discussion of issues rather than memorizing dates or facts about politics or participating in patriotic rituals had higher scores on both the anti-authoritarianism measure and on the knowledge test."[123] A similar study of twenty-four countries found that "schools that operate in a participatory democratic way, foster an open climate for discussion within the classroom and invite students to take part in shaping school life are effective in promoting both civic knowledge and engagement."[124] Practice with managing classroom-type conflicts, such as multiple narratives, can help students manage societal conflicts as well.[125]

Interactions and Continuums

The pathways that conduce to conflict and those that build peace, as just presented, are neither polar opposites nor isolated from one another. It is best to think of each pathway as a continuum on which specific school structures and

[117] See Avery et al. 1999; Avery, Sullivan, and Wood 1997; Bickmore 1999; Bickmore 2008; Houser 1996; Johnson and Johnson 1994; Merelman 1990.
[118] Festinger 1959.
[119] Staub 1989, p. 63.
[120] Harber 2004, p. 43.
[121] Bickmore 2008, p. 447.
[122] For a review, see Johnson and Johnson 1994, p. 126.
[123] Torney-Purta, Schwille, and Amadeo 1999.
[124] Torney-Purta et al. 2001, p. 176.
[125] Gehlbach 2004.

content may be situated.[126] For example, one education system might promote critical thinking more intensely than another.[127]

The pathways also interact. For example, multiple pathways toward conflict can be mutually reinforcing, thereby multiplying their effect. Other times, pathways may work at cross-purposes. Education may simultaneously contribute to creating the underlying conditions for both violent conflict and sustainable peace. For example, an education system might go a good way toward achieving horizontal equity, thus buttressing the peacebuilding side, yet continue to collectivize and stigmatize students into corporate groups, thus reinforcing conflict. The challenge is to figure out the impact of the education system on balance.

Concluding Reflections

In this chapter, I described a number of ways in which education contributes to conflict, or conversely, to peacebuilding. Literature on the causes of conflict relegates education to the margins, and analyses of intergroup conflict in Rwanda often mention education without investigating it in any depth. In contrast, I concentrate on the relationship between education and conflict. I suggest a continuum from a schooling system based on horizontal inequalities that emphasizes essential, corporate identities, and stigmatizes groups to one that promotes horizontal equity, inclusive identity strategies, reconciliation, and critical thinking.

With the tools developed in this chapter, I turn to the real-world setting of Rwanda. I examine the involvement of schools in fostering violent interethnic conflict on the one hand and in building peace on the other. I show that specific mechanisms that help explain conflict in Rwanda manifested themselves in Rwanda's schools. This study thus contributes not only to a more thorough explanation of conflict in Rwanda, but also to a more nuanced understanding of the role of education in conflict and peacebuilding more broadly.

---

[126] For an example of an active to passive education continuum, relating to positive and negative conflict, see the Birmingham International Education Security Index in Davies 2006.

[127] See, for example, Bertrand et al. 2006.

2

Colonial Schooling

When Europeans first described Rwanda, they called it a prosperous "land flowing with milk and honey" where the people lived in "impressive harmony."[1] One colonial administrator described Rwanda as "the safest place on earth. In my time, there was never a gunshot."[2] By 1964, their descriptions had much changed: Rwanda had descended into widespread violence. Thousands of huts were burned and pillaged, 10,000 to 20,000 Rwandans were killed, more than 20,000 were internally displaced, and between 100,000 and 300,000 fled the country.[3] While there were class and regional dimensions, violence was principally between Hutu and Tutsi Rwandans, and those forced to flee were mostly Tutsi.

This chapter attempts to uncover if and how formal education during the Belgian colonial period played a role in the development of this intergroup conflict. First, it familiarizes readers with the historical concepts that are central to understanding ethnic identity and conflict in Rwanda. It then discusses the development of the formal education system during the colonial period. Bringing these two sections together, this chapter then argues that a number of factors underlying violent intergroup conflict in this period were cultivated by Rwanda's colonial era school system. While this chapter covers principally 1919 to 1962, this temporal classification is not entirely satisfactory. Key transformative events upon which I elaborate in the following sections include the revolution and transfer of power to Hutu leaders in 1959, independence in 1962, and widespread continuing violence through 1963–1964. There is thus some overlap between this and the next chapter.

[1] de Lacger 1939, pp. 64–66; The Duke of Mecklenburg (1910) quoted in Lemarchand 1970, p. 143.
[2] Author's interview, Belgian colonial administrator, Belgium, September 27(B), 2006.
[3] On the various sources of these discrepant numbers, see Lema 1993, pp. 37–39; Lemarchand 1970, pp. 167, 71–72.

History, Politics, and Society in Colonial Rwanda

When Canadian General Roméo Dallaire was informed that he would lead a UN mission in Rwanda, he recalls asking, "That's somewhere in Africa, isn't it?"[4] Landlocked in the center of the continent, just south of the equator, Rwanda is one of the smallest states in Africa. It is a stunningly beautiful country, aptly dubbed the land of a thousand hills. Roughly the size of Haiti, or the U.S. state of Maryland, it has a population of more than 11.5 million people (2012 estimate), of which about 84 percent are Hutu, 15 percent Tutsi, and 1 percent Twa, according to conventional wisdom, although these distinctions are no longer publicly permitted or counted in Rwanda today.

Writing a brief overview of Rwanda's past is unusually tricky both because of the level of controversy surrounding the subject and its various political uses.[5] History is contested in most parts of the world, but as Newbury writes of Rwanda, "with an intensity that surpasses the normal clichés, there is no single history; rather there are competing 'histories.'"[6] Even more so than in other countries, in researching Rwanda, one finds "a mixture of fact and fiction designed to offer each community retrospective validation of its own interpretation of the genesis of ethnic conflict."[7] Interpretations of histories change according to the group in power and its ability to decide upon the public transcript. The challenges of historical perspective, accuracy, and manipulation return many times in subsequent chapters. Thankfully, my job is not to come up with a "true" history of Rwanda, but to make sense of this book's research questions in light of the complexity and contestation over Rwanda's past.

When I speak to people who are not familiar with the case of Rwanda, they frequently ask the seemingly simple question: "What exactly are Hutu and Tutsi?" From the precolonial period to today, Hutu and Tutsi have been considered races or ethnicities, as well as castes, classes or socioeconomic groups, and often political identities. Furthermore, consistent with the constructivist approach to ethnicity, the content of Hutu, Tutsi, and Twa has changed over time: "To be Tutsi or to be Hutu, in Rwanda and Burundi, did not have the same sense in 1994, at the time of the genocide, in 1894, when the whites arrived, in 1794, when the former kingdoms were almost at their apogee, and in 1594, when the kingdoms came into being."[8] How identities are shaped in relation to power and internalized by people themselves is crucial to understanding the ongoing construction of ethnicity.

---

[4] Dallaire 2003, p. 42.
[5] For more on the challenges of Rwandan historiography see Chrétien 2003; Eltringham 2004; Lemarchand 1994; Linden and Linden 1977, pp. 5–6, 198; Malkki 1995; Newbury 1998; Vansina 1962.
[6] Newbury 1998.
[7] Lemarchand 1994, p. 19.
[8] Chrétien 2003, p.83. See also Mamdani 1996; 2001. Note that Rwanda and Burundi are demographically similar neighbors that were jointly governed by the Belgians.

Until recently, it had been accepted practice to begin the telling of Rwanda's history as successive waves of migration, and this is how the colonial administrators and missionaries with whom I spoke recounted Rwanda's past.[9] The original inhabitants, the Twa, were deemed of pygmoid origin and were labeled hunters and potters. Hutu were said to have emigrated from Central Africa several thousand years ago. They were believed to be agriculturalists, clearing the land as they moved. The last to arrive – a not insignificant detail – were Tutsi pastoralists. Tutsi were said to have come from Ethiopia with their cows, a valuable resource, sometime after the fifteenth century.

This narrative described precolonial Rwanda as a centralized kingdom in which Hutu, Tutsi, and Twa lived in relatively peaceful coexistence. It said all groups spoke the same language, shared a culture and religion, respected the same king (*mwami*), and lived intermingled on the same hills. Much of this history stems from collaboration between early European historiographers and Rwandan experts in the royal court, and, as discussed in Chapter 4, is consistent with the version of history that the government of Rwanda promulgates today.

While this rosy picture of intergroup relations is overstated, the demarcation between groups in the precolonial period was much less rigid than it would later become. Politically, there was a trinity of chiefs on each hill: a chief of the pastures (always Tutsi), a chief of the land (often Hutu), and a chief of the men (usually Tutsi), leaving space for both Tutsi and Hutu leadership and the ability for peasants to maneuver between chiefs. Clans were often a more important identity than ethnicity, and most clans included Hutu, Tutsi, and Twa.[10] Even the very labels "Hutu" and "Tutsi" varied with time and place in precolonial Rwanda. Prior to colonialism, the terms "Hutu" and "Tutsi" were unknown to some populations outside central Rwanda. At different points, Hutu referred to "boorishness and loutish behaviour," to noncombatant status, and to foreigners.[11] One Belgian missionary told me that he often heard people say "my Hutu," meaning, in fact, "my slave."[12] There were also provisions for social mobility whereby a Hutu who rose through economic ranks could become Tutsi (*kwihutura*) and a Tutsi whose position declined could become Hutu (*gucupira*). Some authors even suggest that one could be Hutu in one relationship yet Tutsi in another.[13]

Socially, there was also much internal differentiation within groups. There were intermarriages and extramarital affairs resulting in group mixing.[14]

---

[9] Centre for Conflict Management 2002; de Lacger 1939, pp. 36–59; Heremans 1971, pp. 3–47; Kagame 1958, pp. 7–11; Lemarchand 1970, pp. 18–22.

[10] Chrétien 2003, p.189; Lema 1993, p. 49; Newbury 1998.

[11] Newbury 1998, p. 74. See also Vidal, who showed that the political use of ethnic designations is actually very recent in De Lame 2005, p. 8; Vansina 2004, p. 134.

[12] Author's interview, Belgian missionary, Belgium, September 20(B), 2006.

[13] Mamdani 2001, p. 101.

[14] Even colonial powers noticed this mixing in their 1926 report. De Lame 2005, pp. 101–102. In contrast, Pottier claims that intermarriages were quite rare. See Pottier 2002, p. 117.

According to Jared Diamond, about one-quarter of all Rwandans have both Hutu and Tutsi among their great-grandparents.[15] Similarities across groups were also common. For instance, the average Hutu and average Tutsi were equally poor.[16] Speaking in 2006, one Hutu man who was educated in the north during the colonial period explained: "My father was a teacher, and he was well-off. So, he spoke to well-off Tutsi and well-off Hutu, without necessarily speaking to poor Tutsi. Because, you shouldn't believe that all Tutsi governed the country – that is false."[17] While, through a process of collectivization, "Tutsi chief" came to be equated with Tutsi in the mid-1950 demographic survey, through the colonial era at least 90 percent of all Tutsi were poor.[18]

This variation in the meaning and salience of ethnicity does not mean that differences between Hutu, Tutsi, and Twa were unimportant, or that they were inventions of the colonial powers, as some have later come to claim. During the precolonial period, there were sociopolitical and socioeconomic distinctions between the groups that hardened during the colonial period. For example, all kings were Tutsi, as were all army commanders and warriors.[19] As mentioned earlier, despite the three-chief system, the highest-placed chief was usually a Tutsi, especially one of the Abanyiginya or Abega clan.[20] The corpse of a Tutsi even had more value than that of a Hutu or a Twa.[21] While not necessarily coinciding, class and ethnicity were entangled. When I asked one man who went to school in colonial Rwanda whether he knew the ethnicity of his teachers, he answered, "yes ... it is easy to know by observing their behavior, their clothing, and [distinguishing] those that were wearing nice clothing [Tutsi] from modest clothing [Hutu]."[22] Groups were also involved in complex patron-client relationships, called *ubuhake*, in which richer Tutsi most often held the patron position, with poorer Hutu as clients. The most burdensome parts of *ubureetwa*, a form of *corvée* labor, were imposed on Hutu only – or at least on farmers rather than pastoralists, which in practice meant mostly Hutu – institutionalizing a hierarchical Hutu-Tutsi distinction and, according to Jan Vansina, serving as the "straw that broke the camel's back" in terms of intergroup relations.[23]

Such evidence points to the ethnic polarization of Hutu and Tutsi as occurring before the arrival of Europeans, not as merely a colonial construct. Some

---

[15] Diamond 2005, p. 318.

[16] Hintjens 2001, p. 30; Prunier 1997, p. 50.

[17] Author's interview, male Hutu, Kigali, April 8(B), 2006.

[18] Chrétien 2003, p. 285.

[19] Maquet 1952, p. 1014.

[20] Prunier 1997, p. 24.

[21] Lema 1993, pp. 52–53.

[22] Author's interview, Rwandan researcher, Kigali, March 13, 2006.

[23] Longman 2010; Newbury 1980; Newbury 1988, pp. 40–41, 75–76, 82, 133–134; Vansina 2004, pp. 134–136.

of the roots of intergroup conflict in Rwanda can be traced back to the reign of King Rwabugiri, which lasted from 1853 to 1894. It was during this time that Hutu and Tutsi became social categories and, subsequently, opportunities for social mobility began to decrease. Indeed, in contrast to the image of a peaceful precolonial Rwanda, Vansina calls the age of Rwabugiri "a nightmare" and argues that this was when the rift between Hutu and Tutsi began to emerge.[24]

Nonetheless, the colonial state played an important role in changing and reinforcing these ethnic identities. When Europeans first arrived in Rwanda in 1894, they were impressed with the politically centralized kingdom they found and were particularly taken by the Tutsi, who appeared to be effective rulers. Having no explanation for how Africans, whom they were coming to "civilize," could develop such a well-functioning state, they devised what came to be known as the Hamitic hypothesis. Championed first by John Hanning Speke, and later by countless others drawing on theories of racial superiority in vogue in Europe, Tutsi were said to be whites in black skin, foreigners from Ethiopia.

Both the Germans (1896–1916) and the Belgians (1919–1962), who ruled the territory of Rwanda-Urundi, espoused Hamitic hypotheses. In 1903, a missionary in Burundi asked of Tutsi: "Did we not see Caucasian crania, admirably Greek profiles, beside quite pronounced Semitic and even Jewish countenances, and even true beauties with bronze-red faces in the center of Rwanda and Burundi?"[25] The Belgian Minister of the Colonies report (1925) stated:

> The Mututsi[26] of good race has nothing of the negro, apart from his colour. He is usually very tall, 1.80m at least, often 1.90m or more. He is very thin, a characteristic which tends to be even more noticeable as he gets older. His features are very fine: a high brow, thin nose and fine lips framing beautiful shining teeth. Batutsi women are usually lighter-skinned than their husbands, very slender and pretty in their youth, although they tend to thicken with age. Gifted with a vivacious intelligence, the Tutsi displays a refinement of feelings which is rare among primitive people. He is a natural-born leader, capable of extreme self-control and of calculated goodwill.[27]

In contrast, it wrote of Hutu as having

> very typical Bantu features. They are generally short and thick-set with a big head, a jovial expression, a wide nose and enormous lips. They are extroverts who like to laugh and lead a simple life.

[24] Vansina 2004, pp. 180–194. See also Chrétien 2003, pp. 79, 190; Lemarchand 1970, p. 39; Newbury 1988.

[25] van der Burgt, Dutch missionary in Burundi (1903), quoted in Chrétien 2003, p. 73.

[26] The prefixes mu- and ba-, which sometimes appear before Hutu, Tutsi, and Twa, refer, respectively, to the singular and plural in Kinyarwanda.

[27] This and the subsequent two statements are quoted in Prunier 1997, p. 6.

It described the Twa as a

> member of a worn out and quickly disappearing race.... The Mutwa presents
> a number of well-defined somatic characteristics: he is small, chunky, muscular,
> and very hairy; particularly on the chest. With a monkey-like flat face and a huge
> nose, he is quite similar to the apes whom he chases in the forest.

As such, Hutu, Tutsi, and Twa came to be seen as "races" by the colonial powers, missionaries, and early historians.[28] The morphological comments on height and noses, as well as the aptitudes attributed to each group, return in subsequent chapters because they left an imprint on Rwandans' self-understandings until at least the 1994 genocide. The *CIA World Factbook*, wherein Rwanda's population is listed as comprising "Hutu (Bantu), Tutsi (Hamitic), and Twa (Pygmy)," is a testament to the durability of the Hamitic hypothesis.[29]

Colonizers in the early colonial period decisively characterized Tutsi as superior foreigners. This label brought short-term benefits but proved disastrous in the longer term. Relying on their Hamitic understanding and indirect-rule strategies, which were said to respect local customs, the Germans – and more significantly, the Belgians who administered Rwanda after World War I – helped Tutsi solidify rule in the country. As one colonial official recalled of his pre-departure education in Antwerp:

> They taught us that we were going to do indirect administration. This involved
> respecting the customary authorities that were in place ... relations that had
> been established for generations.... The cleavage in Rwanda was simultaneously
> racial, economic and political, and the border between the three was difficult to
> determine ... but this cleavage was between possessors of the grass, possessors of
> the herds, and possessors of the land.[30]

Contrary to Rwandans' own perception of themselves, the Belgians saw their colony's population almost exclusively through ethnic lenses and deemed Tutsi as "destined to rule."[31]

Through Tutsi on the ground, the Germans further centralized Rwanda and brought the last outlying areas, the northern kingdoms still ruled by Hutu, under central administration. When the Belgians took control, they decreased the powers of the *mwami* and centralized those of chiefs. The Belgians also helped increase Tutsi power with a significant move in 1926 to place one Tutsi chief in each locale, abolishing the trinity of chiefs and diminishing Hutu political power[32] – a "grave error," looking back, one missionary admitted.[33] While

---

[28] See Classe 1935; de Lacger 1939, p. 36; Kagame 1958, p. 7; Pagès 1930, p. 3.
[29] CIA, 2012.
[30] Author's interview, Belgian colonial administrator, Belgium, September 20(A), 2006.
[31] Ryckmans 1931, p. 20.
[32] Lemarchand 1970, see pp. 44, 48 on customary rule. See p. 73 on the abolition of the trinity of chiefs.
[33] Author's interview, Belgian missionary, Belgium, September 20(B), 2006.

these changes solidified the position of high-ranking Tutsi, reformulations of *ubureetwa* demands in the 1920s increased social differentiation and hierarchy between even lower class, or "*petit* Tutsi," and the average Hutu.[34] In 1933, the Belgians conducted a census that, according to many, crystallized ethnic identity and restricted possibilities for intergroup mobility by having each male Rwandan formally declare an ethnicity. (In my own interviews, Belgian colonial administrators talked about issuing "taxation booklets" in the manner described, rather than "identity cards," and suggested that such booklets may not have been issued to all parts of Rwanda until after 1962, during the First Republic.) While quality of life for Hutu and Tutsi Rwandans differed depending on their region and the behavior of particular chiefs, and there remained similarities between poor Hutu and poor Tutsi, the state generally institutionalized Hutu and Tutsi into distinct and unequal groups. The conditions of the Hutu were "worse under Belgian rule than at any other time in the past."[35] Indeed, Newbury calls Hutu under the Belgians "second class citizens" and deems the situation "dual colonialism."[36]

The Catholic Church played a significant role alongside the state in transforming and crystallizing Hutu and Tutsi identities and the cleavage between them.[37] Although other religious groups, including Protestants, Adventists, Seventh-Day Adventists, and to a lesser extent Muslims, were active in Rwanda, the Catholic Church dominated religion and education. As one Rwandan who had been educated during the colonial period stated, "The church has always meddled in politics. The Catholic Church also upheld the powers that were in place ... when someone colonizes a people, to mark it, to make it submit, they use the politics of dividing, just as the church used religion to divide."[38] When the first Catholic expeditionary mission visited Rwanda, it described the country as one with the rest of the population "absolutely enslaved" to Tutsi.[39] Missionaries saw this as a promising situation, believing that the general population would welcome them, and indeed, by 1910 they had already converted about 4,500 Rwandans, mostly Hutu.[40] In fact, Rwanda became the most Christianized country in Africa, with already 500,000 converts by 1955 and 700,000 by 1960,[41] accounting for between one-fifth and one-quarter of the total population. Soon, however, church leaders too came to support the Hamitic hypothesis, indirect-rule strategies, and Tutsi dominance. Father Classe, who later became the Vicar Apostolic of Rwanda, stated: "Generally speaking, we have no chiefs who are better qualified, more intelligent, more

[34] Mamdani 2001, p. 97–98.
[35] Lemarchand 1970, p. 123.
[36] Newbury 1998; Newbury 1983, p. 254.
[37] For a detailed overview of Christianity and politics in Rwanda, see Longman 2010.
[38] Author's interview, male Tutsi, Kigali, January 30(A), 2006.
[39] Quoted in Linden and Linden 1977, p. 33.
[40] Ibid., p. 79.
[41] Chrétien 2003, p. 272.

active, more capable of appreciating progress and more fully accepted by the people than the Tutsi."[42]

As the Europeans contributed to further hardening group lines through a variety of policies – including those targeting education – Rwandans came to view themselves and each other through much the same lenses. Social-structural exclusions produced bipolarity and stereotypes and gradually moved groups toward more corporate identities. As Gérard Prunier writes:

> The Hutu, deprived of all political power and materially exploited by both the whites and the Tutsi, were told by everyone that they were inferiors who deserved their fate and also came to believe it. As a consequence they began to hate *all* Tutsi, even those who were just as poor as they, since *all* Tutsi were members of the "superior race."[43]

As Tutsi elites consolidated their hold over the instruments of the state, Hutu experiences of intense exploitation during the precolonial and, much more so, the colonial period induced Hutu awareness and solidarity as an identity group.[44] For their part, many Tutsi saw advantages in the European's portrayal of intergroup relations and came to see themselves through the eyes of the Europeans. Many of even the poorest Tutsi considered themselves of higher class.[45]

As the colonial period wore on, rural discontent, especially among the Hutu population, increased significantly. Peasants complained about the unfairness of *ubuhake* and *ubureetwa*. The hardships and humiliation of *ubureetwa*, in particular, were a shared experience among Hutu and induced a "cohesion of oppression," thereby raising Hutu political consciousness.[46] Indeed, a common fate is often a powerful starting point for the construction of a shared identity.[47] While there was variation in time and place in the salience of ethnic identity and anti-Tutsi feelings, resentment played out on increasingly collectivized ethnic lines. Because control over land, labor, education, wealth, and access to the state were concentrated in hands of Tutsi elite, Hutu grievances were juxtaposed to Tutsi privilege.

The administration made a number of political changes to address growing unrest. For instance, they held elections in 1953 and 1956. The elections, however, did not bring about substantial change, because only the lowest positions were directly elected, and Tutsi returned Tutsi to power through indirect elections for the highest positions. The administration abolished patronage relationships of *ubuhake* in 1954, but this too was disappointing for Hutu, as it did not produce meaningful change. Indeed, Tutsi had many other social structures

---

[42] Lemarchand 1970, p. 73.
[43] Prunier 1997, p. 39.
[44] Newbury 1988, p. 209.
[45] Linden and Linden 1977, p. 228.
[46] Newbury 1980; Newbury 1988.
[47] Brewer 2000, p. 119.

of power, gained through colonialism, through which to perpetuate their rule and dominance.[48]

Meanwhile, the experience of other countries that had recently achieved independence also influenced Rwandans. One colonial administrator recalled that "before independence, as in other countries in Africa, people listened to the radio, so there were external influences. So, in '47, British India and a lot of Asian countries gained their independence. Rwanda could not be a stranger to this. As time went by, [Rwandan] officials began to say 'if we want our independence, we have to fight for it'.... [But] there were Hutu that battled against Tutsi."[49]

Indeed, Tutsi and Hutu elites envisioned the transition to independence differently. In preparation for a UN visit, the *Conseil Supérieur du Pays*, a sort of parliament of "overwhelmingly" Tutsi membership, issued *Mise au Point* (Statement of Views) lobbying for a quick transfer of power to the current authorities: themselves. In contrast, the Hutu counter-elite demanded democracy before independence, expecting the majority Hutu to thus take power. They issued *Notes on the Social Aspect of the Racial Native Problem in Rwanda*, better known as the *Hutu Manifesto*, asserting pride and entitlement in the Hutu identity. The fact that the "social aspect" was described as a "racial" and "native" one is a testament to the salience of the Hamitic hypothesis. In this way, Hutu came to see national independence as entailing liberation equally from Tutsi and Belgian colonizers.

In response to these events, and influenced by a growing post–World War II human rights and equality regime and a change of guard among missionaries, the Belgian colonial administration began to shift its allegiance from Tutsi to Hutu. In addition, as one interviewee who was educated in the colonial period recollected, Tutsi "were not appreciated anymore [by the colonial power], because they were asking for independence."[50] The mysterious death of the Rwandan King, *mwami* Mutara III, in July 1959 further contributed to this context of change and uncertainty. While the cause remains controversial today, its immediate effect was to raise ethnic and political tensions, arousing mutual suspicions and decreasing trust.

The *muyaga*, as Rwandans call it – a "strong but variable wind, with unpredictable destructive gusts"[51] – swept through Rwanda in November 1959. Instigated by an attack of young Tutsi militants on a popular Hutu leader, reprisals spread throughout the country, resulting in about 200 deaths.[52] As a former colonial administrator recounted, "All the officials were Tutsi.... In 1959, I think there were maybe two sub-chiefs that were Hutu, one in Umutara and one in Gitarama. And it is like this that I was sent to Gitarama where the violence

[48] Newbury 1988, p. 146.
[49] Author's interview, Belgian colonial administrator, Belgium, September 20(A), 2006.
[50] Author's interview, female Tutsi, Kigali, March 10(B), 2006.
[51] Prunier 1997, p. 41.
[52] Lema 1993; Lemarchand 1970.

broke out. There was a rumor that [Mbonyumutwa, the Hutu sub-chief] had been killed, which was ... false."[53] Violence began against members of the Tutsi aristocracy that held administrative posts, but then spread, through corporatist propaganda, to all Tutsi. As Newbury writes, "Ultimately, an appeal to Hutu solidarity became, for Hutu leaders, the most effective rallying point for revolutionary activity."[54] Tutsi leaders used violence in an effort to maintain the status quo, but the Belgians, with pressure from the United Nations and a new influx of missionaries, supported Hutu. In the end, the so-called Social Revolution or Hutu Revolution of 1959 resulted in the abolition of the Tutsi monarchy, the removal of Tutsi from positions of power and their replacement with Hutu, and the beginnings of widespread violence against Tutsi.

I heard different narratives relating to these events. Hutu generally de-emphasize violence and describe the events of 1959 as a rightful majority overcoming 400 years of political and economic injustice. In fact, a well-known Rwandan phrase for these events, *rubanda nyamwinshi*, refers to the right of the indigenous majority to come to power. In contrast, Tutsi often focus on violence – sometimes calling it genocide – and describe the events of 1959 as driven by a Belgian about-face. The revolution of 1959 thus provides an illustration of divergent transcripts along ethnic lines. Rather than overcome racialized identities, the revolution – and its subsequent interpretations – solidified them. This is hardly unusual; in effect, threat and conflict often harden identities.[55]

The revolution brought about a number of political changes in addition to those already mentioned. As one Rwandan interview participant opined, "Before, we knew nothing [about conflict]. But starting in November '59, there were four political parties. And it is in these political parties, perhaps, that conflict was born."[56] As the possibility of independence loomed, political parties developed largely along ethnic lines, although there were more moderate and activist parties and neither Hutu nor Tutsi were monolithic groups. Numerous interviewees emphasized that ethnicity became much more salient after the revolution. Communal elections were held in 1960 and Parmehutu, the pro-Hutu party, won 70.4 percent of seats. In a response foreshadowing the government's strategy today, the *Union Nationale Rwandaise* (UNAR), a pro-monarchy Tutsi-dominated party, then called on the "Children of Rwanda" to "unite our strengths" and insisted that "[t]here are no Tutsi, Hutu, Twa. We are all brothers! We are all descendants of Kinyarwanda!"[57] This strategy makes sense for an ethnic minority seeking to maintain power. Nevertheless, once in charge of a majority of communal positions, Hutu leaders launched a national coup January 28, 1961 in Gitarama, again largely supported by the Belgians. They proclaimed the Rwandan Republic and elected Grégoire Kayibanda, a

[53] Author's interview, Belgian colonial administrator, Belgium, September 20(A), 2006.
[54] Newbury 1988, p. 213.
[55] Kaufmann 1996; Levine and Campbell 1972.
[56] Author's interview, female Tutsi, Kigali, March 14, 2006.
[57] Lemarchand 1970, p. 161.

one-time primary school teacher, president. Rwanda became formally independent from Belgium, and separate from Burundi, in 1962. The revolution, surrounding events, and subsequent repression resulted in large-scale displacement: between 100,000 and 300,000 Tutsi fled the country.[58]

Independence did not bring an end to Rwanda's struggles. Some of the Tutsi who had gone into exile undertook armed raids to return to Rwanda. Known as the *inyenzi*, or cockroaches (both derogatory and reflective of the stealth in their night-time tactics), the exiles launched more than ten raids during 1963 and 1964. Beginning with attacks on specific individuals and families, the raids eventually took aim at all Hutu officials. The Rwandan government responded with increasingly harsh repression of the general Tutsi population, and violence escalated significantly. As one Parmehutu propagandist announced, "We are expected to defend ourselves. The only way to go about [it] is to paralyze the Tutsi. How? They must be killed."[59] Many of my interviewees recall huts burning during this period as one of their first experiences of political awareness. More than 5,000, and possibly as many as 14,000, Tutsi were killed, individually and in massacres.[60] Bertrand Russell called it "the most terrible and systematic genocide since the genocide of Jews by Hitler," a sentiment replicated by the Vatican.[61] Genocide or not – a question much debated in Rwanda, with the answers depending somewhat on the group in power – thousands were dead and hundreds of thousands were in exile by the end of 1964.

Causes of Violent Intergroup Conflict

Despite these tragic ends, most of my interviewees explained that there were few acute problems between ordinary Hutu and Tutsi during much of the colonial period. As one former colonial administrator summarized, "When I arrived in '48, there were no tensions, no disorder at all.... Then, we could say that within a few years, it exploded. Why?"[62]

The historical overview presented earlier raises a number of proximate causes for the intergroup violence that Rwanda experienced surrounding independence. Imminent decolonization, the death of the king, and deteriorating relations with the Belgians brought to light insecurities about the future of the country for both Hutu and Tutsi groups. Then, the assault on the Hutu leader Mbonyumutwa helped ignite violent conflict. The formation of political parties and their varying demands were also a prime driver of conflict raised by interviewees. One colonial administrator said that much changed on "November 1st, [when,] with instigation of political parties, [Rwandans] started wanting

[58] Ibid., pp. 80–85. Mamdani 2001, pp. 115–116.
[59] Lemarchand 1970, pp. 223–224.
[60] Mamdani 2001, pp. 129–130; Straus 2006, pp. 186–187.
[61] Quoted in Lemarchand 1970, p. 224. See also Linden 1999, p. 363.
[62] Author's interview, Belgian colonial administrator, Belgium, September 20(A), 2006.

to expel one another."[63] Another colonial official, who worked in the education system, and who knew Kayibanda personally, explained that in the late 1950s, Kayibanda would "go on the hills and make speeches that I would call really incendiary. And when he left, not by accident, already all the Tutsi huts would be burning."[64]

Even if these factors were proximate causes of intergroup conflict, they were insufficient to *cause* rural discontent. For proximate causes such as these to turn into acute conflict, there must also be a foundation of underlying causes. Intergroup conflict in this transitional period relied on a foundation of social-structural and psychocultural factors. As one colonial administrator explained, in a statement representative of many, "Political power took advantage of this [ethnic] cleavage, what they called an injustice … little by little, politicians seized upon this."[65] As one elderly Rwandan recalled of his experiences in the colonial period, "They had to draw on something to provoke a movement."[66]

Inequalities between Hutu and Tutsi grew stronger during this period, and socioeconomic relations became increasingly asymmetrical. Alongside, and in part as a result of, increasing inequalities, identity categories were further solidified and increasingly essentialized into all-inclusive groups. Hutu were often collectively stigmatized as inferior to a collective Tutsi group. "It was a regrettable error in my opinion," a Hutu man opined. "Why chant that Tutsi are bad, when instead, I would have chanted that chiefs were bad, that sub-chiefs were bad? That could have attenuated the problem. Because everyone was mad, but everyone was not a sub-chief, and the majority of Tutsi were miserable."[67]

The rest of this chapter argues that the colonial school system, rather that promoting positive intergroup relations, was an important contributor to the horizontal inequalities, increasingly exclusive identities, and stigmatization of the Hutu group in particular, which created a permissive environment for the intergroup conflict surrounding independence. The way that the state and church developed formal education during the Belgian administration of Rwanda played a significant role in advancing divisive social-structural and psychocultural processes.

Formal Education during the Colonial Period

Prior to European arrival, Rwandan education took place primarily at home in the nuclear family and was based on transmitting values and language. Much of this occurred through storytelling, singing, dancing, and poetry – traditions that often live on in families today. During the precolonial period, some formal

---

[63] Ibid.
[64] Author's interview, Belgian colonial administrator, Belgium, September 26, 2006.
[65] Author's interview, Belgian colonial administrator, Belgium, September 20(A), 2006.
[66] Author's interview, male Tutsi, Kigali, January 30(A), 2006.
[67] Author's interview, male Hutu, Kigali, April 8(B), 2006.

education took place at training schools (*amatorero*), particularly for young Tutsi men at the royal court. Students, called *intore*, were trained in militarism, war skills, esprit de corps, and loyalty, as well as iron smith and foundry, basket making, pottery, drumming, dancing, and poetry. [68]

At the turn of the twentieth century, education began to change when the White Fathers – so named for their white cassocks – asked permission from the king to establish a school at the royal court. The king and other Rwandans held strong superstitions against formal schooling, including a myth that missionaries would steal children and put them through a tunnel to Europe. Alternative rumors spread that children taken into school were destined for Mother Death, to whom the *mwami* had promised many Rwandan lives. In fact, the court and the country's chiefs deemed those who went to missionary schools rebels or traitors. [69]

The *mwami* nonetheless granted the missionaries an initial site at Save, in southern Rwanda, and thereafter, the number of schools grew quickly. [70] By 1905 there were ten schools in Rwanda, and by 1913 the number had risen to forty primary schools teaching more than 2,000 children. [71] Because education was unappealing to the highest classes, pupils were from the poorest rungs of the population. Most schoolchildren were impoverished and patronless Hutu who saw possibilities of clientship and protection in the White Fathers. "In the beginning," one White Father told me, "no Tutsi came to these schools. This lasted about twenty-five years. We took the students that came, essentially Hutu." [72] A colonial official specified that this was "not all Hutu. The most intelligent were often kept at home because their parents wanted them to take over one day." [73] Over the years, Tutsi disdain for mission schools softened slightly, and the Germans established a nonreligious school in Kigali for "notable" Tutsi youth. Overall, however, Germans had neither the time nor the means to leave a significant institutional imprint on Rwanda.

The core of the story really begins with the League of Nations mandate, which gave Belgium the right to govern Rwanda-Urundi, including control over all educational institutions. Within their first few years in the country, Belgian authorities opened several official nonreligious schools, first at the royal court in Nyanza, then in four other corners of the country. [74] According to the Belgian administration, these five schools, in operation until 1929, were "strictly reserved for sons of chiefs and for notables of the Tutsi race." [75] This training enabled graduates to take up envied jobs in the public and private sectors.

---

[68] See Vansina 2004, p. 201.
[69] Erny 2001, p. 22; Linden and Linden 1977, p. 35.
[70] Hoben 1989, p. 10; Longman 2010, p. 39.
[71] Erny 2001, p. 24; Ngendahimana 1981, p. 2.
[72] Author's interview, Belgian missionary, Belgium, September 27(A), 2006.
[73] Author's interview, Belgian colonial administrator, Belgium, September 26, 2006.
[74] Erny 2001.
[75] "Rapport Présenté par le Gouvernement Belge au Conseil de la Société des Nations" 1929, p. 62.

In 1926, the Belgian administration allowed Catholic missions an expanded role in education, offering subsidies to religious schools in exchange for some state controls. This resulted in three types of schools: *official schools* or state schools, founded, funded, and administered by the Belgians as the five original ones; subsidized schools (*écoles libres subsidiées*), which constituted the great majority of schools and were run by missionaries but followed the curricular outlines, methods, infrastructural standards, and inspection of the colonial administration; and private schools (*écoles libres des missions nationales*) run by the missions without the help or control of the Belgian administration.

The school facilities themselves were simple. One former colonial administrator described a typical school as "largely a roof to protect from rains and the sun. A roof of straw, mud walls, an open floor, so it was cool inside. And the benches were tree trunks laid on the ground."[76] Another explained that because not all classes had blackboards, students sometimes drew lessons in the dirt, or with a piece of straw on their leg.[77] As in much of Africa to this day, qualified teachers and teaching material were in short supply. Children attended primary schools during the day only, often making a long trek to and from home. In contrast, secondary education in Rwanda developed via boarding schools and largely remains organized this way today. Boarding schools likely heightened school's impact, as students were more isolated from competing forms of socialization.

From approximately 2,000 students in 1915, the number of Rwandan children in schools grew to more than 20,000 by 1925, and more than 87,000 by 1935.[78] It is through the *écoles libres subsidiées* that the colonial administration acquitted itself of almost all moral obligations to educate Rwandans, and that missionaries largely made schools instruments in the pursuit of religious conversion. As one White Father who worked in Rwanda explained, "We did so much for teaching, but it was really to promulgate [the church's] authority and prestige, her pastoral action and her influence."[79] Father Lavigerie, founder of the White Fathers, had for decades propounded the principle that evangelization of Africans would best succeed through proselytization of chiefs. He argued that:

> In a violent society, subdivided in multiple tribes that live in a patriarchal state, what is most important, is to win the spirit of the chiefs.... We will attach ourselves to them in a special way, knowing that by winning over just one chief, we will do more for the advancement of the Mission than in winning over, in isolation, hundreds of poor Blacks. Once the chiefs are converted, the rest will follow.[80]

The church, like the state, framed the category of "chiefs" as solely Tutsi.

[76] Author's interview, Belgian colonial administrator, Belgium, September 20(A), 2006.
[77] Author's interview, Belgian missionary, Belgium, September 20(B), 2006.
[78] Ministère des Colonies, 1925; Ngendahimana 1981, p. 2; Ibid., p. 2; Rubbens 1936.
[79] Author's interview, Belgian missionary, Belgium, September 27(A), 2006.
[80] Quoted in Mbonimana 1978, p. 136.

Although the royal court and chiefs were at first resistant to missionary efforts, they came to highly value them. The first sign of change came in 1924 with *mwami* Musinga's note:

> Through this present letter I announce to you that the Bapadri [fathers] are my friends as they have always been. So if they wish to build schools to teach the people of Rwanda, give them land and help them. I am happy under the rule of Bulamatari [the Belgian Administration, literally the Breaker of Rocks] and for that reason I want there to be Europeans of no other nationality in my kingdom. And you will tell your sub-chiefs what I have told you. It is I, the king of Rwanda.[81]

The most significant change came in 1931, when *mwami* Musinga was deposed for *mwami* Rudahigwa, initiating what is known as "the tornado" of Catholicism. Rudahigwa became the first Catholic Rwandan king. Consequently, conversion to Catholicism became important for all who aspired to political and administrative postings. Chiefs quickly realized that, if not converted, their children would be held back from opportunity. A growing appreciation of the correlation between education and social status led to increased support for schooling in much of colonial Africa.[82] In Rwanda, a rush toward schools ensued as it became imperative to be, in addition to Tutsi, both Catholic and formally educated in order to achieve upward mobility. With time, education became "a commodity as highly valued as cows."[83] The elite and influential *Groupe Scolaire*, analyzed later, was founded at Astrida (now Butare or Huye) around this time. The poorest children, often Hutu, who had originally seen hope and possibility in schooling, were disappointed with their continued lack of mobility and withdrew from school.

In 1938 and 1939, major educational policies were enacted, aiming to better adapt education to the contingencies of African life.[84] This widespread strategy in African colonial education reflected the importance of agricultural development and concern over possible dislocations of rural life brought about by colonialism. It was also based on unease that too much "literary training" may induce "subversive" or anticolonial ideologies.[85] Rwanda's 1938 initiative thus made selection for higher levels of primary school more stringent, with the goal of better matching indigenous Rwandans with the roles the colonial power envisioned for them. As a Flemish missionary wrote in 1940, "The danger is never to teach too little, but to teach too much…. It is our duty to stop the young student as soon as he is sufficiently educated for his environment."[86] I illustrate later in the chapter how the criterion on which scholarly promotion occurred grew increasingly contested.

---

[81] Quoted in Linden and Linden 1977, p. 157.
[82] Windel 2009.
[83] Linden and Linden 1977, p. 239.
[84] For details, see Van Hove 1953.
[85] Windel 2009.
[86] Quoted in Erny 2001, p. 124.

Indeed, politics and schooling had always been entangled in Rwanda. As Rwanda underwent political changes, education was predictably in the limelight. As introduced earlier, in 1957, prominent Hutu graduates from Catholic seminaries published the important *Hutu Manifesto*. Among its many complaints, the Manifesto denounced the "hamitization" of schooling and the administration's indirect support, through schools, for the Tutsi monopoly. Its authors announced, "We want schooling to be particularly watched over," so that the "Bahutu are not the springboard of a monopoly that eternally keeps them in unbearable social and political inferiority."[87] In particular, it demanded that leaders "respect the proportions," meaning that if there were not enough spots in school for all, places should be allocated in proportion to ethnic representation (recognized by identity booklets) in the population. The writers also pointed to the need to better oversee the distribution of scholarships, a great majority of which were funded by Hutu taxpayers.[88] Overall, this text expressed the thoughts of the future leaders of Rwanda and foreshadowed changes that would take place during the First Republic.

When, in 1959, Rwandans organized themselves into political parties, all parties made educational demands. The *Union Nationale Rwandaise* (UNAR), a largely Tutsi party supportive of the monarchy, admitted to an ethnic problem in schools and blamed it on the colonists who used schooling to divide and rule. The *Rassemblement Démocratique Rwandais* (RADER), a Tutsi reform wing, also made recommendations for education, emphasizing free primary education for all. Parmehutu, founded by the authors of the *Hutu Manifesto*, devoted a whole chapter of its party policy to the democratization of education. It supported education for all students in areas served by a school and the suppression of boarding at secondary school, because spots had always been awarded through favoritism. It also advocated several years of free study for the children of Rwandans who had been restrained by *corvée* obligations of various forms by Tutsi authorities and their agents. Significantly, they also announced that all school registration cards would henceforth denote Hutu, Tutsi, or Twa "in the goal of informing all those that are combating racial discrimination in schooling."[89] All of the parties were primarily concerned with the quantity and distribution of education rather than with content.

During Rwanda's transition to independence, education was a controversial issue. Indeed when Belgium handed over educational responsibilities to Rwanda's First Republic, its last Resident General, Jean-Paul Harroy, remarked of the education dilemmas in Rwanda, "This topic, for me, is at the same time a jigsaw puzzle and a viper's nest."[90]

---

[87] Niyonzima, Kayibanda, et al. 1957.
[88] Ibid.
[89] Erny 2001, pp. 202–204.
[90] Ibid., p. 230.

An Assessment of the Role of Colonial Schooling (1919–1962)

When put together, what picture does this jigsaw puzzle of education reveal about the role of schooling in the intergroup conflict that engulfed Rwanda around independence? While the causes of this period of conflict in Rwanda are, of course, multiple, education was a significant contributing factor. In the several decades between the arrival of Europeans and the conflict surrounding independence, education went from being a private, family-dominated affair to one that was shaped enormously by the colonial state. This colonial era school system propagated the social-structural and psychocultural processes that became a part of the foundation for conflict at the end of this period.

Nevertheless, one must be cautious about analyzing historical circumstances through today's lenses. As one former missionary noted, "I think we did well. If we had to start again in 2006 [year of the interview] with the situation exactly the same as in 1930, we could say 'be careful, there are errors not to remake.' But you must not judge in 2006 on events in 1930 or 1940."[91] Similarly, a scholar of Rwanda reminded me that "it is important to note that we are [often] judging [colonial] Rwanda with today's economic standards. In contrast, we must consider our own standards from fifty to sixty years ago. In critiquing schools, we need to think about what we learned fifty or sixty years ago, and there are not so many differences."[92]

With this caveat in mind, it is difficult to make a normative judgment of those who designed Rwanda's educational policy upward of a century ago, or of the logic of its efficacy. Fortunately, this book does not claim to do any such thing. Rather, with the benefit of hindsight, the following historical analysis aims to discern what policies contributed to intergroup conflict, so that future school systems can be structured in a way that avoids the same result.

Access to Primary School

Limited access to schools produced horizontal inequalities, as well as exclusive identities and stigmatization. As one Rwandan interviewee educated during the colonial period explained:

> The education system in Rwandan contributed and went deeply into fostering an inter-Rwandan cleavage during the colonial period because the Catholic missionaries and the German administrators deemed that the best collaborators were Tutsi. Not Hutu. They even came up with a theory that Tutsi were born with a sense of organization, a gift for governing that was innate.... And colonials really collaborated with missionaries to disempower Hutu chiefs ... and to admit Tutsi, not all Tutsi, but the children of important Tutsi chiefs [and to also exclude Hutu from schools].[93]

---

[91] Author's interview, Belgian missionary, Belgium, September 20(B), 2006.
[92] Author's interview, scholar, Belgium, September 25, 2006.
[93] Author's interview, Rwandan researcher, Kigali, March 13, 2006.

It is revealing that Hutu interviewees were, in general, more likely to raise problems in access to primary schools during the colonial period.

In the early colonial period, in state primary schools, Tutsi were significantly more numerous than Hutu. Archival documents from the colonial administration show the five state primary schools as being exclusively for "sons of chiefs and notables of the Tutsi race."[94] By 1929, there were 677 Tutsi students in these schools. As a group of Rwandan historians explained, "We can see here that the future elite of the country was already separated, divided and discriminated from the beginning."[95]

But state schools accounted for only a small number of schools and students and, moreover, they closed in 1929–1930. Around the same period, there was approximately twenty times the number of students in subsidized Catholic primary schools as in state schools, and likely even more in non-subsidized Catholic schools, plus students in schools run by other missions.[96] These primary schools were free, missionaries provided supplies like small chalk boards, and some interviewees even recounted that students were paid in salt to attend.[97] The mere fact of establishing these schools brought Rwandans together. Rwanda was a highly dispersed country with individual homesteads dotting the country's "thousand hills"; according to the colonial administrators with whom I spoke, population dispersal stood out to them as the most striking feature when they first arrived in Rwanda. While hills were already generally quite cohesive, when the church set up a mission post, it brought together people from several hills. One man who began his primary schooling in 1937 recalled that there was just one primary school in Kigali, so children would come together from several kilometers around.[98] "So you see," one Rwandan opined, "where we welcomed a primary school, they established a dispensary, and social cohesion came because people shared."[99] By independence, approximately 250,000 Rwandan children attended primary schools.[100]

In contrast to state schools, Catholic primary schools welcomed more Hutu than Tutsi in the early colonial period. In these schools, Hutu children were admitted to schools alongside Tutsi. One Belgian missionary recounted, "In schools, children were just children. We never wrote students' ethnicities on the students' forms."[101] Contrary to some analyses that date discrimination against Hutu in mission schools to the late 1800s,[102] Hutu were the first to be attracted to mission schools.

---

[94] "Rapport présenté par le Gouvernement Belge au Conseil de la Société des Nations," 1929, p. 62.

[95] Author's interview, group of historians, Kigali, March 27, 2006.

[96] "Rapport présenté par le Gouvernement Belge au Conseil de la Société des Nations," 1929, p. 65.

[97] Author's interview, scholar, Belgium, September 25, 2006.

[98] Author's interview, male Tutsi, Kigali, January 30(A), 2006.

[99] Author's interview, male Hutu, Kigali, April 5(A), 2006.

[100] Hoben 1989, pp. 13–14.

[101] Author's interview, Belgian missionary, Belgium, September 27(A), 2006.

[102] Bush and Saltarelli 2000, p. 10.

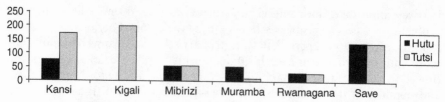

FIGURE 2.1 Number of students by ethnic group in central primary Catholic schools in 1928 (boys). Based on figures reported in L. Déprimoz, Missionary-Inspector on behalf of the Secrétariat National de l'Enseignement Catholique, *Rapport sur les Écoles du Vicariat du Ruanda en 1928 (Année scolaire 1927–1928)*, cited in Mbonimana, "Christianisation indirecte et cristallisation des clivages ethniques au Rwanda (1925–1931)", 1978, p. 143.

With time, however, Catholic primary schools also became more populated by Tutsi. A colonial administrator with much experience in the education system commented, "From '31, it was a rush for schools. This made it such that very soon, schools had a majority of Tutsi, even if Tutsi represented only 15 percent of the population. They rushed schools because they realized … if they wanted to advance … they had to study."[103] By the time of the Belgian administration, church-run schools were predominantly attended by Tutsi. Data from the 1927–1928 report of the *National Secretariat on Catholic Education in Rwanda*, presented in Figure 2.1, shows a majority of Tutsi in several central primary Catholic schools.

The illustrations show a minority Tutsi group, accounting for only about 15 percent of the general population, in nearly all cases occupying as many or even more school places than Hutu. While not providing precise figures, the report also identifies a Tutsi majority in the central primary school in Zaza, "discrimination in favor of Tutsi" in the Rulindo central primary school, and "no discrimination" at the Kabgayi central primary school, although a definition of discrimination is, problematically, not provided.[104] In Figure 2.2, where figures are normalized for proportion of population, Tutsi represent far more than a natural population distribution would suggest.[105]

In general, there were more opportunities for children to become educated in regions closest to larger Catholic missions, although of course this varied from

---

[103] Author's interview, Belgian colonial administrator, Belgium, September 26, 2006.

[104] L. Déprimoz, Missionary-Inspector on behalf of the Secrétariat National de l'Enseignement Catholique (SNEC), *Rapport sur les Écoles du Vicariat du Ruanda en 1928 (Année scolaire 1927–1928)*, cited in Mbonimana, p. 143.

[105] In this normalized figure, a distribution in accordance with the population would show each group representing 50% of students. Any number above 50% indicates that the group is over-represented in the classroom relative to its representation in the population and any number below 50% indicates that the group is underrepresented in the classroom relative to its representation in the population. Tutsi represented more or less than 15% in some regions, so while this figure is illustrative, it is inexact.

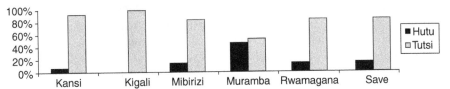

FIGURE 2.2 Number of students by ethnic group in central primary Catholic schools in 1928 (boys) normalized for proportion of population.

mission to mission. Nonetheless, reports also show a significant Hutu-Tutsi gap in branch, or "bush" schools, at least around Kabgayi, where the figures have been reported and are available.[106] Note, however, that it is not clear how these reports defined Hutu and Tutsi, because, as previously discussed, class and ethnicity were often confused. Twa were also severely underrepresented in schools; several interviewees did not remember there being any Twa in their classes.

Furthermore, a few interviewees told me that some rich or prominent Hutu grew up and were educated as Tutsi, which could slightly skew the figures. One White Father shared a story of one of his Tutsi students whom he met again years later, only to learn that he was Hutu. The student told him, "It was important in order to get a place [in school] to say that I was Tutsi."[107] Indeed, ethnic "faking" (*abaguze ubwoko*) continued into independent Rwanda and persists after the genocide. Some Hutu children may have been recorded as Tutsi, either by having their documents formally changed or more informally, through patronage networks. This is very unlikely to have been widespread enough to change the trends. Yet, the direction of faking is an important commentary on social hierarchy. That relatively privileged Hutu could not gain access to schools and other opportunities as *Hutu* is meaningful for understanding the importance of ethnic categories and stigmatization of Hutu.

Tutsi dominance in primary schools declined as time went on. The UN's first mission that visited Rwanda reported that, by then, Hutu were a net majority in the early years of primary school, yet remained a small minority by the end.[108] One research team found that in 1956, Tutsi accounted for 16.59 percent of the population and 32.1 percent of primary school spots and that Hutu comprised 82.74 percent of the population and 67.7 percent of primary school places. They found that Twa represented 0.67 percent of Rwandans but held only 0.2 percent of primary school positions.[109] Another researcher found that in 1962, in the town of Butare, 46 percent of Tutsi and only 13 percent of Hutu had had more than five years of education. My interviewees, who attended school largely during the 1940s and 1950s, all remembered Hutu and Tutsi, at least in Catholic

[106] Mbonimana 1978, p. 143.
[107] Author's interview, Belgian missionary, Belgium, September 20(B), 2006.
[108] Erny 2001, p. 141.
[109] Hanf 1974, p. 140.

primary school, "going to school together, in class seated on the same benches, playing together."[110] Nonetheless, school enrollment remained ethnically unbalanced, even if increasingly less so, throughout the colonial period.

Opinions varied among my interviewees with regard to whether differences in school enrollment by ethnicity, at both primary and secondary levels, should best be described as active discrimination or as an unintentional "situation of fact" reflecting societal conditions. These different transcripts fell largely along ethnic lines. Most Hutu argued that the ethnic tallies presented earlier point to active discrimination by the colonial administration and Catholic Church. As one interviewee explained, "They used the children of the people who had influence. They wanted influence and to get an influential person, you try to befriend him. So that's what the church did. By then, most of the people ruling were Tutsi."[111]

Colonial documents, especially from the 1920s and 1930s, substantiate active discrimination. Monsignor Classe, Rwanda's Vicar Apostolic, who applied Lavigerie's conviction of conversion through chiefs to Rwanda as early as German rule, substituted chiefs in general for Tutsi chiefs, thus adding a new ethnic angle to the policy.[112] In various letters to his missionaries, Classe expounded this idea, arguing that "[w]e must absolutely work to destroy the idea of the governing group that we are the men of the Bahutu,"[113] that "[t]he school of the Batutsi, here, must be ahead of that of the Bahutu,"[114] and that "[i]t is by the conversion of the Batutsi that we will definitively gain the conversion of Rwanda."[115] These convictions, which became known as the Classe doctrine, would prove to have far-reaching ramifications, particularly in the early part of colonial rule. The church and state were also mutually reinforcing. In 1928, Monsignor Classe told his missionaries: "You must choose the Batutsi because the government will probably refuse Bahutu teachers.... In the government the positions in every branch of the administration, even the unimportant ones, will be reserved henceforth for young Batutsi."[116] Classe helped make this true by recommending Catholic Tutsi for positions during the administrative restructuring.[117] Hutu were not entirely left out, and interviewees confirmed that different parishes would have implemented the rules to different extents, but Classe intended to relegate Hutu to education that prepared them for more menial positions in mines and other sites of manual labor.[118] In this way, education reflected existing and desired state structures.

---

[110] Author's interview, group of historians, Kigali, March 27, 2006.
[111] Author's interview, professor, National University of Rwanda, Butare, March 31, 2006.
[112] Mbonimana 1978, p. 136.
[113] Erny 2001, p. 39.
[114] Ibid., p. 101.
[115] Quoted in Mbonimana 1978, p. 140.
[116] Classe Undated; Linden and Linden 1977, p. 163.
[117] Longman 2010, p. 53.
[118] Quoted in Mbonimana 1978, p. 141.

Intentional discrimination by colonial powers was common in divide-and-rule strategies across Africa. In Ghana, for example, a colonial policy mandated that schools in the north should not go past the sixth year of primary, because northerners were particularly useful in cocoa farms and mines. In Sudan, in support of northern Arab/Muslim dominance, southern Sudanese were treated as second-class citizens, excluded from educational opportunities and processes of "Sudanization." In Nigeria, the minority Ibos were favored and treated to a special place in the country via the educational system and posts in colonial government.

In Rwanda, there are additional claims that some Tutsi were instrumental in keeping Hutu out of schools. As one book on Rwandan colonial education recounts:

> In 1958, a Hutu father had painfully saved the required sum to send his son to higher education at the seminary. His *shebuja* (Tutsi patron), who always knew everything in detail, came the evening before the child's departure. Inspection. Reproach: 'My cows are badly cared for. This warrants a fine.' And he set the exact sum that had been saved for school fees.... The son did not go study at the seminary. But soon afterwards, with his father in November 1959, he set fire to the *shebuja*'s hut.[119]

Given that schooling became important for access to positions of power, it makes sense that Tutsi would want to actively hold on to these channels amid a changing environment.

Hutu interviewees often described active ethnically based discrimination in access to schools. While some Hutu interviewees did not find they were discriminated against, as by the 1940s Catholic primary schools were generally open to them, they pointed to stories they had heard about their parents' hardships in accessing school. These mythico-histories amplified their parents' discrimination. In her interviews with Burundian Hutu refugees in Tanzania, Malkki also found that exclusion from education had become a mythico-history.[120]

On the other hand, most Tutsi and Belgian colonial administrators contended that the situation leading to more Tutsi being in schools was merely one of "social fact" rather than an indication of overt discrimination against Hutu. Indeed, class and ethnicity in Rwanda are interwoven. Although schooling was free, and the church even provided scholastic materials, these interviewees explained the Hutu-Tutsi discrepancy as one related to socioeconomics, suggesting that ethnicity was a proxy for status in this relationship. One, for example, explained that Tutsi held power through land and cattle, thus providing them with a status that enabled them to send their children to school. Other explanations were that Tutsi went to school because they had servants to do their chores, whereas Hutu needed to keep their children at home to do

---

[119] Quoted in Erny 2001, p. 232.
[120] Malkki 1995, p. 132.

house- and field-work; that Hutu who were in school had to help their families
work in the evenings, and so were less likely than Tutsi to devote extra time to
their studies, and thus to succeed and stay in school; and that Tutsi had more
access to lighting than Hutu, who could not study after six in the evening,
when it gets dark in Rwanda. Others argued that the upbringing of higher classes would have made their adaptation to schools easier, again complicating and
intertwining ethnicity and class. Some argue that throughout world history, the
socially privileged have been overrepresented in schools.[121]

Colonial officials also downplayed ethnic discrimination. They explained
that their training at the Colonial University in Antwerp explicitly instructed
them to respect customary authorities and to govern indirectly. While avoiding
direct discussion of a preference for Tutsi in education, they seemingly justified
a Tutsi-centric arrangement by arguing that when they arrived in the country, Tutsi were already in charge and that they merely oriented their policies
accordingly.[122]

As an aside, similar de facto justifications were deployed vis-à-vis the relative lack of girls in schools. Although boys were by far more numerous in
schools, interviewees contended that this was not because of a policy of favoritism on behalf of government or churches, but because parents did not send
girls to school. Custom saw girls in the home beside their mothers, and some
worried that men would be reluctant to marry educated girls, as they would
be less easily dominated or may aspire to a higher standard of living.[123] A missionary recalled that after the fact, "There was a lot of criticism that we didn't
open secondary schools to girls quickly enough. But what would have been the
point of this great spending if there was no one to attend? We have to put this
in time context. We didn't halt girls' education.... Educated women often had
trouble finding a place in society. What would have happened if we had forced
girls [to go to school] in 1930? It would have never worked."[124]

In addition to these social-structural explanations for the overrepresentation of Tutsi in colonial schools, some have invoked psychocultural explanations. One colonial study of the education sector in Rwanda claimed that black
children lacked curiosity, the ability to elaborate and abstract, and that "the
Blacks of Ruanda-Urundi are stuck in a neolithic age" that held them back
from attending or succeeding at school. The study was explicit, however, that
these comments did not apply to Tutsi, whom they found inculcated with a
code of honor, initiative, self-confidence, and a sense of responsibility, and who
were much more numerous in schools.[125] Two of the former colonial officials

[121] Ngendahimana 1981, p. 45. See also Erny 2001, p. 220.
[122] Author's interview, Belgian colonial administrator, Belgium, September 20(A), 2006; author's
interview, Belgian colonial administrator, Belgium, September 26, 2006.
[123] Dubuisson-Brouha, Natalis, and Paulus 1958, p. 88.
[124] Author's interview, Belgian missionary, Belgium, September 20(B), 2006.
[125] Dubuisson-Brouha, Natalis, and Paulus 1958.

also asserted that Tutsi simply had a reputation of being more intelligent, or at least more skillful, than Hutu, and claimed that even Hutu preferred to be ruled by Tutsi.[126]

In sum, state schools in Rwanda were exclusive and divisive. Catholic schools, especially under the leadership of Monsignor Classe in the first decades of colonialism, displayed similar tendencies. Some Tutsi and Belgian interviewees contended that while Tutsi were more numerous in schools, this discrepancy was not a result of unfair policy, but of wider societal conditions. Although there was some crossover, Hutu often shared a different interpretation than Tutsi and Belgian interviewees with regard to the intentionality of school discrimination. In either case, many Hutu shared experiences and/or perceptions of horizontal inequalities – a key social-structural factor underlying intergroup conflict during this period. This also led to more collectivized identities and to stigmatization, as the Belgians generally considered Tutsi to be more deserved of opportunities than Hutu. As one Hutu man summarized:

> School favored certain children and authorized certain kids to go to school and left the others aside. I can tell you frankly that at the time I started, there was still some of that.... And the risk really came with the idea that at the end of primary, you had a chance of acceding to secondary school. At that moment, a kid who saw another getting social promotion, but staying a peasant himself, for not having had access to primary school, this really created distinctions between people.[127]

Promotion Past Primary School

Indeed, by the 1940s, when Catholic primary schools were, in principle and in practice, open to all, problems persisted at the secondary level. Educational inequality along ethnic lines deepened in Rwanda at the end of primary school, and many interviewees suggested that this ultimately contributed to underlying intergroup conflict. In response to a question about the causes of violence surrounding the revolution and independence, one answered, "Schooling mattered because a lot of Hutu attended primary school.... But for secondary, Hutu didn't have access ... only very few."[128] According to one colonial administrator, "It was only something like 4 or 5 percent from primary school that had access to secondary. It was really, really minimal. And so, it was absolutely crucial to know who was going on to secondary school."[129]

Preliminary selections were conducted at the end of the fifth grade for promotion to the sixth. An external report of Rwandan education commissioned by the colonial administration reveals that in 1958, there were 17,712 students

---

[126] Author's interview, Belgian colonial administrator, Belgium, September 27(B), 2006; author's interview, Belgian colonial administrator, Belgium, September 20(A), 2006.
[127] Author's interview, male Hutu, Kigali, April 5(A), 2006.
[128] Author's interview, male Hutu, northern Rwanda, March 20(B), 2006.
[129] Author's interview, Belgian colonial administrator, Belgium, September 20(A), 2006.

in the fifth year of primary, but only 3,342 – less than one-fifth – in the sixth year, after the selection process.[130] Even more stringent selections were made at the end of the sixth grade. When the number of secondary schools was already at its peak, less than 10 percent – or, according to some, less than 5 percent – of students finishing the sixth grade were granted places in secondary schools.[131] During much of the colonial period, promotion ratios would likely have been even lower given that there were only three secondary schools in Rwanda: a minor seminary at Kabgayi, the *Groupe Scolaire* at Astrida, and a teacher's school (*école normale*) at Zaza. The authors of the external report remarked on most Rwandans being sent back to the hills after several years of primary school as "one of the sharpest current social problems in Ruanda-Urundi."[132]

The competition for secondary school positions often took place on an ethnic playing field that favored Tutsi. This is particularly true of one location in particular: almost all interviewees mentioned the *Groupe Scolaire* as a site of pro-Tutsi discrimination. Rwandans also hold it up as the best and most elite school of the period. The Nyanza state primary school, which, as seen from the earlier discussion, was reserved for Tutsi, closed in 1930 and its 342 Tutsi students were transferred to Astrida.[133] The Brothers of Charity of Ghent opened the *Groupe Scolaire* as a secondary school in 1932, at which time the school became technically open to all. Its recruitment rules included proving good intelligence, good health, being between fourteen and sixteen years of age (and a minimum height of 1.4 meters), holding irreproachable morality, and succeeding in a selection competition for twenty-five students from Rwanda and twenty-five from Burundi. Significantly, these rules did not apply to "legitimate sons of chiefs" (read: Tutsi chiefs), who could be recruited by the *Groupe Scolaire* without an exam as long as they were of the right age and had finished primary school.[134] Since its inception, it prioritized recruiting sons of Tutsi chiefs and tailored its curriculum to the tasks and skills of future chiefs. Some authors contend that the height requirement, of which my Belgian interviewees denied knowledge, is further evidence of discrimination, because Tutsi are generally taller than Hutu.[135] A colonial interviewee with direct experience with the *Groupe Scolaire* in the 1950s did not remember the admission criteria based on height and denied that there was discrimination based on this stereotype.[136] Despite the ostensibly open competition for *Groupe Scolaire* admission, Tutsi represented a very strong majority throughout the colonial period, as the enrollment records in Figure 2.3 attest.

[130] Dubuisson-Brouha, Natalis, and Paulus 1958, p. 36.
[131] Erny 2001, p. 227; Hoben 1989, p. 14; RoR 1986.
[132] Dubuisson-Brouha, Natalis, and Paulus 1958, p. 37.
[133] Crokaert 1931.
[134] Mbonimana 1978, p. 146.
[135] See Bush and Saltarelli 2000, p. 10. Author's interview, Belgian colonial administrator, Belgium, September 26, 2006.
[136] Author's interview, professor, National University of Rwanda, Butare, March 31, 2006.

Year	Tutsi	Hutu		Congolese
		Rwanda	Burundi	
1932	45	9*		14
1933	21	0	0	0
1934	26	13*		0
1935	41	11*		0
1945	46	0	3	0
1946	44	1	0	8	0
1947	44	2	0	10	0
1948	85	2	0	11	2
1949	85	5	0	9	0
1953	68	3	0	16	0
1954	63	3	0	16	3

FIGURE 2.3 Student enrollment by ethnic group at the *Groupe Scolaire* (1932–1959). Gratefully reprinted from *Rwanda and Burundi*, 1970, p. 138, with permission from René Lemarchand.

Note: Enrollment numbers are reported for the years in which they were available. * indicates that territorial origins are unavailable.

The school was divided into several streams: agronomy, secretariat, medical assistance, veterinary medicine assistance, and administration.[137] Tutsi especially monopolized the administrative stream of the *Groupe Scolaire*. Interviewees who spoke about the *Groupe Scolaire* all indicated that the administrative stream, sometimes called the chiefs-candidate stream, was comprised exclusively of Tutsi. Some said that this stream was exclusively for sons of Tutsi chiefs, and a Belgian administrator recalled that the *mwami* had to approve all nominations.[138] Others argued that while Hutu were not restricted from applying, they knew that they were restricted from government jobs and thus following this stream would have been purposeless. Enrollment in the administrative stream is thus a reflector of wider societal conditions, either de jure or de facto, in that Hutu children understood that they would be excluded from administrative jobs in light of their ethnicity and so tailored their educational goals accordingly. Describing the *Groupe Scolaire* in relation to violent intergroup conflict in Rwanda, one Tutsi man assessed, the school of chief candidates "was the beginning of the division sown between Rwandans. [It sent the message] that Tutsi were capable and the only ones sent to this school. But in other schools, it was mixed."[139] Another man who was educated during the colonial period also singled out the *Groupe Scolaire*, noting that "[t]he question of personal relations between ethnic categories didn't cause a lot of problems between students. But it is another story at the Groupe Scolaire d'Astrida."[140]

[137] Wigny 1941.
[138] Author's interview, Belgian colonial administrator, Belgium, September 20(A), 2006.
[139] Author's interview, male Tutsi, Kigali, January 30(A), 2006.
[140] Author's interview, professor, National University of Rwanda, Butare, March 31, 2006.

Seminaries were virtually the only option for Hutu students who wished to pursue post-primary schooling. Given that not all who attended seminaries went on to priesthood, seminaries were also a route to broader social mobility. Accession to mission-run higher levels of education was formally open to all who wished to write the entrance exam and officially granted to those who best succeeded.[141] "Before independence, we never asked for students' ethnicity in schools," one former missionary recounted. "The church never required ethnicity in primary schools, seminaries, colleges or teachers' schools. We never asked for ethnicity."[142] In the early years of the colonial period, when Tutsi shunned the Catholic missionaries and their schools, Hutu dominated the seminaries. Ian Linden aptly titles his chapter describing the period as one of "Hutu Church and Tutsi Court."[143] Several interviewees reported that there was a growing *Groupe Scolaire*/Seminary divide that took place along ethnic lines: "The seminarists were jealous of what the *Groupe Scolaire* had, of the priorities, and at the *Groupe Scolaire*, they hated the seminarists."[144] The seminaries were at first an outlet for the grievances of Hutu, but they became increasingly dominated by Tutsi, causing acrimony on the side of Hutu and increasing feelings of inequality.

As one colonial administrator reported, while higher schooling was in principle for those with the best examination results, he knew of political nominations and a "political filter" restraining Hutu access.[145] In 1956, although Tutsi constituted 16.59 percent of the population, they held 60.9 percent of secondary school places; Hutu represented 82.74 percent of Rwandans but held just 39.1 percent of secondary school spots.[146] These figures illustrate a marked decline from the ratio of Hutu to Tutsi at primary school around the same time, cited earlier. A UN report from the 1950s judged that ethnic tensions in Rwanda could be reduced by making admission rules easier so that more Hutu would be allowed to move on to high school.[147]

One can imagine the impact of rigorous competition for secondary school in a country with great respect for education and the social mobility it is presumed to bring. Upon graduation from secondary school, Tutsi students were granted jobs in the modern sector and also enjoyed benefits in Rwanda's more traditional economic structures. These opportunities were in part attributable to their qualifications, but also very much because these students were drawn from leading Tutsi families.[148] In many countries, Western-style education was a symbol of modernity and seemed to promise a new lifestyle, yet education

[141] Bigirumwami 1958.
[142] Author's interview, Belgian missionary, Belgium, September 27(A), 2006.
[143] Linden and Linden 1977, Chapter 4.
[144] Author's interview, Belgian colonial administrator, Belgium, September 26, 2006.
[145] Author's interview, Belgian colonial administrator, Belgium, September 20(A), 2006.
[146] Hanf 1974, p. 140.
[147] Erny 2001, p. 141.
[148] Newbury 1988.

reinforced traditional state power.[149] Even educated Hutu had limited social mobility upon graduation in comparison to educated Tutsi, increasing grievances. One interviewee told me, "There was discrimination in employment. Even if you were intelligent, being Hutu, you could not be chief or sub-chief. This isn't really the fault of the Tutsi [who were ultimately blamed], but of colonization."[150] The story of Anastase Makuza, the first Rwandan with a university degree, is a poignant example. Makuza, a Hutu, graduated from Rwanda's Nyakibanda seminary and from the *Congo Centre Universitaire* of Kisantu. Upon his return to Rwanda in 1955 to seek employment, he was turned down by a number of likely employers. He ended up with a typist job in Kibuye, and was promoted a few years later to administrative assistant in Cyangugu and Kigali. As Lemarchand writes, "By then, however, Makuza was already a potential revolutionary.... Like other educated Hutu, he derived a burning sense of grievance from the monopoly exercised by the Tutsi caste over all sectors of the administration and the economy."[151] Indeed, the leaders of the 1959 revolution had received secondary education in seminaries and they emphasized lack of education and social mobility for Hutu as one of their primary grievances. It was not only education, but also this ceiling on the ambitions of educated Hutu, that was a major grievance. "This is what was really hurting Hutu at the time," one man commented. "To see illiterate [Tutsi] ruling over them, even those that had completed secondary school."[152]

In addition to using education for divide-and-rule tactics, colonial powers across Africa have been criticized more broadly for having wanted to curb the development of an indigenous elite that might come to resist them.[153] One colonial administrator explained that Belgian territories typically had more primary and secondary schools than most other African countries, but fewer universities. "We worked education as a pyramid. At the bottom of the pyramid, Belgian territories were a lot wider than other ones. We would have worked up soon."[154] Another Belgian interviewee accused Hutu leader, and later president, Grégoire Kayibanda of explicit efforts to stall the development of Rwandan elites for the same reason.[155] He described how, while working at the *Groupe Scolaire*, he had received a letter from Kayibanda saying "that he didn't need these people of a certain level, that they should go to a more administrative school. For me, it was jealousy because among these students, there were people who had studied more than him.... And he was scared. And he told me very clearly that they didn't need elites and told me, mid-semester, to send the students home."[156]

---

[149] Fuller 1990.
[150] Author's interview, male Hutu, Kigali, April 8(B), 2006.
[151] Lemarchand 1994, p. 139.
[152] Author's interview, male Hutu, northern Rwanda, April 8(B), 2006.
[153] Chrétien 2003, pp. 285–286; Windel 2009.
[154] Author's interview, Belgian colonial administrator, Belgium, September 26, 2006.
[155] Author's interview, Belgian colonial administrator, Belgium, September 26, 2006.
[156] Author's interview, Belgian colonial administrator, Belgium, September 26, 2006.

Advancement past primary school was highly competitive in Rwanda and a source of social strife. In the *Hutu Manifesto*, "the manifesto of my ancestors," offered one Hutu man educated during the colonial period, "they identified a clear discrimination that permitted some children to go to school, and others not."[157] Proportionally to their minority status in the population, many more Tutsi found places in secondary school than Hutu. Tutsi were also the majority in the most elite secondary school in the country. Differential access to schooling along group lines reproduces and enhances divisions, affecting even those – the majority of Rwandans – who did not attend school. The school that one attends in a divided society is a cultural marker,[158] and Tutsi had the upper hand in Rwanda. Some Hutu were able to find places in the seminary, although this only delayed their encounters with the frustration of social mobility until the end of secondary school, when they sought jobs. These horizontal inequalities become a source of resentment and instability when group members feel unable to improve their position in society within the status quo. These conditions also led to increasingly collectivized and stigmatized groups.

Ultimately, the leaders of the 1959 revolution drew on, among other things, a shared experience of difficulties with educational advancement and increasingly greater entrenchment of difference to mobilize the rural masses. At the end of our interview, one Rwandan man noted, "You have forgotten to ask me why Rwanda has a grudge against whites. This is really because whites sowed division here." While acknowledging that the colonial administration brought a number of positive changes to the country, he underlined how schools and the church heightened divisions among the population. Things might have been different "if they arrived here and had left things, but they excluded Hutu. And you can't exclude people and ask them to be happy. You can't exclude them from schooling and power."[159] As one Rwandan university professor explained, "The leaders of the Hutu movement had been discriminated against and were angry about that discrimination. The discrimination was based on real experiences."[160] Interviewees frequently expressed that schools were a part of an overall colonial system in which Hutu felt disadvantaged.

Content and Language

Curricular content also reinforced divisions among Rwandans. In the early years of colonialism, the content of schooling differed by ethnic group. Records indicate that in many Catholic primary schools that had both Hutu and Tutsi students, the two groups were segregated into different streams starting in the

[157] Author's interview, male Hutu, Kigali, April 5(A), 2006.
[158] Davies 2004, p. 76.
[159] Author's interview, male Hutu, Kigali, April 8(B), 2006.
[160] Author's interview, professor, National University of Rwanda, Butare, March 31, 2006.

late 1920s.[161] For example, Tutsi were taught in French so as to prepare them for basic administrative positions, whereas Hutu were taught in the local language.[162] Similarly, French was used in state schools, which were reserved for Tutsi.[163] An aptitude in French was another route through which education contributed to social mobility, especially because secondary school was taught in French. That Hutu had fewer opportunities to learn French would thus have affected their advancement.

Other special treatment for Tutsi in primary schools also helped their societal advancement. Tutsi were given arithmetic classes, which were replaced with singing classes for Hutu. Natural sciences were obligatory for Tutsi but optional for Hutu. Tutsi could be taught without religious instruction, whereas Hutu were educated with the goal of eventual baptism. Sometimes special classes were given for Tutsi on days or times when Hutu were absent.[164] Other authors found evidence of extra subsidies and more qualified teachers in several areas where Tutsi were populous.[165]

In addition to its effect on social mobility, noted in Chapter 1, such segregation reinforces ethnic categorization and contributes to collectivizing difference – both psychocultural factors underlying intergroup conflict – since *all* members of one group have certain entitlements that *all* members of the other do not, merely by virtue of their membership in a particular group. According to interviews in Belgium with colonial era administrators and missionaries, many Tutsi saw themselves as deserving the greater opportunities they were given, and stigmatized Hutu as unworthy of the same opportunities.

The segregated streams system ended by the 1940s and henceforth, Hutu and Tutsi students were taught together. At this time, missionaries privileged the local language, Kinyarwanda, in primary schools, introducing French in the third grade. Missionaries contributed significantly to the creation of written Kinyarwanda grammar books and rules.[166] At the secondary level, only French was permitted. "We were forbidden from speaking Kinyarwanda at the seminary," one interviewee recalled.[167] The interviewees educated during this period had excellent French language skills and were generally very proud of their linguistic abilities. In this way, horizontal inequality between those Hutu

---

[161] Mbonimana 1978, p. 142. In some schools, there were not enough Tutsi to constitute a separate section. For example, my interviewees from northern Rwanda recall there being few, if any, Tutsi students in their schools. Author's interview, male Hutu, northern Rwanda, March 20(B), 2006; author's interview, male Hutu, northern Rwanda, March 20(C), 2006.

[162] Erny 2001, p. 102; Linden and Linden 1977, p. 163; Mamdani 2001, p. 90.

[163] Inspection Générale de l'Enseignement 1929.

[164] Author's interview, female Hutu, northern Rwanda, March 21(C), 2006. See also Erny 2001, p. 102.

[165] Linden and Linden 1977, p. 163.

[166] Author's interview, professor, National University of Rwanda, Butare, March 31, 2006; author's interview, Belgian missionary, Belgium, September 20(B), 2006.

[167] Author's interview, professor, National University of Rwanda, Butare, March 31, 2006.

and Tutsi would have been less than at earlier times, when the groups were streamed into different classes.

What about lessons taught at mixed ethnic schools in the late colonial period? In short, Rwandan history and politics were not taught at primary school during the colonial period. All Rwandan interviewees recalled some teaching of basic European history, but only a few mentioned Rwandan history. "History teaching was rudimentary," one Hutu man from the north recounted, "simply because my ancestors hadn't been to school. So they never wrote ... so the first history we learned was the history of the whites."[168] In contrast to French colonies, or even to the Belgian approach in neighboring Congo, however,[169] an assimilationist European history was not generally taught. One interviewee remembered a teacher who explained the difference between Hutu and Tutsi by pointing to the physical characteristics of the students, although he doubted that this was part of a formal curriculum. Another recalled learning a few short stories about Rwanda's royal family. Yet another remembered a few lessons about the importance of obeying the king, and about whites colonizing Rwanda.[170] While a report from Rwanda's *Institute for Research and Dialogue on Peace* maintains that the theory of successive waves of migration, for example, was taught since the 1940s, including in the sixth year of primary school, interviewees did not remember this.[171] Some of these inconsistencies might be attributable to historical memory. Alternatively, these discrepancies are perhaps accurate representations given that there was no homogeneous national teaching program and each church prepared its own curriculum.[172] What is notable is that no one, except the first interviewee, remembers any history teaching linked to ethnicity or Hamitic theories of Tutsi superiority at primary school.

In contrast, there is evidence that a divisive history was taught at secondary schools, which helped children become aware of their ethnicity while also politicizing it. A textbook used in the *Groupe Scolaire* administrative stream, for example, explains the three ethnic groups by their characteristics and physical traits. In one myth, "the atavistic stupidity of the Bahutu" is highlighted in contrast to the "sage and prudent" Tutsi.[173] In another section, the text details

---

[168] Author's interview, male Hutu, Kigali, April 5(A), 2006.

[169] Vinck 1995. For consistency, I use the name Congo throughout, referring to the now Democratic Republic of the Congo, which has changed names several times in recent history. This should not to be confused with the neighboring Republic of Congo.

[170] Author's interview, male Hutu, Kigali, April 8(B), 2006; author's interview, female Tutsi, Kigali, March 14, 2006; author's interview, female Hutu, northern Rwanda, March 21(C), 2006.

[171] Institut de Recherche et de Dialogue pour la Paix 2005. The citations that support the report's assertion are similarly inconclusive, relying on books that could have hypothetically, but not definitely, been used in primary schools, such as Alexis Kagame's 1943 court history, and on specific curricula from the 1980s. In RoR 1995, the government's review of colonial education says that Rwandan history was not part of the formal curriculum.

[172] Erny 2001, p. 226.

[173] Sandrapt 1939, pp. 139–140.

ubuhake relationships of clientship and how the "backward Bantu popula-tions" were mystified by the Tutsi's cows and the Tutsi's high psychological and political qualities.[174] The two ethnic groups are presented as clearly separate and essentialized. In the Astrida graduates' newspaper, one *Groupe Scolaire* teacher wrote after World War II of how

> the Hamitic people at base have nothing in common with Negroes ... especially in Ruanda-Urundi.... Physically, these [Hamitic] races are superb; despite the inevitable race mixings that are a result of prolonged contact with Negroes, the preponderance of the Caucasian type has remained deeply marked among the Batutsi.... Their elevated height ... the fineness of their traits, and their intelligent expression all contribute to their being worthy of the title that explorers gave them: aristocratic Negroes.[175]

These types of representations, taught in a Tutsi-dominated environment, encouraged categorizing and collectivizing of Hutu and Tutsi identities and pro-moted images of Tutsi superiority, stigmatizing Hutu students. One Rwandan educational expert educated in colonial Rwanda suggested such representations were not uncommon: "In secondary school, you will find a lot of stereotypes of scorn for Hutu, especially at [the Groupe Scolaire]."[176] Texts used in the sem-inaries were indeed similar, such as Father Pagès's *Un Royaume Hamite*, the first written record of Rwanda's "Hamitic" court history. He details the three races/ethnic groups of Rwanda, their physical and personal characteristics, and asserts as "incontestable" the claim that Tutsi are Hamites from Ethiopia.[177] Pagès personally lectured in Gisenyi schools and his students could allegedly self-identify as superior Hamites or inferior Bantu.[178] Moreover, school lessons did not appear to make a significant effort to develop reciprocity among Hutu and Tutsi.

Pedagogy

Through both levels of schooling, widespread colonial pedagogical practices such as teaching by rote and memorization underdeveloped critical think-ing skills and denied children the opportunity to practice managing conflicting perspectives. Schools taught students to be modest and restrained. Teaching in Rwanda has generally been of a learn-by-heart variety, and in some places, pupils were banished to the fields if they were unable to perfectly recall the lesson. One Belgian, formerly involved with Rwanda's schools, recalls that his students knew the courses and texts better than he, "down to the last comma," but had great difficulty putting their lessons into practice. "They knew it, but they knew it by heart. They didn't think about it.... One day the governor

[174] Ibid., pp. 148–149.
[175] Quoted in Chrétien 2003, pp. 282–283.
[176] Author's interview, professor, National University of Rwanda, Butare, March 31, 2006.
[177] Pagès 1930, pp. 5, 28–32.
[178] Linden and Linden 1977, p. 165.

came to our school, to the *Groupe Scolaire*, and asked the students in science what was the definition of two parallel lines. They knew the definition, but when he asked them to go to the board and draw two parallel lines, they didn't know how to do it."[179]

Most interview participants also agreed that they were never welcome to ask questions or disagree with the teachers – "[Y]ou had to listen, swallow the information, and respond to the questions posed by the teacher"[180] – and opined that inculcating obedience to authority was a central part of their school experience. In fact, missionaries often taught their students and followers to respect authorities and one's station in life, and throughout much of Rwanda's colonial period the church emphasized submission.[181] That secondary schools were boarding schools would likely have enhanced the impact of this hidden curriculum. By failing to develop critical thinking skills that can help students peacefully manage conflicts, schools in Rwanda missed an opportunity for peacebuilding.

Conclusion: The Peace and Conflict Role of Colonial Schooling

The structure of the education system contributed to many of the social-structural and psychocultural conditions that underlay conflict during this period in Rwanda. Differential opportunities for schooling along ethnic lines – both in terms of access and streaming – produced horizontal inequalities in education levels and in related social and economic mobility. Discriminatory and exclusive access to school was also a factor in developing the underlying psychocultural processes that may help cause violent interethnic conflict. In this sense, schooling was a reflector of the state's ethnic discrimination and an amplifier of ethnic categorization. Furthermore, by granting and denying opportunities by ethnic criteria, schooling helped harden and collectivize binary identities and stigmatize Hutu as inferior to Tutsi. Conversely, Tutsi developed ideas of entitlement and superiority based on their inclusion.

While one might have predicted school content to have had a similarly negative influence on intergroup relations, I found that this was not the case for primary school history because Rwandan history was not taught. Secondary school history lessons, however, did contribute to categorizing, collectivizing, and stigmatizing Rwandans by ethnic group.

At the same time, the school system did not do a number of the things it might have done to help build peace. For example, it promoted conformity and obedience rather than developing critical thinking skills that might have increased students' agency and helped them peacefully manage conflicts.

---

[179] Author's interview, Belgian colonial administrator, Belgium, September 26, 2006.
[180] Author's interview, female Tutsi, Kigali, March 14, 2006.
[181] For a reflection on the Church's selective teachings during the colonial period, see Aelvoet 1962.

Of course, the argument is not that education on its own led to the multiple episodes of violence that broke out in Rwanda around the time of independence; a constellation of other factors were also required to drive discontent and mobilization. Schooling did, however, in contrast to predominant optimism regarding the peacebuilding role of education, foster a number of the mechanisms that mattered in underlying conflict in this period in Rwanda. Social inequalities grew and festered during this period, provoked in part by well-recognized factors such as the increase in power for Tutsi chiefs, but also by restrictions on schooling and social advancement for Hutu. Grievances over inequalities, created in part by unequal access to schooling, and increasingly binary, essentialized, and stereotyped understandings of Hutu and Tutsi identities, promulgated through school access and content, also gave ethnic entrepreneurs material to work with.

Schooling may also have played a more direct role in violence between 1959 and 1964. Hutu graduates of higher education were frustrated at the gap between their expectations of social mobility and the realities of Tutsi power. It was this Hutu counter-elite who shared the experience of blocked mobility that wrote the *Hutu Manifesto*, who were able to channel the grievances of the rural population, and who began the revolution that eventually led to violence in Rwanda.

Moving beyond the usual preoccupation with peacebuilding to consider the ways in which education contributes to conflict is essential if we wish to understand and improve the impact of education. In the next chapter, which focuses on the lead-up to the 1990s civil war and genocide, many of the same colonial era schooling patterns prevail.

3

Schooling under the Rwandan Republics

When I visited the church in Nyamata, where 10,000 Rwandans were killed during the genocide, its entry was draped with a banner reading "*Iyo uza kwimenza nanj ye ukamenya ntuba waranyishe*": "If you had known me, and known yourself, you would not have killed me." Indeed, understandings of identity and attitudes toward the other – gained in part through schooling – are central to explaining the 1994 genocide that claimed the lives of approximately 800,000 Rwandans.[1] In just a hundred days, Hutu extremists, with the participation of a great number of ordinary Rwandans,[2] murdered nearly 75 percent of Rwanda's resident Tutsi population as well as tens of thousands labeled "Hutu moderates." The killings crossed boundaries that are difficult to comprehend: neighbors killed neighbors, coworkers killed coworkers, and even families were sometimes torn apart along victim-perpetrator lines.

This chapter shows how leading explanations for intergroup violent conflict in Rwanda rely on an underlying foundation of which schooling was a key part. Picking up historically where the previous chapter left off, it first presents a brief survey of post-independence Rwanda through its First and Second Republics, reviewing some of the major causes of the genocide. It highlights, in particular, how these explanations hinge upon the role of horizontal inequalities, exclusive groups, and stigmatization. After reviewing major educational policies and programs implemented between 1962 and 1994, I argue that the content and structure of schools reflected and amplified horizontal

---

[1] The exact number of deaths is unknown and contested. The widely accepted UN estimate is 800,000 dead including Hutu and Tutsi. Des Forges puts the figure of Tutsi civilians killed at 500,000 and estimates the number of Hutu killed in the genocide at 10,000. The Rwandan government puts deaths, both Hutu and Tutsi, at 937,000 to 1,000,000. "Rwanda Census Puts Genocide Death Toll at 937,000," by Arthur Asiimwe, *Reuters*, April 4, 2004; Des Forges 1995; Des Forges 1999, pp. 15–16. For a discussion of these figures, see Straus 2006, p. 51.

[2] Jones 2001, p. 41; Mamdani 2001, pp. 7, 266; Straus 2006, p. 117.

inequalities in society and contributed to categorizing, collectivizing, and stigmatizing Hutu and Tutsi into exclusive groups. As in the colonial period, these processes contributed to a foundation on which violent intergroup conflict became possible.

In this case, my findings also suggest that the combined impacts of the structure of schooling and its content were far more powerful than either one might have been alone. As one former student recalled,

> They took it personally, not as a history.... So the way the teacher could teach a history, was not really a history, but hatred history. You know, what they [Hutu and Tutsi] did. The kingdom belongs to Tutsi and they did this. And the Hutu, they were slaves to the Tutsi.... And then they were seeing the teacher getting angry. Hating those Tutsi who were there [in the classroom]. You know, at that time they were asking the Tutsi to stand up as if those Tutsi at the present are the ones who did that.... And it's so embarrassing and so frightening.[3]

Teaching about historical differences while highlighting current differences can accentuate the impact of school experiences on students. Recall that combined head-first (which aims to change beliefs in order to then change behavior) and feet-first (which aims to change behavior in order to then change beliefs) approaches may have the strongest effect on students.

Politics and Society during the Rwandan Republics

Understanding intergroup conflict in Rwanda, as well as the role of education, requires some knowledge of politics and society during the Rwandan Republics. This section aims to provide this background. In fact, Rwandan independence brought important changes to intergroup relations in the country. As we saw in the last chapter, Grégoire Kayibanda was elected the first post-independence president, inaugurating Rwanda's First Republic, which lasted from 1962 until 1973. A Hutu, Kayibanda oriented his government and policies to represent the Hutu masses, and equated fulfilling the interests of the demographic majority to democracy. His government chased, imprisoned, or assassinated all former Tutsi leaders and opposition Hutu who would not join the Parmehutu party.[4] Parmehutu became a single-party government, and Hutu replaced Tutsi as the dominant group in Rwanda.

At the same time, many colonial trends remained the same after independence. In terms of politics, one monoethnic power replaced another without any meaningful transformation in the style of government or the roles of its major players. Like the former kings, the president was in many ways unaccountable and autocratic, and the prefects and burgomasters of the First Republic much resembled the chiefs and sub-chiefs of the colonial era.[5] As one

---

[3] Author's interview, female Tutsi, Kigali, February 10(C), 2006.

[4] Uvin 1996, p. 8.

[5] Lemarchand 1970, pp. 265–286.

colonial administrator explained, "Even if Kayibanda was not a customary chief, they put him really at the top. And once he took command, everyone obeyed him."[6] Independence did not radically change society either. Tens of thousands of Tutsi remained in Rwanda, often comparatively well educated and relatively wealthy, although many remained poor. The lives of most Hutu did not change much: "[T]hey were as poor and powerless after 1962 as they had been before."[7] Some of the ethnic intermingling that had occurred during the precolonial and colonial periods also continued. As one Tutsi interviewee told me: "There were mixes of Hutu and Tutsi in my extended family. My aunts married Hutu men, my uncles married Hutu women."[8]

History and ideology underwent inversion without wholesale transformation. Interpretations of the country's history, which, as we saw in the last chapter, had been central to politics and the self-understanding of Rwandans, remained the same except that their meanings were turned upside down. Whereas the colonial powers viewed Tutsi as foreigners and thus superior and better suited to rule than Hutu, the Kayibanda government considered Tutsi to be foreign invaders. The country was thus presented, including in schools, as belonging to Hutu – "its true inhabitants." Hutu and Tutsi identities were thereby further solidified, and Kayibanda described Rwanda as "two nations in one state."[9]

Throughout the Kayibanda years, Parmehutu became increasingly dominant, as well as both ethnically and regionally exclusionary. One missionary who worked in colonial Rwanda explained that the new government "said that Tutsi had [previously] taken power and now we are going to exclude them. So, in their heads, they were going to do exactly the same thing as Tutsi [had done]: exclude Tutsi from government and take their places."[10] The government imposed quotas to limit the number of Tutsi in schools and the civil service through a policy called *iringaniza*, which roughly translates as social justice. Some Tutsi feared a recurrence of violence. As one Tutsi interviewee told me, "Because my parents were always telling me stories about 1959 ... I became scared to see war again like that one."[11]

Kayibanda also favored his home region of Gitarama, in Rwanda's south-center. Soon, power struggles developed within Parmehutu and corruption and nepotism grew. The majority of the population experienced a psychological letdown as the expectations of the revolution went largely unfulfilled. Key complainants were Hutu graduates of primary schools who felt entitled to employment yet found themselves unemployed, as well as those in the

---

[6] Author's interview, Belgian colonial administrator, Belgium, September 26, 2006.
[7] Uvin 1998, p. 20.
[8] Author's interview, female Tutsi, Kigali, February 6(A), 2006.
[9] Lemarchand 1970, p. 169.
[10] Author's interview, Belgian missionary, Belgium, September 27(A), 2006.
[11] Author's interview, male Tutsi, Kigali, January 30, 2006.

north who had historically resisted "Tutsi" state centralization and who felt disadvantaged by Kayibanda's southern favoritism.

By February 1973, complaints turned into unrest. Anonymous self-appointed "Public Safety" committees expelled Tutsi students from Rwandan schools and administrative posts. One Tutsi interviewee who had been a student at the time explained this period of history as follows:

> They started to eliminate the Tutsi. They burned my parents' house, they ate all of our cows, then we had to spend several months in the bush. Then, we had what they called peace and then a change of power with a coup d'état. But, that is really the moment when people showed that there was hatred between the two ethnic groups. And I was a victim. Upon returning to school, there were the children of those who had eaten our cows, the children of those who had burned our home, in school with me, which caused a lot of distance.[12]

These committees targeted Tutsi in high schools, the National University of Rwanda (NUR), and the seminaries, which were still perceived as "havens of Tutsi ascendancy." Alongside Tutsi, they attacked children of mixed marriages and sought out ethnic "fakers" who had changed their identity to gain admittance into schools. One Hutu woman told me about her sister who had been killed at school in this way: "She was Hutu, and she had a Hutu identity, but her face, they would say 'no, she's not Hutu.' Because here in Rwanda, we always look at the face."[13] Tutsi teachers, too, were sometimes targeted. One interviewee told me, "I remember, it was my grade five class. The teacher was teaching and when he saw a vehicle pass, near class, he had to hide. I did not understand. It was only afterwards that he told us that he was scared that they were coming to kill him."[14] Tutsi were attacked with impunity and many fled. Approximately 500 to 600 Rwandans were left dead as a result of this unrest.[15]

In July 1973, Juvénal Habyarimana, a Hutu general from Gisenyi in northwestern Rwanda, launched a coup and ushered in the Second Republic. One Hutu from the north, thirteen years old at the time and now in prison on genocide charges, explained this historical event:

> When President Habyarimana removed President Kayibanda from the south, there were a lot of people who thought of peace. Because they saw that now we are liberated from meanness, from those with a view from the south.... And when Habyarimana took the regime ... I remember that people applauded him, because he was going to bring peace to the children of Rwanda. Because there had been massacres between students, there were all kinds of problems burning houses of Tutsi.[16]

---

[12] Author's interview, male Tutsi, Kigali, January 20, 2006.

[13] Author's interview, female Hutu, Kigali, March 10(A), 2006.

[14] Author's interview, female Hutu, southern Rwanda, March 16, 2006.

[15] Linden 1999, p. 375. Mamdani 2001, p. 147. For a personal account of these events, see Umutesi 2004, pp. 11–13.

[16] Author's interview, female Hutu, Kigali, April 5(C), 2006.

Indeed, many people initially welcomed Habyarimana as a protector of all Rwandans. He replaced the institutions of the First Republic with the Committee for Peace and National Unity, then the National Republican Movement for Development (MRND), a single party of which all Rwandans were members. Systematic harassment of Tutsi became less common, and some of my interviewees recounted that ethnic tension between the two groups had significantly subsided by the 1980s. Some Hutu even charged President Habyarimana with favoring Tutsi.[17] Lemarchand, writing in 1974, suggested that "the prospects of a Hutu-Tutsi rapprochement, both within and outside Rwanda, have never been brighter since independence."[18]

Although one tends to rethink everything that occurred during the Habyarimana period through the lenses of its genocidal outcome, during much of the Second Republic Rwanda was a darling of the international aid community and considered a model developing country.[19] The Habyarimana government was particularly adroit at legitimating itself internally and internationally through reminders of the innate justice of the social revolution. It was also successful at championing the "myth of apolitical development," wherein the state's sole goal was perceived to be economic growth. His actions diverted attention from "dirty politics," legitimated the state's intrusions into social and political life, and deflected attention from continuing differential treatment of groups. Habyarimana's actions were not entirely smoke and mirrors; it is widely agreed that Rwanda during the late 1970s and early 1980s experienced social and economic improvement in all important areas, including education. In many ways, the government of Paul Kagame today is reminiscent of Habyarimana's in its skill at advancing an image of progress and apolitical development, as the next chapter discusses in more detail.

Nonetheless, a number of familiar political issues persisted. The Habyarimana government killed many of the power holders of the First Republic and is best described as an autocratic military dictatorship. Elections returning the president to power with more than 98 percent of the vote were a mere charade, and criticism was harshly repressed.[20] Like Kayibanda, and the colonial administration before him, Habyarimana also maintained ethnic divisions. He aimed to concretize the gains of the revolution by formalizing Kayibanda's quotas for education and jobs. Moreover, he wanted to unite Hutu by reserving most opportunities for them. While Tutsi were allowed limited participation in the state, and perhaps more so than in Kayibanda's government, Hutu still dominated the army and local politics.[21] One interviewee described the reality of this time period: "I saw [someone of a different ethnicity] as my friend, and he

---

[17] Jefremovas 1997.
[18] Quoted in Mamdani 2001, p. 140.
[19] The information in this paragraph is from Uvin 1998, pp. 40, 45.
[20] Uvin 1996, p. 8.
[21] Prunier 1997, p. 75.

saw me as his friend ... but you could easily hear someone say that 'you are from this or that group, get out of here. Go on, you shouldn't be in my country.' Conflict was not open, but at the same time, it wasn't hidden."[22] Also like his predecessor, Habyarimana favored his home region, this time the northwest.

In the late 1980s and early 1990s, Rwanda encountered trouble on several fronts. Economically, GDP per capita fell from US$355 in 1983 to US$260 by 1990.[23] At the same time, the government was implementing structural adjustment and devalued the Rwandan franc amid significant inflation. The poorest segments of the population felt the adjustments most harshly, reinforcing class divisions. Compounding problems, the population in Rwanda more than doubled during the Habyarimana years, from 3 million in 1970 to nearly 7.5 million by 1991. Population density grew to average more than 400 inhabitants per square kilometer by about 1990.[24] As one Hutu woman opined, "In Rwanda, it is a big challenge because it is a small country and there are a lot of people.... This is probably one of the big causes of conflict."[25]

A number of political events also destabilized the country. The Habyarimana government began facing internal criticisms of corruption and a loss of legitimacy. Grievances were mainly along class and regional lines among Hutu factions, because Habyarimana had continued to favor his northwestern home region. Then, in October 1990, the government faced an armed invasion from Uganda by a group of Tutsi exiles called the Rwandan Patriotic Front (RPF). One Tutsi woman explained that "[w]hat they called the *inyenzi* [cockroaches] were refugees from Rwanda who had fled the country and who were living in the surrounding countries and wanting to come back. But, they were trying to come back armed. Each time they tried to come back, the government killed people inside the country."[26] A civil war ensued and lasted approximately three years, providing Habyarimana both a challenge to his government and the opportunity to use an external enemy to consolidate Hutu into a cohesive group and to rebuild his support.

In 1991, under pressure from both Rwandan pro-democracy activists and the international community, which tied its continued aid to democratic reform, the Habyarimana government half-heartedly initiated multipartyism.[27] The MRND changed its name to the MRND-D, adding the second "D" for "democracy," although in reality, Habyarimana stalled democratization and altered few of his practices. Opposition parties were united in opposition to these tactics, but also cleaved along both regional and ethnic lines. As one Hutu man said, "Even though they were all Hutu, there were still problems. They belonged to different political parties." For instance, as around the time

[22] Author's interview, male of unknown ethnicity, Kigali, February 7, 2006.
[23] Erny 1994, p. 81; Uvin 1998, p. 54.
[24] Linden 1999, p. 394; Newbury and Newbury 1995, p. 8.
[25] Author's interview, female Tutsi, Kigali, March 14, 2006.
[26] Author's interview, female Tutsi, Kigali, January 27, 2006.
[27] This paragraph is based on Des Forges 1999, pp. 121–158.

of independence, Hutu from near Gitarama, Kayibanda's hometown in central Rwanda, were often pitted against those from the north, Habyarimana's home region. Moreover, he continued, "some were thought to be RPF sympathizers."[28] In March 1992, radical Hutu created the *Coalition pour la Défense de la République* (CDR) and critiqued the governing party for not taking a harder line against the RPF and Tutsi more broadly. Some political parties became increasingly radicalized and turned to violence in an effort to achieve their goals. In addition to massacring Tutsi, the government also orchestrated attacks on Hutu that it then blamed on Tutsi. Those in power used violence to reinforce Hutu in-group solidarity and to stigmatize Tutsi as an out-group of RPF collaborators. While the opposition pressed forward and a coalition cabinet was formed in 1992, the government continued to resist efforts to separate the regime from the state and its benefits. Some elements within various parties became known as "Hutu Power," referring to an ideological movement across party lines that embodied ethnic solidarity and extremism. The CDR and MRND-D formed youth militias; the latter's was known as the *interahamwe*.

Habyarimana's government also seized on events in neighboring Burundi to stigmatize Tutsi and to present them as a threat. In 1993, the Tutsi-led Burundian army assassinated the country's first Hutu president, Melchoir Ndadaye, initiating fighting between the Hutu militia and the Tutsi army, widespread killing, and a flood of 300,000 Hutu refugees into Rwanda. These events provided Habyarimana with a concrete illustration of the Tutsi threat and helped bring together Hutu from different political factions and those who had been divided along regional lines.

Having been at war for nearly three years, facing internal political pressures, and with threats of discontinued funding by the international community, the Habyarimana government came to a negotiated settlement with the RPF in Arusha, Tanzania, in August 1993. The accords set out a power-sharing agreement for a broad-based transitional government with rules for the respect of law and human rights, the integration of the two armies, the non-conditional repatriation and reintegration of refugees and internally displaced Rwandans, and for a neutral international peacekeeping force.[29] Hard-liners in both the MRND-D and opposition parties claimed that the provisions were too favorable to the RPF and to Tutsi in general. Indeed, a core group of elites that had profited under Habyarimana were not willing to forfeit the benefits they had reaped.

On April 6, 1994, returning from a meeting on the implementation of the Arusha Accords, Habyarimana's airplane was shot down as it approached the Kigali airport. The genocide was set in motion. Within a few hours, Habyarimana's closest associates began killing off their opposition – both Hutu and Tutsi – then targeting Tutsi more generally. Many ordinary Hutu

[28] Author's interview, male Hutu, northern Rwanda, March 19, 2006.
[29] Des Forges 1999, pp. 123–125.

Rwandans joined in the killing, although not all Hutu participated, and not all who did participate did so to the same degree. The United Nations downsized its peacekeeping contingent, which had been present to support the implementation of the Arusha Accords. Then, with insufficient forces and a limited mandate, it watched genocide more efficient than Nazi death camps engulf Rwanda.[30]

Causes of Violent Intergroup Conflict

The now standard explanations of the genocide locate the driving causes in the economic and political events of the 1980s and early 1990s described earlier in the chapter. Scholars generally agree that the killings, rather than erupting through primordial ethnic hatred, were organized in advance by specific Hutu hard-liner elites who feared a loss of power.[31] My interviews substantiated this analysis. Interviewees, especially Hutu, often blamed the authorities for fomenting intergroup conflict and placed little responsibility on the population. "The major problem was political," one Hutu woman declared, in a statement representative of many I heard. "Not in the population. The population is poor. The population is rural. So, even if we identified Hutu and Tutsi among ourselves, it [violent conflict] was a political problem."[32] A man I interviewed in the Central Kigali Prison went even further, saying, "I think that really only politicians were able to manipulate the people, but the majority of the population didn't have those [extremist] tendencies."[33] Interviewees, especially Tutsi, nonetheless felt that that perpetrators' participation in the genocide was virtually "automatic." As one teacher commented, "[A]ccording to what I saw, my students liked each other and visited each other, but when killings started, it was like a whistle blowing. When the authorities said to [kill], they began putting themselves into groups and acting. 'I have to do this because it is demanded by the state.'"[34] These views are consistent with instrumentalist theories of ethnic conflict contending that conflict arises when ethnicity is mobilized and manipulated by elites for political purposes.

Because people are not automatons, these explanations inadequately explain how the genocide became possible or what underlying foundations allowed such a large number of Rwandans to be mobilized so readily. In contrast to those who attribute to them a culture of obedience,[35] Rwandans had often used ethnicity for their own purposes and disobeyed orders from above.[36] To turn into acute conflict, proximate causes such as economic and political changes,

[30] Dallaire 2003, pp. 251–255.
[31] Barnett 2003; Des Forges 1999; Prunier 1997; Straus 2006.
[32] Author's interview, female Hutu, southern Rwanda, March 15(A), 2006.
[33] Author's interview, male Hutu, Kigali, April 5(A), 2006.
[34] Author's interview, female Tutsi, Kigali, January 27, 2006.
[35] Prunier 1997; Reyntjens 1996, p. 6.
[36] Eyoh 1999; Uvin 1998.

mobilization by ethnic entrepreneurs, and the plane crash need to become activated on an underlying foundation. In other words, for Rwandan political conflicts to become violent conflict, for political, ethnic, class, and regional conflicts to play out predominantly along ethnic lines, and for effective mobilization to occur, the social-structural and psychocultural material to do so needed to be there. In the Cambodian genocide, the Khmer Rouge framed and justified violence in such a way that it drew on familiar, existing knowledge and ideology.[37] Similarly, in Rwanda, while different perpetrators had different motivations for acting,[38] preexisting experience and knowledge created a foundation that allowed calls for mobilization by elites to be more resonant and thus more effective. This groundwork also provided ordinary people with an outlet through which they could scapegoat and direct blame for their continued and growing misery.[39]

If horizontal inequalities, exclusive identities, and stigmatizing groups were part of the groundwork for violent interethnic conflict in Rwanda, the question follows: how did these underlying social-structural and psychocultural factors develop? The rest of this chapter turns to education to demonstrate that formal schooling played an important role in this underpinning.

Formal Education under the Rwandan Republics

From 1959 until 1966, several laws and policies gradually brought schooling under national control. In the fall of 1959, the would-be governing party, Parmehutu, issued an educational manifesto that introduced the first national commitment for expanding primary education to universal levels. It also decreed that all national educational reports henceforth needed to indicate the "racial" proportion of Hutu, Tutsi, and Twa in schools,[40] and introduced ethnic quotas for promotion past primary school. The *Constitution of the Republic of Rwanda* (1961) and the *Loi Scolaire* (1966) further pronounced primary education to be obligatory and free for all. As I show, however, practice differed.

Throughout the period from the late 1950s to mid-1960s, Rwandans began replacing Belgians as school principals and administrators and the *Loi Scolaire* centralized Rwanda's education system under state, rather than ecclesiastical, control. A Rwandan man who oversaw this process as a school inspector told me that "teaching was now ... imposed by the government, diplomas were given by the state, and exams were the same in all schools."[41] The law also set out government standards for personnel, admissions, textbooks, and curriculum. [42] While one of my interviewees, a missionary and colonial school

---

[37] Hinton 2005, p. 29.
[38] Des Forges 1999, p. 770; Straus 2006.
[39] Uvin 1998, p. 217.
[40] Ngendahimana 1981, p. 58.
[41] Author's interview, male Hutu, northern Rwanda, March 20(B), 2006.
[42] Lemarchand 1970, p. 258.

principal, described this process as peaceful and cooperative,[43] the transition brought great controversy between church and state, and the church deemed this law unconstitutional. The two sides were ethnically polarized as the Hutu government against a mostly Tutsi clergy. Parmehutu circulated a manifesto charging church authorities with continued Tutsi favoritism, promoting Hutu-Tutsi divisions, and trying to discredit the government.[44]

Neither independence nor new laws, however, significantly changed the educational system inherited from the Belgians. The newly independent government took over primary schools serving about 250,000 students, secondary schools serving just 4,000, and only one post-secondary institution, the major seminary in Nyakibanda, with the National University (NUR) to be added shortly thereafter in 1963.[45] Although the quality of teaching declined "catastrophically,"[46] the physical school structures, teachers, teaching methods, and curriculum marked important continuities from the colonial period through the First Republic.[47] Primary schooling remained six years: a first cycle of three or four years focused on literacy and a second cycle of two or three years provided more general training. The first cycle was taught in Kinyarwanda, and the second in French. At the end of the sixth year, students took a national exam for admission to secondary school. Primary schools continued to be of three types – official, subsidized, and private – although near the end of the Kayibanda regime the meaning of private changed from religious to secular parents' schools. While its role was constrained, the church remained an important educational institution, alongside the family and the state, and retained its control of most secondary education. The church regained much of its role in primary schools in the 1980s when budget shortages plagued the government.[48] Educational challenges also remained similar: inadequate financial resources, a shortage of qualified teachers, a lack of pedagogical materials, an insufficient number of schools, and a high dropout rate.

On the other hand, the Kayibanda regime did make some changes to schooling policies and practices in post-independence Rwanda. It committed itself first and foremost to expanding educational opportunities. Having made the Hutu majority's lack of education one of its central criticisms of the colonial regime, improving this situation had to be at the forefront of the newly independent government's political agenda. Failing to do so would risk a loss of credibility. It also introduced Rwandan history in primary schools, for the first time, through a course called *causeries*, and in secondary schools as its own subject. Written history teaching material from the First Republic was, however, scarce or nonexistent.[49]

---

[43] Author's interview, Belgian missionary, Belgium, September 26(A), 2006.
[44] Lemarchand 1970, p. 259.
[45] RoR 1989; Hoben 1989, pp. 13–14; Ngendahimana 1981.
[46] Author's interview, scholar, Belgium, September 25, 2006.
[47] See, for example, Karangwa 1988, p. 39.
[48] Linden 1999, p. 364; Ngendahimana 1981, p. 68.
[49] Gasanabo 2004, pp. 75–77.

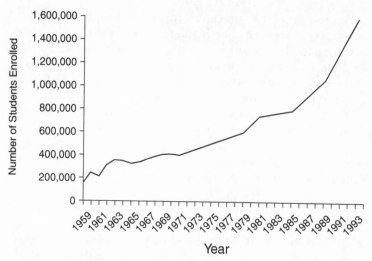

FIGURE 3.1 Number of students enrolled in primary school (1959–1960 to 1993–1994). *Sources*: Hanf 1974, p. 30; Hoben 1989, pp. 34, 37; Obura 2003, p. 40; RoR Undated, p. 9.

The population responded to these changes and primary school registration grew quickly, as illustrated in Figure 3.1. The government had to introduce double shifts – where one teacher taught some students in the morning and a different group of students in the afternoon – to accommodate the influx. However, the rate of population growth surpassed the rate of increase of available spots in school for much of the period, so that schools were unable to keep up with the demand for enrollment.[50] This can be seen by comparing Figure 3.1 to Figure 3.2.

Moreover, opportunities for post-primary education did not grow in tandem. This resulted in frustration, which leaders feared might lead to social unrest. As under the colonial regime, Rwandans continued to see schooling as intricately tied to social mobility and access to wage employment in the city. In 1970, in an effort to address dissatisfaction, the Kayibanda government instituted a network of *Centres d'Enseignement Rural et Artisanal au Rwanda* (CERAR) for boys and a few similar programs for girls. CERAR taught a two-year post-primary program to train farmers "capable of being agents of development, to improve the living conditions on the hills and to permit each to meet his/her potential."[51]

Resentment also began to grow in relation to the growing disparity between the rhetoric of social justice and the reality on the ground in both class and ethnic terms. Primary school teachers earned on average only about 750 RWF

[50] Hoben 1989, p. 34; Obura 2003, p. 40.
[51] Ngendahimana 1981, p. 66.

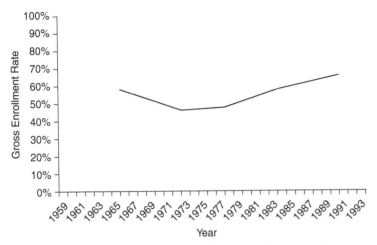

FIGURE 3.2 Primary school gross enrollment rate (1966–1991).

Sources: Hoben 1989, p. 34, Obura 2003, p. 40.

Note: Gross enrollment rate (GER) is the total number of pupils enrolled in primary school, regardless of age, expressed as a percentage of the population in the theoretical age group for primary education. Since many students join primary school very late, or drop out and reenroll, GER can theoretically be over 100 percent. In contrast, net enrollment rate (NER) is the total number of pupils in the theoretical age group enrolled in school expressed as a percentage of the total population in that age group.

(Rwandan francs) monthly (at the time, about US$7.50), whereas the minister of finance earned approximately US$1,200 per month.[52] Indeed, in my interviews, many teachers complained that their pay – then and now – was inadequate to meet even their basic needs. The Hutu population also increasingly accused the government of inadequately addressing inequalities, arguing that there was a colonial carryover attitude of Tutsi favoritism, and of providing better opportunities for educated Tutsi.[53] Complaints culminated in the 1973 Tutsi expulsions from administrative and educational positions, discussed in the previous section.

When Habyarimana took control of the government, he made clear that education was central to the Second Republic's goals. Over the next several decades, he consistently presented education as the "cornerstone of the general development of Rwanda."[54] The government backed up his words with action, continuing to spend significantly on education. At this time, it was common for African countries to spend one-fifth to one-sixth of their national budget on education. Rwanda spent approximately one-quarter of its national

[52] Lemarchand 1970, p. 238.
[53] Hoben 1989, p. 15; Lemarchand 1970, p. 260.
[54] RoR 1979, p. 40.

budget on schooling and thus ranked among the top three or four spenders on education in Africa. The head of the Ministry of Education was held to be the most important political figure after the president, at least during the mid-1980s, further illustrating the significance of education for Rwandans. Most of the education budget – 70 percent in the mid-1980s – was spent on primary schooling. According to a World Bank survey, only two (Djibouti and Yemen) out of seventy developing countries spent a higher proportion of their education budget on primary education.[55]

In addition to supporting higher primary school enrollment rates, the Second Republic made two key changes to education that were designed to rectify other shortcomings of colonial schools. First, in response to colonial era imbalances and to charges of continued Tutsi overrepresentation in higher levels of education, Habyarimana's government introduced a complex quota system. Primary school remained ostensibly open to all regardless of class, ethnicity, gender, and geographic origin. The quotas formalized Kayibanda's practice of allocating secondary and post-secondary school spots according to ethnicity. As Tutsi represented between 9 percent and 15 percent of the Rwandan population, they were to be granted only 9 percent to 15 percent of positions in schools (different sources put the quotas at different numbers between these extremes).[56] Charging the First Republic with using education for regional and familial patronage, and thus with creating regional inequality, Habyarimana added the criterion of regional origin of students and rural/urban provenance to quotas. This time, the north, especially the provinces of Gisenyi and Ruhengeri – not coincidentally Habyarimana's home region – was favored at the expense of formerly advantaged provinces in the south, such as Butare, Gikongoro, and Gitarama. As one Hutu woman, who had been a student at the time, remarked, "Habyarimana made it such that Gisenyi, his home town, was favored, saying that those [students] had to get in to schools, because there, they hadn't studied."[57] The multidimensional quotas – with not only ethnicity, but also region, as decisive criteria – reflect the fact that conflict management "is a two (at least) level game," with both inter- and intragroup competition.[58]

The quota policy included the following criteria for secondary school admission:

- school records and national examination scores, to which all other elements are subordinated;
- ethnic equilibrium, based on quotas established on the basis of the proportion of each ethnic group's representation in the entire population of the country;

[55] Hoben 1989, p. 57.

[56] 2004. "The Road out of Hell," *The Economist*. Available at: http://www.economist.com/node/2535789; Chrétien 2003, p. 309; Hanf 1974, p. 140; Hoben 1989, p. 98; Linden 1999; Mamdani 2001, p. 139; Newbury 1992, p. 198; Obura 2003, p. 44; Prunier 1997, p. 60.

[57] Author's interview, female Hutu, Kigali, March 10(A), 2006.

[58] Ross 2007, p. 19.

- a regional balance that corrects the accumulated disequilibrium of opportunities for schooling in certain regions to the detriment of others and permits equitable distribution of admissions to secondary school in all prefectures;
- sexual balance, based on demographic distribution of males and females; and
- the rectification of anomalies by a correction of 5% of school places reserved for distribution by the ministry.[59]

As I demonstrate in the next section, my own interviewees, as well as those interviewed by others, believe that for secondary school, ethnicity trumped other criteria for admission, such as records and exams,[60] and that there were also serious concerns about regional favoritism.

These quotas made significant strides in addressing representation at post-secondary levels. Tutsi dominance in tertiary institutions drastically declined from the 1960s through the 1980s. In the 1960s, close to 90 percent of students at the National University of Rwanda were Tutsi. From 1981 to 1987, with quotas having been in effect for about two decades, Tutsi represented 10–14 percent of students at the National University of Rwanda.[61] One report from 1982–1983 states that only 28 of 424 students were Tutsi, representing just 6.6 percent.[62] Scholarships for university education in Rwanda and abroad were mostly reserved for Hutu.

Habyarimana's second major educational reform attempted to "ruralize education."[63] He made each educational cycle a "terminal cycle" and added lessons on the skills needed for rural life to schools' academic programs. This was because more than 83 percent of youth exiting primary school returned to their traditional rural setting, and yet were ill-prepared and unwilling to do so.[64] In fact, a 1988 World Bank study found that out of thirty-nine Sub-Saharan African countries, Rwanda accepted the lowest proportion of primary school graduates into secondary school.[65] The reforms therefore aimed to better match Rwandan schooling with Rwandan "realities" and to "orient youth education onto the path drawn by the Manifesto of the MRND."[66] This kind of programming was relatively common in Africa at the time, illustrated, for example, by Nyerere's "Education for Self-Reliance" policies in Tanzania.[67] In Rwanda, some saw this as an effort to dampen ethnic conflict as well by fostering reciprocity and a shared future. The government intended to inculcate Rwanda's youth with a rich national culture and to encourage the participation of all in the development of the country. My interviews show, however,

---

[59] MINEPRISEC, 1986, quoted in Hoben 1989, p. 104.
[60] Ibid., p. 104.
[61] Munyantwali 1991, p. 304; RoR 2006b, p. 189.
[62] Mugesera reported in McLean Hilker 2011, p.270.
[63] Hanf 1974.
[64] Karangwa 1988, p. 46; RoR 1979b, p. 49.
[65] Hoben 1989, p. 48.
[66] RoR 1979b, p. 50.
[67] Samoff 1990, pp. 229–230.

that these reforms did nothing to change the intensity of competition over access to secondary school.

There were several other elements to the reforms that emerge as important in my analysis of the peace and conflict implications of schooling during this period. The reforms also added two additional years to primary school for practical training (retrenched in 1991), changed the language of instruction at all levels of primary school to Kinyarwanda, universalized mixed-gender primary schools, expanded post-primary rural training programs, and took steps to increase secondary enrollment from roughly 8 percent of primary school entrants to 10 percent.[68] Primary school teaching of history as its own subject began in 1979 and teachers' manuals were created by 1982.[69]

While recognizing that "schooling is not a magic wand to liberate the country from poverty, misery, ignorance and other constraints of under-development," the Habyarimana government emphasized schooling as a "pillar" of Rwanda's "overall system of development."[70] In return, Rwanda was a favorite of the international donor community, especially under Habyarimana, for significantly expanding primary school enrollments and achieving gender parity in primary schools by 1990.[71] What remains to be examined is the impact of these efforts on the relationships among Rwandans.

An Assessment of the Role of Schooling (1962–1994)

In assessing the role of schooling in peace and conflict during this period in Rwanda, I heard two main narratives. The first, and most common overall, was shared by nearly all Tutsi that I interviewed, some Hutu, and educational experts. As a professor from Rwanda's National University phrased it, "[E]ducation really rendered a disservice to generations." He elaborated:

> There are certainly many factors that contribute to conflict in Rwanda, but in my opinion, schools are among those factors. In classes, they asked Hutu, Tutsi, and Twa to stand up [according to their ethnicity].... This frustrated the students that lived this. At the end of primary school, we did an unfair exam [to access secondary school]. Also, history was taught to render a part of the population apathetic to the situation of the other.[72]

These are the key themes of the rest of this chapter and the argument that I develop: that access to schooling, history curricula, and classroom practices under the Rwandan Republics created some of the social-structural and psychocultural mechanisms that underlay violent interethnic conflict in Rwanda. The horizontal inequalities, exclusive identities, and stigmatization that were

[68] Hoben 1989; Karangwa 1988; RoR 1979b.
[69] Gasanabo 2004, pp. 77–78.
[70] RoR 1979b, p. 50. See also Karangwa 1988, pp. 54, 56; Simpenzwe 1988, p. 32.
[71] See RoR "La Scolarisation Féminine," undated, p. 9.
[72] Author's interview, education administrator, northern Rwanda, March 17, 2006.

reflected, amplified, and produced in schools contributed to the groundwork on which proximate causes took effect.

The counterargument to this narrative presents an additional explanation of events that cannot simply be shunted aside, despite the fact that only a minority of interviewees expressed it. These interviewees suggested the others merely reproduced the official discourse of today's Tutsi-dominated government, which claims that education during Kayibanda's and Habyarimana's Hutu-centric regimes fostered intergroup conflict. Hutu interviewees also often highlighted the current government's interest in making the link between previous education and interethnic conflict in order to demonize the previous Hutu governments and to bolster its own support. As one Hutu man in the north of the country told me:

> Politicians use several ways to convince people that it is he who has the men [support of the population]. I don't think that you can train people to genocide, nor to war, because normally children don't know what authorities or their parents are doing.... The current regime is saying that to show that the old regime is bad and that everything done in those moments is bad. So for me, [the role of schooling in conflict] is not true.[73]

More generally, many Hutu interviewees were hesitant about the overall contribution of education to conflict. They often took my questions more literally, reflecting on the fact that education did not teach them explicit hatred. As one interviewee answered me, "Never did a teacher bring us together in class to tell us, 'you, Hutu, hate Tutsi!'"[74] To overcome this challenge of discrepant narratives, I triangulated interviews and documents. Nonetheless, I take seriously the different perspectives, group transcripts, and mythico-histories of those with experience of the Rwandan educational system and living within today's political context.

Access to Primary School

As previously noted, by law proclaimed at independence, primary school became ostensibly open to all regardless of gender, ethnicity, and geographic origin. A few interviewees suggested that the mere act of bringing children together into nonsegregated schools may be considered peacebuilding, although others pointed out that mixed classrooms were not significant factors given that Hutu and Tutsi lived intermingled on the same hills, played in their communities, sat together in church, worked adjoining fields, and interacted at markets. No interview participants raised unprompted problems in access to primary school.

On the other hand, when specifically asked, most interviewees were of the opinion that access to primary school was not equal for all Rwandans, with inequalities emerging along class, gender, and ethnic lines. First, poor children

---

[73] Author's interview, male Hutu, Kigali, March 22(C), 2006.
[74] Author's interview, female Hutu, Kigali, April 5(C), 2006.

had less access to education. One man who had been a student in the colonial and postcolonial periods recalled that "even when primary schooling was obligatory and free, there were households living in such misery that they couldn't send their kids to school."[75] Parents still had to pay indirect costs including uniforms and school material, and had to make up for lost hands around the home. One man who taught primary school from 1983 to 1993 assessed that "[j]ust over half of children went to school since there were those that couldn't, who didn't have uniforms, that couldn't pay for notebooks, for school books, or who simply didn't want to. A lot of parents said 'no, you stay here, look after the cows or the goats. Studying isn't good for anything.'"[76] In addition, school fees were reintroduced by 1988 and the cost of primary school soon amounted to more than US$18 per child per year at a time when GDP per capita was only about US$255.[77] This was an unbearable sum for many Rwandans, considering that an average family had six children. Additionally, the currency devaluation and inflation that accompanied Structural Adjustment Policies made fees more harshly felt. This phenomenon was common throughout Sub-Saharan Africa and has been observed in such places as Ghana, Kenya, Malawi, and Nigeria.[78]

Dropout rates were also linked to poverty. Primary school dropout rates are reported to have ranged from 13.2 percent to 18.8 percent between 1966 and 1972 and from 7.8 percent to 10.9 percent between 1986 and 1990. Even at the time of my interviews, I observed that primary schools often had up to six grade-one classes, but only a couple of grade-six classes. Fifty percent of dropouts, at least around 1990, were motivated by general poverty, school fees, and/or the cost of uniforms.[79] Another study found that urban students stayed in school longer than rural-based students,[80] perhaps because schools were closer to urban students, although rural poverty is a plausible alternate explanation.

Second, girls also had unequal access to school. As one interviewee explained, in a statement representative of many, "The number of boys was very high in relation to the number of girls. Because people had a mentality that it was boys who have to study and that it was girls who had to stay home to help the family. The girls of an age of maturity left to find husbands and didn't come back to help their families. So, [for both reasons] parents in that time wanted to send their boys to school more than girls."[81]

Third, many interviewees felt that Tutsi access to primary education had not been equal to that of Hutu students. There were no formal ethnic restrictions

---

[75] Author's interview, male Hutu, Kigali, April 5(A), 2006.
[76] Author's interview, male Tutsi, Kigali, January 20, 2006.
[77] Musabimana Undated, p. 33; Ngendahimana 1981, p. 60; RoR 1991, pp. 9–17.
[78] Sefa Dei et al. 2006, p. 20.
[79] For 1966–1972 rates, see Hanf 1974, p. 37; Musabimana undated, p. 33; For 1968–1969 figures, see Ngendahimana 1981, p. 60; RoR 1986, pp. 1–2.
[80] Hoben 1989, p. 106.
[81] Author's interview, male Hutu, Kigali, March 22(C), 2006.

on primary school. Figures from the Ministry of Education (1989–1990) report that Tutsi represented 7.4 percent in the first grade of primary schools, while Hutu represented 91.4 percent. On the other hand, considering grades one to six collectively, Tutsi represented 9.4 percent and Hutu represented 89.9 percent of students in primary schools by 1990.[82] If Tutsi represented the common estimate of 15 percent of the population, they would have been underrepresented at all primary levels. Based on the 1978 census, which considered the population to be about 9.5 percent Tutsi, 90 percent Hutu, and less than 1 percent Twa, Hutu would have been slightly overrepresented in primary schools, especially in the early years.

Rather than legal restrictions on access to schools for Tutsi students, I heard more often about restrictions on symbolic access and negative practices affecting the educational experience for Tutsi students that indirectly affected their access to schools. As one Hutu man put it, reminding us that schooling is an instrument of the state, "There are white sheep, black sheep, and brown sheep. They mostly get along, but the shepherd has his favorites."[83] As another man, a Tutsi teacher during the two Republics, explained, "There were children who were frustrated, who didn't come back to school, especially when school talked about Tutsi.... There are some that said it felt like torture and they went home, especially the Tutsi."[84] One Hutu man who was a student in the Kayibanda years reported that "Tutsi were seen as mean people. They called them snakes," and that this made children uncomfortable at school.[85] A Tutsi woman who had been educated during the same era expressed similar themes: "[Tutsi were seen as] venomous snakes. And they chased Tutsi everywhere. Really, if you were Tutsi, you couldn't be calm at school."[86] In this way, hostile learning environments may have contributed to fewer Tutsi deciding to pursue an education.

Promotion Past Primary School

Whereas access to primary education was not generally limited along ethnic lines, more problems arose at the end of primary school. Nearly every interviewee – Hutu and Tutsi, male and female, and Rwandans from all regions of the country – raised the issue of inequality of access to secondary school and felt that this inequality was detrimental to relations among Rwandans. Access to higher levels of education in Rwanda is intricately tied to perceptions of social mobility, actual social mobility, and average rate of pay, as it is in most of the world. Problematically, however, there were (and still are) only very few secondary school positions in Rwanda. Indeed, the school system was pyramidal, with exceptionally narrow top layers, as shown in Figure 3.3. Different

---

[82] MINEPRISEC figures in Obura 2003, p. 44.
[83] Author's interview, male Hutu, Kigali, February 12, 2006.
[84] Author's interview, male Tutsi, Kigali, January 20, 2006.
[85] Author's interview, male Hutu, Kigali, January 29(B), 2006.
[86] Author's interview, female Tutsi, Kigali, January 29(A), 2006.

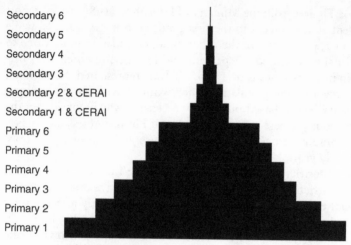

Secondary 6
Secondary 5
Secondary 4
Secondary 3
Secondary 2 & CERAI
Secondary 1 & CERAI
Primary 6
Primary 5
Primary 4
Primary 3
Primary 2
Primary 1

FIGURE 3.3 The educational pyramid in the 1980s.
Source: Based on Susan J. Hoben, *School, Work and Equity: Educational Reform in Rwanda*, 1989, pp. 36–37.

sources put the number of primary school students accepted into secondary school between just 6 percent and 9 percent.[87] There were additional spots in post-primary farmer-training programs, but enrollment in them progressively declined as students and parents realized that they would not lead to salaried jobs.

A key explanation for inequality in access to secondary schools was that entrance exams were graded in light of ethnic identity and ethnic equilibrium policies: in other words, policies in favor of Hutu. The quotas were justified on the basis that the secondary school pie was of limited size and had to be divided proportionally to the Rwandan population in each ethnicity and region. As one Hutu man from the north argued, "Power holders have to behave in a certain way to raise literacy as soon as there is too much demand and not enough capacity."[88] He explained of the period after independence:

> Independence was a moment when we saw the majority of a certain ethnicity [Tutsi] who had until then pursued their studies with just a minority from the other group, see their roles reversed. We found the majority presence [in secondary schools] go to the majority group.... Then, the majority of people who found themselves in secondary school in the '70s found themselves at university. They found the others [Tutsi] who were used to being alone over there. So you see these people [Hutu] who had long had a brake on their ambitions arrive like a flood of water, and the others [Tutsi] were a little bothered.[89]

[87] Hoben 1989, p. 48; Obura 2003, p. 41; RoR 1991, p. 4.
[88] Author's interview, male Hutu, Kigali, April 5(A), 2006.
[89] Ibid.

It is difficult to judge the quotas implemented by the First and Second Republics in the hindsight of the genocide. Considering that Tutsi were significantly advantaged in access to many schools during the colonial period, establishing quotas, ostensibly to improve horizontal equity, is understandable. Indeed, many countries support affirmative action in an effort to redress past discrimination and to ameliorate equality of opportunities in education and employment. When I asked about counting spots by ethnicity, a Hutu man replied, "Well, we had to. Wouldn't you? One group had been previously disadvantaged.... Hutu had been disadvantaged for four hundred years. Tutsi had been the leaders and gaining benefits. Nineteen fifty-nine was to try to stop the injustice. Then, we had to count to ensure that previous injustices didn't recur."[90] The quotas may also be regarded in a positive light as ensuring minority rights, and some Tutsi did consider the quotas as positive guarantees of a minimum number of higher education spots. Consultants who visited Rwanda under Habyarimana "noted with approval that access to schooling appears unusually equitable," and thereby dismissed possible problems.[91] The Catholic bishops in Rwanda, as late as 1990, also praised Habyarimana's policy of ethnic equilibrium.[92]

Yet, most interviewees felt that quotas ultimately contributed to conflict among Rwandans. "It absolutely created a complex for the people that were discriminated against," one Hutu woman in southern Rwanda, now a teacher, argued. "It impeded them from getting to higher jobs, even if they believed themselves to be capable. And it affected children from a young age. It created separate camps, and it is probably those camps that evolved all the way to what we experienced in '94."[93] Another Hutu woman from the south expressed similar sentiments:

> If the child knows that he is from this or that ethnicity, that he comes from this or that region, and for example, at the end of the exams to go to secondary school, he finds himself deprived of his right to education [for these reasons], of course there are frustrations that rise in the mentality of children.... There were a lot of frustrations because [the policy] was not based on justice. There were a lot of injustices.[94]

Indeed, Tutsi generally saw the quotas in this light – not as a way to level the playing field, but as a form of discrimination. Witness these representative statements:

> When we were children, it was Hutu who had the chance to go to secondary school. Tutsi, they said that they were a distrusted people.[95]

> To go to secondary school, they would say that you need perhaps 80 percent [on the exam], but for Tutsi it was 90 percent, so as to diminish the number of Tutsi that could enter secondary school.[96]

---

[90] Author's interview, male Hutu, northern Rwanda, March 20(B), 2006.
[91] Daniere and Meyer 1981 and Le Thanh Khoi 1985, cited in Hoben 1989, p. 104.
[92] Longman 2010, p. 149.
[93] Author's interview, female Hutu, southern Rwanda, March 15(A), 2006.
[94] Author's interview, female Hutu, southern Rwanda, March 16, 2006.
[95] Author's interview, female Tutsi, Kigali, January 29(A), 2006.
[96] Author's interview, male Hutu, Kigali, January 29(B), 2006.

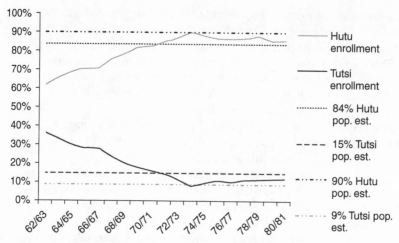

FIGURE 3.4 Over- and under-representation of ethnic enrollment at secondary school in relation to population (1964–1980).
Source: Based on figures from RoR 1986.

Figures substantiate the fact that many fewer Tutsi were admitted to secondary school than passed the exam.[97] Some Tutsi students who were unable to go to public secondary school sought access to seminaries, but recounted the same ceilings on their ambitions. As one man told me, "The only reason that I did not have access to a scholarship for theology was my ethnicity. I was even told by a pastor responsible for national-level church affairs that I couldn't get a scholarship because I am Tutsi."[98]

Whether or not figures match up with the ethnic quota policy goals depend on one's estimate of the ethnic proportions – and recall the political importance vested in under- and over-estimating census data the world over[99] – as well as the number of students that were able to bypass the quotas. Figure 3.4 illustrates that if Tutsi constituted the low estimate of 9.5 percent of the population, as per the 1978 census, their overrepresentation declined over the Hutu Republics and only once, in 1973, did they become underrepresented in secondary schools. If, on the other hand, Tutsi constituted the high estimate of 15 percent of the population, they remained overrepresented in secondary schools for much of the First Republic, then became slightly underrepresented in the Second Republic. In either case, the early overrepresentation may simply correspond to the decade it took for quotas to take effect. The lowest points of Tutsi representation correspond to the 1973 persecutions of Tutsi.

[97] RoR 2006c, p. 148.
[98] Author's interview, male Tutsi, Kigali, January 20, 2006.
[99] Anderson 2003.

Regardless of actual enrollment rates, school exclusion became part of a Tutsi narrative, or mythico-history, among exiles as well as those within Rwanda. One publication wrote that "Tutsi don't study" and that since 1975, no public school was supposed to welcome Tutsi. Another alleged that "the installation of the ethnic equilibrium policy is a cultural genocide that constitutes the civil death of Tutsi."[100] People are generally more sensitive to losses relative to where they start and overvalue losses relative to comparative gains.[101] Therefore, Tutsi perception of their relative deprivation and Hutu perceptions of injustice and entitlement exacerbated the cleavage between groups, even if the quota system moved Rwanda toward proportional equity in ethnic access to secondary school. Horizontal equity relies on acceptance of remaining inequalities by the population.

In response to reduced access to public secondary schooling, Tutsi engaged in several alternative strategies to pursue their education. Some Tutsi students turned toward private schools. Many private schools were even known as "Tutsi schools" and Hutu were significantly underrepresented in them.[102] However, Hutu that "were on the wrong side politically, especially those from the south" as well as the children of Hutu who had married Tutsi, also frequently attended.[103] In general, these private schools were considered second-rate in comparison to public schools.[104] Another strategy to combat Tutsi exclusion was to send one's children to Burundi, Congo, or Uganda.[105] While these strategies slightly advanced Tutsi access to education, their continued separation from Hutu students in Rwanda further entrenched ethnic divisions and prevented cross-ethnic cohesion.[106]

A repeated complaint among Tutsi who were allocated a spot in public secondary schools was that their ethnic identity limited their access to the undesirable streams of study, especially, somewhat paradoxically, to the study of primary education. Primary teaching required fewer years of study than other streams, graduating teachers were sent to unwanted rural outposts, and primary teachers in Rwanda are often looked down upon in comparison to those with government or private-sector jobs. As one Tutsi primary school teacher told me, rather than offer students the opportunity to pursue longer secondary school programs, "They would put us in classes of two or three years and nearly all Tutsi were streamed into education."[107] Another Tutsi teacher explained, "You had to go into education. All the Tutsi had to go into education. You were

---

[100] *Impuruza* December 1989 and *Le Patriote* February 1989, respectively, quoted in Munyantwali 1991, p. 306.
[101] Levy 2000.
[102] Munyantwali 1991, p. 304.
[103] Author's interview, Belgian missionary, Belgium, September 27(A), 2006.
[104] Hoben 1989, pp. 52–56.
[105] Author's interview, female Tutsi, Kigali, February 8(G), 2006.
[106] Muhimpundu 2002, p. 200.
[107] Author's interview, female Tutsi, Kigali, February 2(B), 2006.

not supposed to become a doctor ... and they sent you back to your birth hill. You didn't get to work in the city like the others."[108] A Government of Rwanda report suggested that women, more than men, were also streamed toward primary teaching for the same reasons.[109]

In addition to the ethnic dimension, I frequently heard that regional quotas provoked grievances. Interviewees identified region of origin – region was the second quota component under the Habyarimana regime – as a restrictive and unfair factor in secondary school admission. Indeed, Hutu especially emphasized the regional aspect of quotas because, while the ethnic dimension of the quota policies was felt most strongly by Tutsi, Hutu were more likely to be adversely affected by the regional dimension. Grievances emerged among Hutu because preferential treatment frequently results in intragroup competition over the distribution of benefits and antagonism from those who are ineligible for preferences.[110] Interviewees described the situation as follows:

> The equilibrium policy wasn't really centered on ethnicity, but regionalism ... And for that we found a lot, a lot of the population of young people from the region of the north, the region of the president of the Republic [getting admitted to schools].[111]

> All I know is that while there were ethnic problems, there were also regional problems. This means that we could see in the southern region, where I was a student, perhaps a sole student going to secondary school, or none at all. Meanwhile in the northern province, from where the president of the Second Republic came, we could find a whole class that obtained places in secondary school. I myself was victim of this regional equilibrium.[112]

Hutu from the north were also favored for opportunities to study abroad.[113] As one of Longman's interviewees from southern Rwanda expressed, "it was like we were colonized by the people from the north."[114] In the 1980s, students from Gisenyi and Ruhengeri represented 12 percent and 14 percent, respectively, of admissions to university, although these regions account for much less of the population.[115]

Regional issues also arose between Hutu and Tutsi. The combination of regional and ethnic quotas made access to secondary school particularly difficult for some Rwandans. Rural-based Tutsi, for example, were particularly hard-hit by regional quotas.[116] Moreover, in the complications of overlapping

[108] Author's interview, female Tutsi, Kigali, February 10(A), 2006.
[109] RoR Undated, p. 23.
[110] Weiner 1983.
[111] Author's interview, male Hutu, Kigali, March 15(D), 2006.
[112] Author's interview, female Hutu, southern Rwanda, March 16, 2006.
[113] Longman 2010, p. 121.
[114] Ibid., p. 121.
[115] RoR 2006c, p. 190–193.
[116] De Lame 2005, p. 62.

ethnicity and region, Hutu from the south sometimes felt themselves considered Tutsi – and thus to be disadvantaged – again making ethnicity a central dividing line of identity and entitlement. In this way, regional quotas also contributed to the hardening of ethnic identities.

As with the ethnic dimension of quotas, some Rwandans found ways to circumvent restrictions. One Hutu man, ultimately educated in the north, explained, "Say I arrive in grade six, I do the exam to go to secondary school and I fail. I change districts. Say I was in district A, I go to district B. The year ends and I write the exam. I fail. But then I do it again in district C and this time I change my name too. I change my identity, even my parents."[117] Children from cities such as Kigali and Butare sometimes applied to secondary school as if they lived on their parents' home hills, thus increasing their chances and causing "rural" spots to be occupied by urban students.[118]

Wealthier and well-connected Rwandans were also better able to navigate the political and academic systems and gain admittance to higher levels of schooling despite the restrictions of ethnic and regional quotas. Indeed, interviewees expressed strong opinions in regards to the corruption that pervaded the education system. As one Hutu man put it, "It was the friends of the well-placed that got access."[119] Another maintained that "[t]he children of the ministers did the exams before.... They had the exams before they were given!"[120] Others paid bribes to get a spot in secondary school. After she did well on her exam but was not on the list of those admitted to public secondary school, one Tutsi interviewee, who had been a student at the time and is now a teacher, recounted:

> I was at home crying for almost a week. I was sad and frustrated. [Officials] were telling me nothing. Then, I remember, I gave some money. I remember my parents told me that I would go give 50,000 francs to an old lady, the mother-in-law of the minister of education, because she lived near us on the hill.... We gave those 50,000 francs and two weeks later, another list arrived on the hill.... This one was not the people who succeeded [on the exam and equilibrium], but the people who were admitted without succeeding.[121]

However, class politics also contributed to ethnic inequalities and highlighted the new higher social station of Hutu. A Tutsi woman illustrated the ethnic dimension of class, noting that "there were a lot of people who went looking, negotiating. I already had good grades, but I had to have someone push me, a Hutu behind me who would go ask for a spot for a Tutsi child."[122] Alternatively,

---

[117] Author's interview, male Hutu, Kigali, February 6(B), 2006.

[118] Hoben 1989, p. 106; Newbury 1988, p. 226.

[119] Author's interview, male Hutu, northern Rwanda, March 20(A), 2006. See also De Lame 2005, p. 63; Hoben 1989, p. 107.

[120] Author's interview, female Tutsi, Kigali, February 2(B), 2006.

[121] Author's interview, female Tutsi, Kigali, February 10(A), 2006.

[122] Author's interview, female Tutsi, Kigali, February 8(G), 2006.

wealthier Rwandans sometimes had their ethnic identity cards changed. "Often enough," one man explained, "Tutsi gave money to change their ethnicity. So we were Tutsi, but we wrote Hutu on the identity card. We gave maybe a cow to become a friend, and then they gave a Hutu card in return."[123]

Another way that class overcame quotas was during the part of the Second Republic when secondary school boarding was temporarily suppressed: a "catastrophe for peasants," deemed one scholar of Rwanda with decades of experience in the region. She explained that within boarding schools, Rwandan students of all classes were ensured at least basic necessities. When boarding was suppressed, and students were still sent to far-away secondary schools, peasants would sell a cow to pay for the first year. After that, having nothing left to sell, poor students would drop out, leaving their spots open for richer Rwandans. This left peasants "very sour and justly so," fostering resentment.[124] Thus, while the quotas restricted access, political clientship left room for maneuvering. Some say that there is a "fourth ethnic group" in Rwanda, comprising those who have education, "European savoir faire," and the ability to circumvent rules.[125]

Overall, however, relatively few Rwandans were able to get around quotas, and many continued to feel that access to secondary education was ethnically unequal. Horizontal inequalities are most problematic when the opportunity for mobility from one group to another is low. Although quotas were meant to help the historically disadvantaged Hutu, they did so by restricting opportunities for Tutsi. This type of situation, wherein one group can achieve its goals only at the expense of the other group, often leads to negative attitudes, hostility, and discrimination[126] and has been characteristic of access to education in Rwanda. Inequalities in policies between Hutu and Tutsi reinforced ethnic categories and increased feelings of stigmatization. In addition, while higher-class Rwandans and those with ties to the government could circumnavigate the policies, others felt stuck in their ethnic and regional positions. In these cases, inequalities became a source of social instability and resentment against Hutu, who were ostensibly advantaged by these policies, as well as against Tutsi, who were still seen as receiving more than their share of benefits.[127]

In contrast to the colonial period, however, there were not obvious horizontal inequalities between Hutu and Tutsi in jobs and income. While Hutu had more access to civil service jobs, they were not necessary overrepresented vis-à-vis their proportion in the population,[128] and moreover, Tutsi still managed to occupy important positions throughout the country, especially in private business. However, when strong *intra*group differentials exist, for example between rich

---

[123] Author's interview, male Tutsi, Kigali, March 11, 2006.
[124] Author's interview, scholar, Belgium, September 25, 2006.
[125] De Lame 2005, p. 97; see also Destexhe in Uvin 199, p. 128.
[126] Sherif 1967.
[127] Stewart 2002, p. 5.
[128] Uwizeyimana, cited in RoR 2006c, pp. 140–141.

and poor Hutu, or between Hutu from different regions, as they did during the First and Second Republics, leaders may exploit *inter*group differences to avoid animosity being directed at them.[129] Access to schooling served well in this regard.

While Hutu, especially from the north, gained from educational changes, Tutsi could still be perceived as having too much, thereby fostering grievances among Hutu and leaving space for the government to scapegoat Tutsi. The impact of preferential policies need not be proportional to the grievance; minor preferences often result in significant resentments, even among those who do not actually lose out.[130] Because justice is often in the eye of the beholder, an improvement in objective conditions, such as in access to school for Hutu in this period, may still be interpreted in a way that supports negative feelings toward the other group.[131] The governments of the First and Second Republics continued to blame Tutsi for Rwanda's problems, invoking stigmatization and drawing attention away from other, nonethnic inequalities.

In sum, many Rwandans raised the issue of promotion past primary school as unfair, with quotas based on ethnicity, region, and class standing out as important dimensions. On a social-structural level, by controlling promotion past primary school, the state controls the production of a middle class and may – as in Rwanda – thereby produce horizontal inequalities. On a psycho-cultural level, Tutsi feelings of loss, Hutu feelings of entitlement, and a feeling among some Hutu that Tutsi were still getting too much likely strengthened in-group solidarity and out-group derogation on both sides, hardening, essentializing, and polarizing groups, despite the fact that access to school may have been fairly equitable on an ethnic basis. Just as awareness of their common discrimination increased Hutu cohesion in the colonial period, group exclusion or entitlement to schooling played a similar role in emphasizing and solidifying groups during the two Republics.

Even among those who understood the original rationale of quotas in Rwanda, some lamented that they went on for too long given the rancor they caused. In the early 1990s, U.S. aid agencies, for instance, discussed getting rid of ethnic identity cards.[132] In April 1992, when Agathe Uwilingiyimana became minister of education (she was later prime minister and among the first killed in the genocide), one of her first acts was to abolish quotas and to replace them with an exclusively merit-based system. More specifically, merit would be judged at the district level, so that students were compared to others who studied under the same conditions as them.[133] She received widespread support for this courageous, yet ultimately unsuccessful, effort to diffuse tensions.[134]

129 Stewart 2002, p. 11.
130 Sowell 2004, p. 18.
131 Coleman et al. 2008.
132 Uvin 1998, p. 39.
133 RoR 2006c, p. 164.
134 Des Forges 1999, p. 17; Prunier 1997, pp. 145–146.

Language

As discussed earlier in the book, access to language skills is another way in which competition for schooling is a potential grievance between groups. During this period, access to secondary school was particularly important because it meant access to learning French, an international language of commerce, and opportunity within the Rwandan economy as well.[135] Through the 1960s and 1970s, the lower years of primary school were taught in Kinyarwanda, with the upper years taught in French. In 1979, as part of Habyarimana's reforms, the language of instruction for all of primary school was changed to Kinyarwanda, thereby restricting access to French. As one Rwandan man who had studied in the decades after independence explained, "When I was in primary school, we studied in French.... We had a lot of recitations of texts from La Fontaine, difficult stuff. But by the time I became a teacher, they had changed the curriculum.... [W]e taught in the maternal language and things were at the level of the child. But, this very much contributed to lowering linguistic abilities."[136] Both Hutu and Tutsi parents and students were disappointed with the policy change to instruction in Kinyarwanda. French was considered linguistic capital to which they were being denied access.

Changes away from French-language teaching at primary school made secondary school even more important for social mobility. Because secondary school continued to be taught in French and access was restricted by quotas, some interviewees felt the ethnic, regional, and class dimensions of access to learning French were unfair. Tutsi and other Rwandans from the south often felt that the policy was especially unjust. "There were schools for the rich," one Tutsi woman told me, "where they studied in French, and schools for other Rwandans in Kinyarwanda. Normally, the children that went to rich schools, it was them that were able to get to the top. And they were Hutu."[137] As with quotas, these differences in access to language increased competition, helped solidify ethnic and regional groups, and amplified horizontal inequalities between them.

Pedagogy and Classroom Practices

Classroom practices and pedagogy also affected intergroup relations. As has been alluded to in previous sections of this chapter, interviewees very frequently highlighted an additional experience – of having to publicly self-identify according to ethnic identity in class, at both primary and secondary school – as problematic for the relationship among Rwandans. One long-time Tutsi teacher admitted, "I myself I did it, I did it to students. I asked 'Hutu go there, Tutsi go there.'"[138] While several interviewees claimed to have already known their

[135]   Des Forges 1999, pp. 62, 93.
[136]   Author's interview, male Tutsi, Kigali, January 20, 2006.
[137]   Author's interview, female Tutsi, Kigali, January 29(C), 2006.
[138]   Author's interview, female Tutsi, Kigali, January 27, 2006.

ethnic identity and that of their classmates, this activity categorized students and sent them the implicit message that it was appropriate to be divided in this way. Some interviewees date the beginning of this practice to about 1959, or even 1957–1958, when power began to flow into Hutu hands. Interviewees recall its significance both in terms of categorizing and collectivizing Hutu and Tutsi into groups, and in terms of entitlements that followed – especially spots in secondary school.

Moreover, a good number of interview participants claimed that they did not know their ethnic identity when asked in class. Many identified primary school as the site where they first concretely learned their ethnic belonging:

> When I was at primary, they would ask us, "you are of what ethnicity?" ... Like me, personally, my parents were devout Catholics; they did not teach me that. But when I arrived at school, they asked me, "you are from what ethnicity?" I was little, I didn't know, so I went to ask Papa, so he told me, "you belong to this ethnicity," and I went to tell them. At school they said that Tutsi had a refined nose ... Hutu had a big nose. So me, since I have a big nose, [I thought] I am Hutu. But when I asked my parents, they told me that I am not Hutu, I am Tutsi. So at that moment I was frustrated because the majority were Hutu and I was on the side of the Tutsi. It's like that that I learned that I was Tutsi, but I didn't know.[139]

> They asked us [our ethnicity] but sometimes we were mistaken, we went in such a group because you see your friend there.... We didn't know exactly to which group we belonged.[140]

I spoke with one interviewee about the fact that ethnic consciousness could also come through family socialization and the wider community. He replied, "When we learn it at school, it becomes even more delicate." He explained that while he did learn about ethnicity on his hill, it was reinforced and validated at school.[141] Schools are not the only places where Rwandan children learned ethnicity, yet they are an important site and, given the age of primary school children, sometimes the first place, as illustrated by the preceding quotes. Furthermore, because schools are seen by Rwandans as official and respectable, this categorization is legitimated. Schools marked ethnicity as an important, and moreover exclusive, classification in interactions with the state.

Some interviewees further argued that ethnically labeling students brought negative attention to the minority, and several recalled it being paired with an exercise wherein the teacher explained the physical traits of Hutu, Tutsi, and Twa:

> Especially the problem [the roots of conflict] came when we did the "census" at the beginning of the year. During that period, there were misunderstandings. ... People didn't have confidence in others. We came to understand that we are different and that we cannot trust the other.[142]

139 Ibid.
140 Author's interview, male Hutu, Kigali, March 12, 2006.
141 Author's interview, male Tutsi, Kigali, March 11, 2006.
142 Ibid.

So the teachers would teach ... and speak about those different ethnic groups. They
were Twa and Hutu and [Tutsi]. And then that period came.... "Who is Hutu?
Who is Tutsi?" ... And I think from there, it contributed [to conflict] because ...
teaching that period, that ideology of differences to the children, it contributed to
children understanding that there is a difference between those different people. If
you say in a group of Mutwa those are Tutsi or those are Hutu, maybe they will
say, "Ah, maybe I'm not the same as her or the same as this one. Maybe I'm different? Maybe I have to get these privileges because I belong to this group."[143]

I taught what are the qualities of the Hutu? What are the faults of the Tutsi? We
taught that. Even me I taught it because it was in the state's curriculum. I had to
say it despite myself.[144]

Several interviewees, Tutsi in particular, explained that this experience made
them feel fearful, inferior, or humiliated, and that it was often tied to teasing
or harassment. One woman recounted her experience at primary school under
the Habyarimana regime:

When we arrived at school, they said Hutu stand up, Tutsi stand up. And Hutu
didn't really have any problems. But Tutsi had problems in relation to Hutu. And
they would tell us in class, when they knew that you were Tutsi, that you didn't
have the right to speak. After making the list of Hutu and Tutsi, they would call
the Hutu to the front and they would take the seats in front, and us Tutsi, we had
to sit at the back.... So there, we really started to know who we were. And some
Hutu didn't want to sit beside you.[145]

A few interviewees claimed that these ethnic identification practices did not
happen in their schools. This claim was especially salient among Hutu from the
north, some of whom maintained that the practice would not have been necessary because it was well known that all students were Hutu. Others from the
north, as well as elsewhere, remembered the counting practice unfolding differently. When I asked one Hutu man whether students had to stand up according
to ethnic identity in his class, he replied, "We didn't do it. They simply asked
us to bring our parents' identity cards and the teachers filled out the forms.
We were not aware of the [political] situation."[146] One man, now in prison on
genocide charges, denied the existence of the practice all together: "That story
[of having to stand up], it is a story invented today, by the big people in power
who are accusing the Second Republic. The people in power today invented
this story to accuse the Republic that they abolished because the assassinated
president [Habyarimana] had what we called 'ethnic and regional balance.'"[147]
The vast majority of Hutu and Tutsi interviewees, however, recalled being ethnically identified in class.

---

[143] Author's interview, male Hutu, Kigali, February 10(B), 2006.
[144] Author's interview, female Tutsi, Kigali, January 27, 2006.
[145] Author's interview, female Tutsi, Kigali, January 29(A), 2006.
[146] Author's interview, male Hutu, Kigali, March 22(C), 2006.
[147] Author's interview, male Hutu, Kigali, April 5(A), 2006.

Once it was discovered that a student was Tutsi, some Hutu teachers and students made life unbearable for him. As one Tutsi woman told me, "When you were Tutsi, you were scared to raise your hand," showing me that she would raise a small part of her finger, then shrug it back. "And then, the other students would tease you, because there would only be two or three Tutsi in class."[148] Another Tutsi woman explained that "[w]hen you were Tutsi, you had to sit with other Tutsi on the same bench."[149] One Tutsi student recalled how he begged his father to allow him to change primary schools from Kigali to a more Tutsi-dominated community in the south after his classmates identified him as Tutsi and began to systematically harass him.[150] A Hutu man who was a secondary school student, then teacher, during the Kayibanda and Habyarimana governments even reported hearing allegations from Tutsi students that "so and so teacher from the other ethnicity hits us a lot."[151]

As in their experience of primary school, many interviewees observed that the educational environment at secondary school cultivated horizontal inequalities, exclusive identities, and stigmatization. As one Tutsi woman who was educated in Kigali explained, "When I arrived at secondary school ... I was persecuted by my math teacher because I was Tutsi. That was the only reason. So, each time I was first in my class in that subject, I always got a zero. And I couldn't say anything, and he [the teacher] just looked at me, and mocked me." She further noted that because Tutsi women are often stereotyped to be tall, beautiful, and have long hair, "you would see maybe girls whose hair was growing very well, and they had hair just to here [she points to her back]. They got very bad grades because they were pretty girls. They were persecuted only for this. They were made to shave their heads to please the Hutu women." [152]

One former student explained how these experiences terrified her and her parents. "If you go home and ask your parents ... why they call you like that [by ethnicity in class], your parents – like my parents they were survivors [of violence surrounding 1959] – begin to panic. They were starting to think there was a plan to be killed."[153] However, a few interviewees, especially Hutu, claimed that there was no ethnic favoritism, reminding us that schooling was not a singular experience, as well as of the existence of divergent narratives.

In addition to knowing their peers' ethnicities in primary and secondary school, nearly all interviewees also claimed that they knew the ethnic identity of their teachers. "We too were threatened," one Tutsi teacher who worked in southern Rwanda told me. Her students would sometimes sing "Tutsi, Tutsi" and make it such that she did not want to go to work.[154]

---

[148] Author's interview, female Tutsi, Kigali, February 2(A), 2006.
[149] Author's interview, female Tutsi, Kigali, February 10(A), 2006.
[150] Author's interview, male Tutsi, Kigali, January 30, 2006.
[151] Author's interview, male Hutu, northern Rwanda, March 21(B), 2006.
[152] Author's interview, female Tutsi, Kigali, February 8(G), 2006.
[153] Author's interview, female Tutsi, Kigali, February 10(C), 2006.
[154] Author's interview, female Tutsi, Kigali, February 2(B), 2006.

I also spoke with interviewees about pedagogy. Rwandans noted that, as I demonstrate in the section on history later in the chapter and as was the case during the colonial period, multiple perspectives were never taught. Most interviewees said that they were not allowed to question or disagree with the teacher. As one Hutu man who was a student, then teacher, commented on the pedagogical culture, "The teacher has to teach what he wants you to learn and what he wants to teach you. So if you disagree, he will say, 'Hey, I'm a teacher, so you have to understand like this. Because I'm here to teach you.'"[155] Interviewees described class as copying notes and having to memorize them. One woman who had been a student in the Habyarimana era commented, "The teacher can just teach. It is very rare that students asked questions."[156] That secondary schools were boarding schools, and thus constantly exposing youth to both explicit and hidden curriculum, heightened the intensity and impact of pedagogy and hidden curriculum.[157] In short, schools cultivated a "spirit of submission" consistent with the church and wider society's doctrine of submission to the government and fear of authority.[158] Through these practices, children lost out on the possibility of learning critical thinking, gaining exposure to different perspectives, and having experience with conflict management, which were opportunities that could have helped, even in small ways, build sustainable peace.

I asked interviewees about other practices that went on at school but outside of the classroom. During primary school, I was told that children usually played together regardless of ethnicity. "Children of different ethnic groups played together even though teachers, even myself, had to write ethnicity on the files. But at recess, there were no differences. The children liked each other, they were friends. To have friends we did not make cliques with ethnicity. That is to say that children played together. There were no problems. Apparently."[159] Others recognized that while children played together, some Tutsi students were teased for their ethnicity. A few Tutsi students recalled being physically and verbally harassed at recess or on their walk home from school, particularly during the early years of the Kayibanda government and the latter years of the Habyarimana regime. Even among those who reported that all children played together, a number of interview participants recollected that outside influences filtered into schools, and that problems arose whenever violence began to take place in the country. This is a common finding in the peace education literature.[160] "Remember," one professor from the National University told me, "school is not an island."[161]

---

[155] Author's interview, male Hutu, Kigali, February 10(B), 2006.
[156] Author's interview, female Tutsi, Kigali, February 6(A), 2006.
[157] Author's interview, education administrator, northern Rwanda, March 17, 2006.
[158] Longman 2010; Muhimpundu 2002, pp. 168–169; Ndura 2006, p. 199.
[159] Author's interview, female Hutu, southern Rwanda, March 16, 2006.
[160] Kuppermitz and Salomon 2005.
[161] Author's interview, professor, National University of Rwanda, Butare, February 14(A), 2006.

Interviewees also reported that by secondary school, there were more pronounced differences between ethnic groups. One interviewee thought, for instance, that while there were few problems among the youngest children, there were interethnic problems, even hatred, among students by the upper years of primary school. She told me that "[a]t secondary school, you had a tendency to group your friends by ethnic group, and also by region, because region also became very, very strong, especially northerners who were the people in power.... We didn't show it, because [under Habyarimana] we weren't supposed to sow divisions, but we certainly felt it indirectly."[162]

Classroom practices collectivized and essentialized students into exclusive identity groups, sometimes even teaching students their ethnicities, and sometimes developing ethnically based stigmas as well. At the same time, pedagogy did not develop critical thinking – a missed opportunity for peacebuilding.

History Teaching

Alongside issues of school access and practices, many Rwandans believed that history lessons were problematic for intergroup relations. In contrast to the colonial period, this is true of both primary and secondary levels. History lessons highlighted historical divisions and enmity between Hutu and Tutsi, thereby entrenching collectivized and stigmatized ethnic groups. Interviewees recall Tutsi being portrayed as the source of past injustices, further stigmatizing this group. European and Rwandan historiography, on which the curriculum is based, never simultaneously valued both Hutu and Tutsi.[163]

Interviewees consistently highlighted their learning about three historical events as contributing to negative relations between Rwandans: lessons concerning the arrival of Rwanda's populations, *ubuhake* patron-client relations, and the 1959 revolution. The specific details of the narratives they remembered learning were generally consistent with each other's answers, although there were some differences in the specific elements that Hutu remembered, in contrast to Tutsi. This is not unusual; people experience and remember things differently and these discrepancies also offer insight into each group's public transcript. A few Hutu interviewees disagreed that history lessons helped underlie conflict, mostly reasoning that the historical narratives that were taught were true, and thus could not cause problems. One man from the north advocated, "It was in history, not things that the teacher invented. It was written. There are books!"[164] Another explained that they "just studied history" and that "I don't think that could have contributed to the crime against humanity that was committed in Rwanda, the genocide."[165] Yet another said, "They just taught us facts, not to hate."[166] This was, however, a minority opinion.

[162] Author's interview, female Tutsi, Kigali, February 8(G), 2006.
[163] Gasanabo 2004, p. 257.
[164] Author's interview, female Hutu, Kigali, April 5(C), 2006.
[165] Author's interview, male Hutu, Kigali, April 5(B), 2006.
[166] Author's interview, male Hutu, northern Rwanda, March 19(G), 2006.

As a result, it was particularly useful to compare interview data with curricular documents. The recollections that I heard in interviews were also consistent with the 1980s primary school curriculum documents. There were, nonetheless, some minor inconsistencies in interviewees' versus documents' foci, which I highlight. These divergences could stem from multiple sources. Many interviewees' experiences predate the available texts; during the Kayibanda years through to the end of the 1970s, teachers had to find and develop their own material based on high school experiences for those that had had them, on personal research, or on learning within their communities. Alternatively, teachers may have strayed from the texts, students may have interpreted the lessons in their own ways, or, in some cases, interviewees' opinions may reflect the current government's official transcript – or group transcripts – rather than actual recollections.

History Lessons: The Arrival of Rwanda's Populations

All of the interviewees that I asked recalled learning about "the arrival of Rwanda's populations" at school. Two interviewees recounted such lessons:

> Ah, well, at primary school they told us that it was the Twa that came before, hunting. So, the second were the Hutu, cultivating. And the Tutsi, they told us that they were Nilotic people that came with herds of cows. So, they told us that they came from Ethiopia, eh? So they said that Rwanda was for Hutu. They are Rwandan. The others, it is for them to stay in Ethiopia.[167]

> We learned that the first people were the Twa. And that they had the activity of making pots. And that the second people were Hutu, that had the activity of cultivating. And that the last people were the Tutsi that had pastoral activity. That is what we learned. And, we learned that when the Hutu arrived they had kings. And when the Tutsi arrived, they started a system of slavery.[168]

While both Hutu and Tutsi interviewees' historical narratives showed remarkable consistency, group narratives also emerged. Tutsi interview participants were more likely than Hutu participants to mention that they learned Tutsi were last to arrive, that Tutsi colonized and subjected Hutu to 400 years of oppression, that Tutsi took over the country, that Tutsi had less of a right to the country than others, and that Tutsi were from Ethiopia. Hutu were more likely than Tutsi to mention the Tutsi monarchy.

The sixth grade curriculum document explored "ancient" (precolonial) Rwanda and dedicated a full section to "how Rwanda was inhabited." This narrative matched interviewees' recollections. The curriculum repeated the order of arrival – that Twa were first, Hutu second, and Tutsi "last to arrive in Rwanda" – several times. Further, the first sample exam question provided for teachers involved identifying the chronological order of arrival of groups in

---

[167] Author's interview, male Hutu, Kigali, January 29(B), 2006.
[168] Author's interview, female Tutsi, Kigali, February 6(A), 2006.

Rwanda.[169] This text also detailed the occupations of each group – Twa were hunters and potters, Hutu farmers, and Tutsi pastoralists – and the regions from whence they came – Hutu from Central Africa, Tutsi from Sudan or Ethiopia. In this way, primary curriculum taught the Hamitic hypothesis, but did not make any explicit claims about entitlement to the country. It noted that Hutu had family links to other Bantu and that Rwandan Tutsi were related to Tutsi in Burundi, Hima in Uganda and Tanzania, and Massai in Kenya.[170] There was no reference to common Hutu and Tutsi heritage. The curriculum described interaction between Hutu and Tutsi upon Tutsi arrival as "friends" who "intermarried," and claimed that Hutu agreed to be Tutsi's subjects and to work with them to conquer other Hutu and Tutsi lands.[171] Interviewees, however, did not mention the cooperative aspects of the interactions, illustrating the salience of the negative aspects of the relationship in their understandings, as well as potential issues of recall or memories being filtered through historical experience.

There are significant nuances in the interpretation of this narrative in contrast to how it was taught in the colonial period. During the colonial period, Tutsi were presented as foreigners, better suited to rule. During the two Republics, Tutsi were presented as foreigners with less entitlement to the country. The secondary school textbook critiqued the "Hamitic myth" – that Tutsi were superior – calling it "false and stained with racial prejudice,"[172] but accepted that Tutsi were foreigners from Ethiopia. As one Tutsi woman recalled, "They taught the Nilotic [Tutsi], in contrast to Bahutu. All the while showing that you were a foreigner. It was the Nilotics that came and that they were not really indigenous. They were not people of the country. And then, whenever you'd say something, they'd say 'oh, you're Tutsi'," suggesting that she had less right to speak given her ethnic status. "Then, things got a lot graver when I started university in '92 because there were really threats. They'd say 'Ah, my sister. You invaded the country, now you'll pay.'"[173]

History Lessons: Ubuhake

Everyone with whom I spoke about school lessons on *ubuhake*, variously translated as vassalage or cattle-clientship, remembered having learned a similar narrative:

> The Tutsi minority race possessed cows. The majority of Hutu were cultivators. So, they worked ... to get manure, to get milk. Since authority came from Tutsi during that time, even before the arrival of the whites, the Hutu had to come to get cows. They were like, I don't want to use the word slave, but servants. They had to spend years and years to get a cow.... It was hard to work years and years to get only one

---

[169] RoR 1985, pp. 137, 39.
[170] Ibid., pp. 135, 37.
[171] Ibid., p. 137.
[172] RoR 1987, p. 18.
[173] Author's interview, female Tutsi, Kigali, February 8(G), 2006.

cow. This was not good. I can say that it was very painful. It was what incited, for them, the hate towards the Tutsi race. We [Tutsi] are conscious of this.[174]

Tutsi were richer so they could dominate over us [Hutu]. So the Hutu went to do *ubuhake*. So we went to be servants for a cow. We spent four or five years. If you made a mistake when they had given you a cow, they took it back. Yes! That's what we learned at school! But our parents also lived this.[175]

The quotes above employ mythico-historical narratives, bringing the past into the present with clear ethnically based references to "we" and "they." Interview participants emphasized that Tutsi had cattle and that Hutu worked for Tutsi. Both Hutu and Tutsi also highlighted that the relationship, which constituted virtual slavery, disadvantaged Hutu.

The fifth grade history curriculum introduced this narrative of *ubuhake*. This lesson was repeated, almost verbatim, in the eighth grade curriculum. While most of the text's messages were consistent with interviewees' remarks, highlighting, for example, "that ubuhake included many bad things,"[176] the official lesson on *ubuhake* notably never mentioned Hutu or Tutsi. It defines the practice as "conventions between a person that wanted a cow and protection and a person who was very rich," without defining the positions ethnically.[177] Yet only a couple of interviewees explained the practice this way, whereas the rest described it as a relationship between Hutu and Tutsi, consistent with several references in the secondary school textbooks.[178] The official primary school material explained only the negative aspects of this relationship; it did not emphasize the relationship of exchange highlighted by today's government.

History Lessons: The Revolution of 1959
All of the Rwandans with whom I discussed lessons about 1959 also recalled learning a very consistent narrative.

Well, the Tutsi exploited the Hutu, and the Hutu couldn't evolve [the same word as Rwandans use for the modern, educated class], so they had a revolution. It was so that the Hutu could evolve and everything.[179]

The period of 1959 was presented as Hutu didn't want *ubuhake* any more, didn't want the king, the *mwami*, because the king was oppressive, and they revolted against the Tutsi. So the power of the *mwami*, the power of the Tutsi, was presented as an oppressive power, from which the Hutu had to free themselves. Yes. That is what we learned at school. And then, the oppressors left, and went to

---

[174] Author's interview, female Tutsi, Kigali, January 27, 2006.
[175] Author's interview, female Hutu, southern Rwanda, March 15(C), 2006.
[176] RoR 1983, p. 155.
[177] Ibid.
[178] RoR 1987, p. 96; RoR 1989, p. 70.
[179] Author's interview, male Hutu, Kigali, February 6(B), 2006.

many of the countries in the area, and the good ones were left, the Hutu that had vanquished the bad ones.[180]

Most interviewees – Hutu and Tutsi – specified that the events of 1959 were a "revolution." Many recollected learning that this revolution overthrew the Tutsi monarchy and that Rwanda became a Republic, that the majority took power in the spirit of liberation, justice, and democracy, and that the revolution overthrew feudalism and *ubuhake*. A few interviewees recalled learning that Tutsi went into exile and were killed during this period. All of these details are consistent with the curriculum documents.

The Revolution of 1959 was probably the history lesson that interviewees could recall in most detail. This is not surprising given that it received more attention in official curricula than the two issues described in the preceding subsections; there were four full primary school lessons on 1959.[181] Another lesson on "Independent Rwanda" was also related to this narrative. These five lessons appeared in the fifth and eighth grade curriculum documents, illustrating the centrality of this narrative. Hutu and Tutsi were highlighted as different throughout this chapter. Furthermore, Tutsi were stigmatized for wanting to continue practices of "injustice and oppression" in Rwanda.[182]

In at least two of these three prominent lessons, as taught at primary school, Hutu and Tutsi were presented as collective and essentialized categories, and Hutu were presented as the long-time victims of Tutsi. Hutu and Tutsi were not always collectivized in these texts, however. In several paragraphs, the text referred to "some Tutsi," who came from "important families," and the "children of these Tutsi,"[183] as having special privileges, thus differentiating between Tutsi of disparate classes. On the other hand, this curriculum did say that Tutsi held most state jobs, and that only Tutsi owned properties and pastures,[184] without making any distinctions among them. By not including the grievances of poorer Tutsi, the text collectivized Tutsi as all members of the elite. The narrative also collectivized the Hutu population, stating, for example, that "Hutu too wanted a role to play in government."[185] Secondary school texts elaborate on details, sometimes distinguishing among Tutsi but at other times collectivizing them. For instance, the secondary school material notes that a few progressive Tutsi shared a sentiment of change with Hutu. On the other hand, it also collectivizes Tutsi, noting that the *Hutu Manifesto* was to overcome the political, economic, social, and cultural monopoly of the Tutsi group.[186]

---

[180] Author's interview, female Tutsi, Kigali, February 8(G), 2006.
[181] "The Hutu Manifesto;" "The Reasons that Provoked the Revolution of 1959"; "Towards the Revolution of 1959;" and "The Revolution of 1959 and its Consequences." RoR 1983, p.115.
[182] Ibid., p. 157.
[183] Ibid., p. 159.
[184] Ibid., p. 157.
[185] Ibid., p. 160.
[186] RoR 1989, pp. 109–110.

From History Lessons to Conflict

Interviewees also recollected lessons that do not appear in the official curriculum documents and highlighted these lessons as stigmatizing Tutsi. For example, a number recounted the story of the wicked Queen Kanjogera that they had learned at school: "Each time she [Kanjogera] stood up, they said that she had to kill a child."[187] Another elaborated:

> To show us that Tutsi were very bad, the teacher told us that there was a queen called Kanjogera.... Each morning when she went to stand up, she placed her sword [on the body of a Hutu child] and pressed herself to standing [thereby impaling the child]. This showed that she was mean.[188]

This story portrays Kanjogera as an evil Tutsi and interviewees remembered this lesson as stigmatizing *all* Tutsi as wicked. A Hutu woman from the north recollected, "Sometimes we even cried when teachers told us what they did to Hutu, how they would get up with lances on Hutu lying on the ground! That is really something moving, and children would go home crying."[189] It appears that this narrative was taught by some teachers both before and after a written history curriculum was established. Teachers clearly played an important independent role in the selective transmission of knowledge and in shaping children's identity more broadly.[190]

There are other specific examples of curricula that stigmatize Tutsi. In her book, Barbara Coloroso recounts, "On a recent trip to Rwanda, a young woman showed me a worksheet she had completed when she was a child at primary school in the 1960s. One of the math problems reads, 'If you have ten cockroaches in your town and you kill four of them, how many do you have left to kill?'"[191] As noted in the last chapter, Tutsi exiles that attempted to return to Rwanda after the 1959 Revolution were referred to as cockroaches, and during the civil war and genocide the term expanded to refer to all Tutsi. While I did not encounter evidence of this type of overtly anti-Tutsi teaching, the example reminds us that it is not only the content of *history* classes that can affect intergroup relationships. Coloroso refers to a similarly stereotypical and discriminatory question posed in an early 1930s German math class: "If three Jews robbed a bank, and each got a part of the loot proportionate to their ages ... how much would each get?"[192]

Furthermore, what is omitted from the curriculum may be as important as what is included. A few interviewees noted that Rwandan primary schools did not adequately teach "love of the other," and the notion of a common good was not developed. Instead, lessons were primarily about the responsibilities of

---

[187] Author's interview, female of mixed ethnicity, Kigali, January 29(E), 2006.
[188] Author's interview, male Hutu, Kigali, January 29(B), 2006.
[189] Author's interview, female Hutu, Kigali, April 5(C), 2006.
[190] Samuels 1977, pp. 95–117.
[191] Coloroso 2007, p. 58.
[192] Ibid.

the state and the need for students to respect officials by simple virtue of their positions.[193]

In hindsight, I did not inquire enough in interviews about history lessons that may have been supportive of peacebuilding. Interview participants did not raise these memories on their own; perhaps in part because the now-prevalent transcripts do not do so either, but likely also because, given the genocide, these memories are not dominant. A review of the curriculum documents, however, reveals a few lessons that could be interpreted as building reciprocity and a shared future. In the sixth grade curriculum document, for example, all sections except the one on Rwanda's original inhabitation talked about Rwandans collectively rather than as Hutu and Tutsi. The sixth grade material also included a lesson on friendship among Rwandans. The fourth grade material focused on national symbols such as the flag and the anthem. Overall, however, both Hutu and Tutsi remember the history curriculum as more problematic than positive for intergroup relations.

Indeed, many interviewees highlighted how ethnic identities were collectivized and stigmatized. Tutsi in this period, for instance, were often presented as needing to bear collective responsibility for past Tutsi actions. One Tutsi woman explained:

> They would teach us that Tutsi were bad, and that in history the colonizers were associated with Tutsi, meaning that they [Tutsi] were the governing class.... And I too was convinced that the feudal system was bad for the country and oppressed Hutu.... But I didn't feel that I was directly concerned, me and my family, because it was other people [that oppressed them].... So when they taught us in school, I accepted that the Tutsi that governed the country were bad. But for Hutu, all the Tutsi were bad, you see.[194]

Others explained how history stigmatized Tutsi and scapegoated them for the country's problems, even turning regional grievances into ethnic ones. One Hutu man, a long-time school inspector in northern Rwanda explained:

> I'd conclude that the curriculum that we taught, especially in civic education and history, contributed to genocide because it engaged with ethnicities in a particular way. So it advanced especially ideas that there was one ethnicity, that I can call Tutsi, that was at the head of the country for four hundred years and that Hutu were not allowed to say a word. You can see how that would contribute [to violent conflict]. There were also divisionist ideas about the people from the north, or more that the people from the south were like Tutsi and had influence with Tutsi. That too contributed in some way to genocide.[195]

Narratives, such as those taught in history lessons about the arrival of populations, *ubuhake*, and the revolution of 1959, became mythico-histories, serving

---

[193] Muhimpundu 2002, pp. 154–156.
[194] Author's interview, female Tutsi, Kigali, February 8(G), 2006.
[195] Author's interview, male Hutu, northern Rwanda, March 20(A), 2006.

as "emotionally significant connections" over time so that the past may be evoked in order to respond to the experiences and fears of the present and future.[196] Representations of the past can be seen as "umbilical cord[s] to the present and future,"[197] securely connecting people and feeding them, even over generations. History lessons in this period were taught as if they were a justi- fication for the actions of the government of the day: they divided Rwandans, collectivized ethnic identities, stigmatized, and sometimes scapegoated Tutsi.

The specific history lessons mattered for underlying conflict as well. Genocide was, one long-time Tutsi teacher commented, "a call to history from what I see. That history, we learned it at school. They taught us that our parents were poor because of you [Tutsi], that you took our fields and our goods.... That's what we learned at school. If we hadn't learned that at school, they couldn't have done this [genocide]."[198] A Tutsi man similarly opined that, "This history had an influence on Rwanda because politicians used it to political effect."[199]

In fact, popular media, including magazines and the radio, as well as people engaged in face-to-face coercion, employed messages that were resonant with school lessons that predate 1994. The May 1991 issue of the Hutu extremist *Kangura* magazine wrote: "The Tutsi found us in Rwanda; they oppressed us; and we put up with this. But now that we have left serfdom and they want to reinstall the morning chicotte [whip]. I think that no Hutu will be able to endure this. The war Gahutu leads is just. It is a battle for the republic."[200] Propagandist Leon Mugesera's infamous 1992 speech referred to a conver- sation in which he warned a member of the Liberal Party (PL) that "your home is in Ethiopia, that we are going to send you back there quickly, by the Nyabarongo [River]." The Nyabarongo feeds into the rivers of the Nile watershed and hence is supposed to permit passage to Ethiopia. As Des Forges explains, "For the audience, 'member of the PL' could not have meant anything other than Tutsi, and the mention of transportation by the Nyabarongo had to be understood as killing the people in question and dumping the bodies in the river, a usual practice in past massacres of Tutsi."[201] In personal coercion, Straus quotes one perpetrator-leader saying, in response to a question about what was said to motivate other Rwandans to join in violence, "They [Tutsi] killed Habyarimana, our parent ... no one could stay [home] without joining the attacks ... the Tutsis were fighting to retake the country as it was before 1959."[202]

Previous experience with stigmatization also facilitates group-based scape- goating among ordinary people, who may rely on scapegoating to help make

---

[196] See also: Barnett 1999, pp. 8, 14; Ross 2002, p. 306; Volkan 1997, pp. 81–82.
[197] Barnett 1999, p. 14.
[198] Author's interview, female Tutsi, Kigali, January 27, 2006.
[199] Author's interview, male Tutsi, Kigali, January 30, 2006.
[200] Chrétien 2003, p. 324.
[201] Des Forges 1999.
[202] Straus 2006, p. 141.

sense of the economic and political problems that pervade their lives.[203] One Hutu woman that I interviewed explained how societally resonant stigmas were invoked: "The [RPF] war to come back to Rwanda did some harm. It allowed [government] voices to say of Tutsi, 'they want to dominate Rwanda, they are coming again with *ubuhake*, they will do lots of bad things'. All of the population, they then know that if it's a Tutsi, it's an evil spirit. And, if it's a Hutu, it's on the side of Habyarimana."[204] A Tutsi man who had fought with the RPF similarly explained that when the RPF attacked Rwanda in 1990, the government "made people believe that we were foreigners, not Rwandans, even though we were."[205] One Hutu man convincingly argued that it was politically expedient to teach this history curriculum. "They had reason to teach it, because it was the moment [to do so]. Just as today," as I show in the next chapter, "the current regime teaches that all of the previous regimes were bad, because it replaced the other regime."[206] The narratives reviewed in this chapter formed an underlying foundation for violent conflict; it would likely have been more difficult to mobilize Rwandans without them.

Conclusion: The Peace and Conflict Role of Schooling during the Rwandan Republics

Schooling in Rwanda contributed to laying both the social-structural and psychocultural conditions that helped underlie violent interethnic conflict in this period. School structure was a key part of these processes. Exclusive or preferential access to state resources, such as education, often produces conflict between groups and leads to competition over scarce resources. While there were no formal restrictions on who could attend primary school, many interviewees spoke about restrictions in symbolic access owing to the difficult experience of primary education for some Tutsi. Moreover, nearly all interviewees had strong concerns about the unfairness of promotion past primary school. Under Kayibanda, access was regulated by ethnic quotas, which continued under Habyarimana with the addition of regional elements. Unequal access served as a constant reminder of differences, keeping ethnic and regional distinctions prominent and hardening in-group/out-group distinctions by vesting them with political meaning. Restricting access to schooling also promoted collectivization, with ethnicity as one's central defining feature, regardless of individual merit, and contributed to the creation of stigmas, because entitlement followed directly from identity. The inequalities in access were also a point of contention themselves, with each side arguing that they were losing out. Because schooling was tied to upward mobility, demand for education

---

203 Staub 1989, p. 48.
204 Author's interview, female Hutu, Kigali, March 10(A), 2006.
205 Author's interview, male Tutsi, Kigali, March 11, 2006.
206 Author's interview, male Hutu, Kigali, March 22(C), 2006.

engendered much competition. Access to school was also linked to access to French, the language of opportunity. While Tutsi felt disadvantaged, they often remained, or were reported to be, overrepresented in secondary and tertiary education and in the high-status positions that schooling was presumed to bring. This allowed the Hutu governments to divert attention away from their own privileges, scapegoating Tutsi and blaming them for the country's troubles.[207]

According to interviewees, school content, including classroom practices and history curriculum, also contributed to underlying conflict. The classroom practice of asking and, in some cases, even teaching students their ethnicity accentuated differences and collectivized ethnic groups. Some students also experienced stigmatization based on these practices. As discussed in Chapter 1, many consider other classroom practices, such as adherence to a single and exclusionary narrative, the failure to develop critical thinking skills, and the promotion of conformity, to be missed opportunities for peacebuilding.

Contrary to faith and hope in the positive power of schooling, this chapter makes the case that during the Republics, education's key effect was to produce subtle psychocultural and social-structural processes that facilitated conflict in Rwanda. The post-genocide government thus faced an enormous challenge. The next chapter assesses the post-genocide government's successes and failures at reforming post-genocide education to improve intergroup relations in Rwanda.

[207] Lemarchand 1970, p. 239; Uvin 1998, p. 137.

4

Schooling after Genocide

I have made the case that schooling in both the colonial period and the two Republics helped underlie conflict in Rwanda. However, just as education affected conflict, Rwanda's school system was also severely affected by the violence that engulfed the country. The last normal year of schooling was 1990 and schools closed completely during the 1994 genocide. Much of the educational infrastructure was destroyed. Schools themselves were often sites of mass atrocities. About 75 percent of teachers were killed, fled the country, or were imprisoned on genocide charges.[1]

As students returned to post-genocide schools, they faced a multitude of challenges. A very high proportion of children had witnessed a death in the immediate family. More than 1.2 million children were left orphaned, representing 16 percent of the entire population, or nearly one-third of all children. More than 100,000 children lived in child-headed households.[2] Some children returned from a life in exile, while others fled the country to refugee camps, to return a few years later with often horrific experiences. They brought with them different languages and varied educational backgrounds. As one Rwandan student summarized, "It was very serious. We were mixed because we had people that came from other countries: from Tanzania, from Burundi, from Congo. Some spoke Swahili, others English, others French. All in one classroom!"[3] Many Rwandans spoke of trauma: "It was terrible. There were those that had lost their parents, others that didn't know where their parents had gone. There was a lot of famine and a lot of problems with school fees. No stability. And we were still scared that war would return to the country."[4] As a

---

[1] RoR 1997, p. 13.
[2] Geltman and Stover 1997. See also Obura 2003, p. 50; Obura 2005, pp. ix, 19.
[3] Author's interview, female Tutsi, southern Rwanda, February 14(C), 2006.
[4] Author's interview, female of unknown ethnicity, southern Rwanda, February 14(D), 2006.

teenage boy commented in a disturbingly casual tone, "I was a bit traumatized. I saw a lot of macheteing and such."[5] Overall, the new Rwandan government inherited an education system in serious trouble.

The government made schooling a top priority. Explicitly blaming the past education system, particularly the curriculum, for the "self-destruction of the country," it centered its efforts not only on reconstruction, but also on innovation.[6] Education was quickly assigned a dual role in post-genocide Rwanda as part of both the development and national unity agendas.

How has education fared in post-genocide Rwanda? This chapter considers the peace and conflict role of schools after the Rwandan genocide. First, it briefly reviews Rwanda's recent post-genocide history and its current political context. Second, it examines educational developments in Rwanda since the genocide ended in July 1994. Third, this chapter analyzes the role of schooling in post-genocide Rwanda and presents a mixed picture for the contribution of present-day education to peace or conflict.

Politics and Society in Post-Genocide Rwanda

Rwanda's genocide lasted approximately one hundred days and ended with a military victory of the Rwandan Patriotic Front (RPF) in July 1994. The new government took charge of a country in shambles. Of a pre-genocide population of about 7 million, between 500,000 and 1 million Tutsi and moderate Hutu were dead. Fearing reprisals, about 2 million Hutu had fled to neighboring states, the largest concentration ending up in dismal conditions in Goma, Congo; most returned en masse in 1996. About 1 million Rwandans were internally displaced by violence. Approximately 500,000 Tutsi returned from life in surrounding countries, many exiled since the first round of ethnic violence in 1959. The country's economy and infrastructure were destroyed, including its education system. GDP per capita fell nearly US$200 from 1990 levels to an average of US$80 per year, with about 95 percent of the population living on less than US$60 per year. Many psychologists and medical practitioners assessed Rwandans as a deeply traumatized population; 80 percent of children interviewed by UNICEF, for example, experienced a death in their family, 91 percent thought they would die, 36 percent saw other children participating in violence, and 16 percent had, at some point, hidden under dead bodies. The Human Development Index (HDI) ranked Rwanda 174th out of 175 countries in 1994; only war-torn Sierra Leone might have been a worse place to live.[7]

[5] Author's interview, male Tutsi, southern Rwanda, February 14(B), 2006.
[6] RoR 1995, pp. 5, 16, 25, 44, 56; RoR 2002a, p. 5.
[7] See World Bank figures reported in Gourevitch 1998, p. 270 and UNICEF figures in Obura 2003, p. 50. The HDI ranks nations according to their citizens' quality of life. Measures are life expectancy, adult literacy, enrollment at the primary, secondary, and tertiary levels, and income. See UNDP 1997.

The RPF made quick progress on political stability. Despite the challenges, it managed to establish basic order and a new government took office on July 19, 1994. It appeared committed to many of the principles of the Arusha Accords, including, most crucially, power sharing. Pasteur Bizimungu, a Hutu member of the RPF, became president, Faustin Twagiramunga, a Hutu from the *Mouvement Démocratique Républicain* (MDR), became prime minister, and Paul Kagame, a Tutsi commander of the RPF, became vice-president and minister of defense. This transitional government, due to last five years, named itself the Government of National Unity. In 1999, it extended the transitional period but held local elections. In March 2000, after a turbulent period of internal power struggles, Bizimungu resigned, along with several other key political figures. Paul Kagame, who still holds power today, assumed the presidency. The government passed a new constitution in 2003 and Kagame was reelected, albeit in flawed elections, in 2003 and 2010. According to the 2007 Ibrahim Governance Index, Rwanda was the most improved Sub-Saharan African nation in terms of governance performance over the past five years.[8] Since the genocide, Rwanda's leaders have also made a strong political commitment to women's participation in government and Rwanda now holds the world record for the highest proportion of women in parliament, at 56 percent in the lower house.[9]

In addition to these political initiatives, the new government soon implemented a variety of policies to address other challenges of Rwanda's post-violence context. In terms of security and justice, it quickly moved to arrest and imprison suspected genocide perpetrators; 10,000 Rwandans found themselves in jails by November 1994. This number peaked at 130,000 several years later.[10] While the international community introduced the International Criminal Tribunal for Rwanda (ICTR), the government resuscitated its national courts, then introduced a modern adaptation of *gacaca* courts, a traditional model of dispute resolution, literally meaning "judgment on the grass," to relieve prison congestion and to foster restorative justice and reconciliation.[11] Throughout this time, the government managed to uphold basic security and to stave off large-scale violence on Rwandan soil, despite incursions from Hutu extremists based in the Congo.

The government also worked on social relations. The RPF blames the genocide on societal ignorance, "bad governance of previous regimes," and "a genocide ideology that showed itself before and after the massacres." It promotes a return to an allegedly harmonious precolonial golden age, blaming the colonial powers for divisions among Rwandans.[12] Therefore, in an effort designed to

---

[8] "Rwanda 'Most Improved' in Africa," *BBC News*, September 25, 2007; Rotberg 2007.

[9] See Inter-Parliamentary Union 2012. The global average is 20% while the Sub-Saharan African average is slightly less than 19%.

[10] Tiemessen 2004, p. 58.

[11] For an overview, see Schabas 2008.

[12] RoR 2006a, p. iii. For renditions of this narrative, see Lemarchand 1994, pp. 19–20; RoR 2000; RoR 2002d; RoR 2004a; RoR 1999; Penal Reform International 2004; Sebahara 1998; Shyaka undated.

foster reconciliation, the government banned ethnicity by removing its mention in identity cards and discouraging public use of "ethnicist ideology." In addition, by the fall of 1994, the RPF prioritized the rewriting of history books and placed a moratorium on teaching history in Rwanda's schools. It also engaged in commemorative genocide projects and recognized the first annual mourning week, which began April 7, 1995. In 1998, it established the National Unity and Reconciliation Commission (NURC) with a mandate to rebuild the unity of Rwandans, to "monitor the adherence of the population to policies of national unity," and to research "the real causes of the genocide."[13] In 2007, it added the National Commission for the Fight Against Genocide. The government also implemented *ingando* solidarity camps to educate certain segments of the Rwandan population on what it means to be Rwandan. *Ingando* camps aim to facilitate the social reintegration and reeducation of most Hutu, notably demobilized soldiers, former insurgents, refugees who fled to neighboring countries in 1994, and released prisoners. They also reeducate incoming university students and local officials, many of whom are RPF loyalists, as well as church leaders and *gacaca* judges, who are largely Tutsi.

In economic terms, Rwanda averaged impressive 7 percent growth rates in the years immediately after the genocide (1994–1997) and over the past six years (2006–2012) has continued to grow an average of 8.4 percent per annum.[14] It has also made significant strides in terms of infrastructure and attracting private investment. In 2000, Rwanda's government introduced Vision 2020, a comprehensive framework for Rwanda's economic development based on the UN Millennium Development Goals, and in 2002 and 2008 it introduced poverty reduction strategies as road maps for reaching these goals.[15] Rwanda joined the East African Community in 2007 and the British Commonwealth in 2009. Rwanda's membership in the latter is a particularly notable development in light of the absence of any prior historical ties between it and the United Kingdom; the accession to the Commonwealth was viewed in Rwanda as "recognition of the tremendous progress [it had] made in the last 15 years."[16] Since the genocide, Rwanda's HDI rating has risen twenty places, to twenty-first from the bottom, although at least some of this is accounted for by other countries' declines.[17] Poverty rates have decreased from about 77 percent in 1995, to 57 percent in 2006, to 45 percent in 2010–2011 – an achievement rendered more impressive in light of population growth – although the national poverty line is around just US$0.44 per day.[18]

[13] RoR 2004c, pp. 19–20.
[14] United States Department of State. "Background Note: Rwanda," Available at http://www.state.gov/r/pa/ei/bgn/2861.htm#econ; Lootsma, 2012.
[15] RoR 2000, 2002c, 2007a.
[16] Josh Kron, "Rwanda Joins the Commonwealth," *The New York Times*, November 28, 2009.
[17] UNDP 2007c, 7; UNDP 2011.
[18] UNDP 2007c, 6; RoR, 2012.

Rwanda's government has shown significant initiative in addressing the main pillars of peacebuilding – security, political institutions, economic development, justice, and reconciliation – and this image of stability and progress dominates international reporting. Examples abound: *The Toronto Star* featured "A Picture and A Thousand Words" with a photograph showing two Rwandan men hugging and smiling. The byline read: "The man on the right killed the sister of the man on the left. Today, they're best friends."[19] *New York Times* columnist Nicolas Kristof presented Rwanda as a positive model of economic development and was so optimistic about Rwanda's future that he offered "an investment tip: Buy real estate in ... Rwanda."[20] Philip Gourevitch praised Rwanda's progress and leadership in *The New Yorker* and Stephen Kinzer authored a book-length homage to Rwanda's post-genocide government in *A Thousand Hills: Rwanda's Rebirth and the Man Who Dreamed It.*[21]

But the foregoing is a very partial account. Much as I highlighted the continuity from colonial to postcolonial regimes in the last chapter, there are marked similarities between Rwanda's pre- and post-genocide periods. Several authors argue that positive assessments of post-genocide Rwanda stem from the guilt of the international community at having failed to stop the genocide; consequently, there has been ready international acceptance of reality as being "what Rwanda's political leaders, as moral guardians, tell the world ... it is."[22] Indeed, the RPF has successfully presented itself as the representative of genocide victims and, as such, not open to challenge. The Kagame regime uses a "genocide credit" to silence critique.[23] It is also extremely adept at presenting an "easy-to-grasp, seemingly uncontested narrative" that many in the international community seem happy to swallow. The government further makes meaningful investigation of many topics in Rwanda very difficult, with those propounding something other than the accepted narrative potentially facing expulsion, punishment, or even death.[24] A couple of NGOs with whom I am in regular contact asked that I not report their comments for fear of their work being discontinued by the government.

When one examines Rwanda's post-genocide record without RPF lenses, or what Pottier calls their effective "spin-doctor[ing],"[25] the picture changes quite dramatically. First, there is increasing concentration of power around a small group of former Tutsi exiles, largely from Uganda. As of January 2009, Tutsi hold at least as many key governmental positions in government as Hutu, despite their still being a minority in the population. Moreover, the number of Tutsi in key governmental positions that have spent a significant amount of

---

[19] Debra Black, "A Picture and a Thousand Words," *The Toronto Star*, August 26, 2007.

[20] Nicholas Kristof, "Africa: Land of Hope," *The New York Times*, July 5, 2007.

[21] Gourevitch 2009; Kinzer 2008.

[22] Pottier 2002, p. 207.

[23] Ibid., p. 199.

[24] See, for example, Thomson 2009; HRW 2004; Julianne Kippenberg, "Rwanda: Still in Our Human Rights Blind Spot," *The Observer*, July 25, 2004; Longman 2012.

[25] Pottier 2002, p. 52.

time in exile (ex-refugee) is more than three times the number of non-ex-refugee Tutsi.[26] Reyntjens calls this group a "new *akazu*"[27] (little house), reinvoking the term used to describe Habyarimana's closest associates.

Second, Rwanda is currently much closer to authoritarianism and dictatorship than to democracy. Under only a veneer of pluralism, the Rwandan government arrests or sends its opponents into exile and keeps civil society and the press under tight control. To rid the country of allegedly pervasive "genocide ideology," it charges and jails citizens with "divisionism," increasingly a synonym for disagreeing with the government.[28]

Third, the RPF has committed vast human rights abuses.[29] Reports indicate that the RPF committed widespread killings during the civil war (1990–1993) and during the genocide. Since 1994, the RPF has also engaged in killings and other violations of human rights in two wars in the Congo (1996–1997, 1998–2003) and in massacres in Rwanda, such as at the Kibeho camp for the internally displaced in April 1995. In 2012, several bilateral donors cut aid to Rwanda in response to accusations that the Rwandan government continues to support a rebel group in Congo.[30] Human rights organizations further condemn the RPF's day-to-day infringements on human rights, including the unfairness of *gacaca* and poor prison conditions. In contrast to its strong emphasis on justice for Hutu perpetrators of the genocide, the RPF downplays or ignores its own violations and thus reigns with impunity.

Fourth, even with economic progress and a rising HDI rating, the vast majority of Rwandans still live on subsistence agriculture in grueling poverty. For instance, the original copy of the 2007 UNDP report (thereafter rejected by the Rwandan government) found marked and growing inequality among Rwandans.[31] Indeed, Rwanda's Gini coefficient (a globally used measure of inequality) has increased dramatically since the 1980s, and the richest 20 percent expend as much as the other 80 percent of the population.[32]

Finally, there are deep and multiple cleavages in Rwanda that are hidden by most popular accounts. Just as the meaning and content of Hutu and Tutsi changed over time through precolonialism, colonialism, and independence, they changed again through the genocide. Starting in April 1994, to be a Tutsi was to be a target. To be a Hutu was to be a perpetrator, although possibly one coerced into action with death threats by extremist Hutu. Post-genocide efforts at outlawing ethnicity also transformed these categories. In some ways – as I

---

[26] Ansoms 2009b, p. 294.

[27] Reyntjens 2004, p. 187.

[28] Amnesty International 2009; Reporters without Borders 2009; RoR 2003b, articles 9, 54, 179; RoR 2007a.

[29] Amnesty International 2007; Burnet 2012; Des Forges 1999; Eltringham 2004; Freedom House International 2006; Pottier 2010.

[30] UN Security Council 2012.

[31] See James Munyaneza, "Rwanda: I Didn't Read UN Report before Launch – Musoni," *The New York Times*, August 24, 2007; UNDP 2007b; UNDP 2007c.

[32] Ansoms 2009a, 13; CIA 2012.

argue is the case in scholarships for education – these categories were put underground and invested with new implications, but not erased. People have found new ways to use these old categories. To the government, "survivors" refer to Tutsi, "perpetrators" to Hutu; "old case load refugees" refer to Tutsi that fled Rwanda pre-genocide, and "new case load refugees" denote Hutu that left during and after genocide. Staff at one international agency that I visited used "trees" (Tutsi) and "bushes" (Hutu) as code words. One taxi driver, presumably Hutu, described himself to me as "of those not liked in Rwanda." Ordinary Rwandans also still understand each other in ethnic terms. Most of my interview participants shared their ethnic identity with me or gave me strong clues to ensure that I understood it, and referred to others ethnically. It is a valid concern that researchers continue to use these terms and thus keep them alive. However, the fact that my interviewees identified themselves and others as Hutu or Tutsi without me having to ask indicates that these categories remain salient identity markers for Rwandans themselves. There are also, of course, categories that cut across ethnicity, such as clans, religion, rural/subsistence, and urban/market economy, although even population patterns have shifted as rural areas have becoming increasingly Hutu and urban areas increasingly Tutsi.

The post-genocide period has also brought new societal schisms. For example, there are important differences between Tutsi that grew up outside of Rwanda and those that spent their lives in the country. There have been public denunciations by *Ibuka*, the largest survivor organization, that the mostly Tutsi government, many of whose members only recently returned to Rwanda after years abroad, is ill-equipped to represent their interests.[33] Tutsi that stayed in Rwanda are sometimes suspected by new arrivals of having been genocide collaborators.[34] Tutsi from different countries of exile also find themselves to be markedly different; growing up in Uganda or Congo or Burundi makes for distinctive experiences, and language learned in exile has created new cleavages. Hutu also have vastly different experiences of exile and innocent Hutu are frequently grouped in with the guilty. Life is particularly difficult for those of mixed ethnic parentage, who are often refused acceptance by all sides. In some ways, while the Rwandan government has strived for unity in homogeneity, in an all-encompassing "Rwandanness" not to be disaggregated, it has, in fact, to confront unprecedented diversity.

Consistent with outsiders who have called Rwandans particularly obedient to authority,[35] the current government is working on a presumption that it can tell Rwandans what to do and that they will do it – that it can engineer a new reality relatively easily. The logic of the Kagame regime seems to go as follows: tell them to reconcile and the population will do so. Teach them a new history and they will embrace it. Notify them that Hutu, Tutsi, and Twa no longer exist and it will be so. While on the surface, ordinary Rwandans may appear to embrace these initiatives, my interviews revealed deep disagreement. As one

---

[33] See Vidal 2001, p. 44.
[34] Colletta and Cullen 2000, p. 44; Prunier 1997, p. 206.
[35] Gourevitch 1998, pp. 23, 318; Prunier 1997, p. 57.

Rwandan woman described, "When one goes in the street, he says 'hello, hello, all is well' (*smiling*), but he does not dare reveal his real opinion or else they will imprison or kill us."[36]

From what looked to be a promising start after the genocide, the political situation in Rwanda has progressively deteriorated. Many expatriate aid workers and scholars with experience in the region share a dismal prognosis of Rwanda and are particularly concerned about the possibility of renewed violence. As one NGO worker remarked, "The thought from those that have been here a long time is that the same thing that happened in 1994 will happen again [with]in the next twenty years."[37] Reyntjens provided a similar warning: "For someone like the present author, who warned against massive violence during the years leading up to 1994, it is frustrating to wonder whether, in two, five or ten years from now, the international community, again after the facts, will have to explain why Rwanda has descended into hell once more."[38] Recent personal communications with Rwandans and others working in the region suggest particular concern for violent conflict around the time of the next presidential elections (2017) at which time President Kagame is, according to the constitution and his personal promises, due to step down. Might education help mitigate against such an outcome? Or, will education continue to foster the same perverse intergroup trends as in the past?

Schooling after Genocide

Rwanda has great aspirations for its post-genocide education system. Despite blaming schooling for exacerbating intergroup relations in the past, the Kagame government has tremendous hopes and plans for both formal and informal education.

In terms of development, education is thought to be "the only factor that is likely to support the sustained modernization and diversification of modes of cultivations and systems of production."[39] In some ways, the government's emphasis on the developmental potential of schooling is similar to Habyarimana's approach reviewed in the last chapter. Today, however, schooling is also presented as a crucial step for achieving Vision 2020 and the goal of Rwanda becoming a knowledge-based economy.[40] The government ambitiously, yet unrealistically, asserted that by 2012, 50 percent of primary school students would have access to "one laptop per child."[41]

---

[36] Author's interview, female Hutu, northern Rwanda, March 21(C), 2006.

[37] Author's interview, NGO representative, eastern Rwanda, March 9, 2006.

[38] Reyntjens 2004, p. 210.

[39] RoR 1997, p. ii.

[40] RoR 2000, p. 13. The report emphasizes information technology and a number of interview participants also raised its importance.

[41] RoR 2007a.

At the same time, schooling is assigned a key role in the wider unity and reconciliation package. According to the government, schooling in the "new Rwanda" is aimed at "training citizens free of any type of discrimination, exclusion and favouritism and thus contributing to the promotion of peace, Rwandese and universal values of justice, solidarity, tolerance and respect for the rights and duties of human beings."[42] It is charged with the "detoxification" of youth and with the restoration of "recently eroded Rwandan values."[43] Education is also considered a "structure to neutralize the ideology of genocide."[44] This national unity agenda includes formal schooling, non-formal education, non-school-based education such as *ingando*, and popular education such as radio programs.

Along with education, youth are invested with great hope and responsibility for Rwanda's future. Hope in the next generation was a common topic among interviewees:

> I see that we are on the right road, the right track. If the big [those with power and status] and we the old do not get mixed up in these affairs, [if] we don't teach our own children [about ethnicity], and even at school we don't talk about it [ethnicity] anymore, I hope that the next generation will be better.[45]

> The policy of the current government is that newborns learn that they are all the same. We are counting on those that are currently being born! It is hard for the old, and it is also hard for the young because they are being born amongst the contaminated.[46]

The new social studies texts, discussed later in this chapter, similarly note that "older people find it hard to change a way of life. Some were brought up to believe they were better than others."[47]

In many ways, Rwanda's expectations for education have been matched by inputs. Recent figures put government spending on education at 18.2 percent of the federal budget, down from a high of 27 percent 2006, but up from 15 percent in 1996. By the mid-2000s, education represented the single largest expenditure in the national budget, double that of health care, although the relationship has since reversed.[48] In 2010, the Rwandan government spent 5 percent of GDP on education. To contextualize, as of 2006, Sub-Saharan African countries spent a median of 4.4 percent of national income on education and the global average as of 2010 was 3.8 percent.[49] The majority of funds have tended to be allocated to primary education, although the gap between primary

---

[42] RoR 1997, p. 23.
[43] RoR 1995, p. 12.
[44] RoR 2006a, p. 219.
[45] Author's interview, female Tutsi, Kigali, January 27, 2006.
[46] Author's interview, male Tutsi, Kigali, March 11, 2006.
[47] Bamusanire 2006a, 105.
[48] Bridgeland, Wulsin, and McNaught 2009, p. 19; UNDP 2007c, p. 23; UNESCO 2010.
[49] Education For All Global Monitoring Report team 2011, p. 2; UNESCO 2009; UNESCO 2010.

and higher levels of education is narrowing and Rwanda is now one of the top higher education spenders in Africa.[50] The United Kingdom's Department for International Development is the government's largest bilateral partner and is providing significant ongoing support for education.[51] Rwanda is also part of the World Bank and Global Partnership for Education's *Education for All Fast Track Initiative* and has thus received a catalytic fund grant.

The government's first focus after the genocide was access to education. It reopened primary schools by mid-September 1994 and began reopening secondary schools in October 1994.[52] It organized exams for promotion past primary school, in several languages, by March 1995, at the same time as it reopened most private secondary schools. The remaining public secondary schools and the National University (NUR) reopened by April 1995, just a year after the genocide had begun. Following its *Education for All* commitments,[53] the government aimed to rapidly expand primary school intake via (re)building schools, more equitably distributing schools across the country, attracting more teachers, and promoting enrollment.[54] The 2003 Constitution made explicit that "every person has the right to education" and declared primary schooling "compulsory" and "free in public schools."[55] At first, the government maintained the basic structure of education at six years of primary, six years of secondary (or two to three years at technical centers), and four years of tertiary education. In 2009, the government added three years of schooling to "basic education," rendering "ordinary education" a nine, rather than six, year program, and making "lower" secondary school accessible and just three years.[56] There are now talks of extending basic education to twelve years.[57]

The government's second priority was improving the quality of teaching and learning. When I spoke to people about the improvements they would like to see in Rwandan schools, the most-mentioned answer had to do with the quality of schools: classrooms are too full; the quality of rural schools lags far behind those in urban areas; teachers need to be better trained and better paid; and schools require more material and better infrastructure.[58] Many classes consist of only a blackboard and children do not have textbooks. Some "schools," especially in the east of the country, do not have physical structures,

---

[50] Bridgeland, Wulsin, and McNaught 2009, p. 19; Schendel, Mazimhaka and Ezeanya 2013, p. 19; UNESCO 2010.

[51] Kanyarukiga et al. 2006, p. xi. Between 2000 and 2005, about 5% of all British aid to Africa went to Rwanda, totaling approximately 168 million pounds sterling. The United Kingdom remains the largest bilateral donor to Rwanda alongside the United States.

[52] Bridgeland, Wulsin, and McNaught 2009, p. 7.

[53] UNESCO 1990, 2000.

[54] RoR 1995, p. 18; RoR 1997, p. x.

[55] RoR 2003b, art. 40.

[56] RoR 2007a, pp. 22–23.

[57] Rodrigue Rwirahira, "12-year basic education program to start in February," *The Rwanda Focus*, January 23, 2012.

[58] RoR 2002a, p. 6.

and, in 2006, I frequently heard about children being schooled outside in the shade of trees.[59] In a Rwandan survey of households, 49.6 percent said they were dissatisfied with education and 91.2 percent of these said the reason was lack of basic educational and school materials.[60]

The third post-genocide educational concentration was the amelioration of the management of primary education. Examples include the consolidation of the multiple ministries responsible for education and subsequent efforts at decentralization.[61] Parent-teachers associations have also become much more common and active in the post-genocide period.

Additionally, the government wanted to improve curriculum, to which it continues to make broad reforms.[62] As noted earlier, Rwanda's government suspended history teaching from schools in 1994. This suspension was not unusual for a post-violence environment, but the formality of the moratorium was somewhat unique. The government placed the rewriting of history among its priorities and suggested the need to "publish a manual of Rwanda's history that will permit to rehabilitate certain historical truths that had been sacrificed for the sake of ideological manipulation."[63] The history curriculum has remained on the agenda for the National Curriculum Development Centre since it was established in 1996. In 1999, the government suggested that history should be taught in schools for two hours each week but did not offer substantial guidelines, or any textbooks or teaching material, thereby continuing a de facto moratorium. Four initiatives, discussed later in this chapter, are moving Rwanda away from this moratorium.

Similar to its approach to ethnicity in the wider Rwandan context, the post-genocide government has outlawed ethnic identity from schools. Students are no longer asked their ethnicities in class. The government also repealed the law instituting secondary school quotas, thus officially banning "all forms of discrimination and favoritism" and instituting a meritocracy.[64] It also created the National Examination Council to ensure fair standards. At the 1995 Policy and Planning meeting for the education sector, participants asked the international community to "never again make reference ... to the ethnicization of Rwandans" and asked UNESCO to help them "ban, in all international media, the division of the Rwandan people through ethnicization."[65]

The new government also changed the language policies of Rwanda's schools.[66] As previous chapters explain, prior to 1994, French and Kinyarwanda

[59] See, for instance, RoR 2004b, p. 19.

[60] RoR 2002a.

[61] Kanyarukiga et al. 2006, p. 3; RoR 1997, pp. iii–xi, 31; RoR 1998, pp. 14–17.

[62] See, for example, Charles Kwizera, "Rwanda: Education Body Unveils New A Level Curriculum," *The New Times*, May 29, 2009.

[63] RoR 1995, p. 48.

[64] Ibid., p. 21.

[65] Ibid., p. 51.

[66] RoR 2010a, p. 14.

had been the mediums of instruction. From 1994 to 2008, the Rwandan government aimed for a trilingual society, adding English as a third official language and dedicating approximately 45 percent of the primary school week to learning languages.[67] The first three years of primary school were taught in Kinyarwanda, with English or French as subjects. In the latter three years, the language of instruction was French in about 95 percent of Rwanda's primary schools, with English as a subject.[68] English was the primary language of instruction at some of the country's most elite schools. Tertiary education took place in both French and English. In 2008, Rwanda announced plans to make English the medium of education and to fully integrate it into all levels of both public and private schools by 2011.[69] French would be considered only an "additional language."[70] All exams for access to secondary school would also be written in English only. English-language teaching is said to be good for improved international commerce and trade, especially as Rwanda joined the English-speaking East African community. Similarly, the importance of English-language teaching is increasing in places like China, Pakistan, and South Korea.[71] Yet, the change may also reflect the Rwandan government's desire to distance the country from France, accused of arming and training *génocidaires*. Less publicly recognized, the inclusion of English reflects the importance of Rwandan English speakers, particularly from Uganda, and the move toward English in schools helps legitimate this dominant form of linguistic capital. According to my contacts in the teaching cadre, actual implementation of the English-language policy has been uneven with a persistence of French and increased reversion to Kinyarwanda as well.

Overall, the United Nations Development Program commends the education sector as "in many ways, an example of what well-planned, coordinated and targeted investments can achieve in terms of human and economic development."[72] But have these changes eliminated the harmful social-structural and psychocultural processes that plagued Rwanda's schools in the past?

An Assessment of the Role of Schooling (1994–Present)

In this section I examine access to primary and secondary school, history teaching, pedagogy, and how ethnicity has been addressed in classrooms. I argue that despite some developments that are consistent with peacebuilding, the

---

[67] RoR 2002a, p. 27.

[68] Kanyarukiga et al. 2006, p. 35.

[69] Scott Baldauf, "Rwanda Says 'Au Revoir' to French, Turns to English," *The Christian Science Monitor*, September 25, 2007; Gwynne Dyer, "Rwanda Abandons French Language," *Straight. com*, October 17, 2008; Moses Gahigi, "Rwanda: English Language Teaching Kicks Off," *The New Times*, November 30, 2008; Edwin Musoni, "Rwanda: Minister Explains Choice of English," *The New Times*, October 28, 2008; Samuelson and Freedman 2010.

[70] RoR 2010a, p. 14.

[71] Samuelson and Freedman 2010, p. 204.

[72] UNDP 2007c, p. 22.

post-genocide government is again creating the types of social-structural and psychocultural mechanisms that contributed to conflict in Rwanda's past.

Access to Primary School

The Rwandans with whom I spoke felt that access to primary school was equal for all. Promisingly, no interviewees claimed discrimination or inequality on ethnic grounds. They reminded me, in fact, that parents can be punished with a 10,000 franc fine [about US$20] for failing to send their children to school.[73]

Rwanda has enjoyed success at raising the enrollment rates at schools. From a primary net enrollment rate (NER) of 65.3 percent in 1997 and 73.3 percent in 2001, the NER rose to approximately 93 percent in 2004 and 94.2 percent in 2008, although provincial disparities in registration are significant.[74] The *Education for All Monitoring Report* states that NER in Sub-Saharan Africa averaged 70 percent by 2006, putting Rwanda admirably well above average.[75] Nonetheless, the percentage of children that complete primary school is much lower (different figures put this at 50–75 percent in recent years) and was, at least around the mid-2000s, below the Sub-Saharan African average.[76] On the positive side, Rwandan schools have achieved gender parity in primary enrollment, and in a reversal from just a few years ago, more girls complete primary school than boys, although girls generally perform less well than boys at primary school.[77] This gender parity achievement is particularly significant as less than 30 percent of the thirty-nine Sub-Saharan African countries studied by UNESCO have achieved gender parity in primary education.[78] Rwandans seem to appreciate the government's concern with growing the educational pie and recognize good access to basic education as a peace dividend. During my 2009 visit I found students and parents to be very optimistic about the addition of three supplementary years of "basic education," although several with whom I met were unsure whether they would really be able to take advantage of this change.

To be sure, while access to schools is greatly improved over previous periods, hidden costs seriously hinder access, especially for the poor, orphans, and child heads of households.[79] As interviewees told me:

> It is too expensive. For example, here our students pay 2000 francs [about US$4] for chalk and classroom material to come to this school. But many don't find it.[80]

---

[73] Ingelaere 2009, p. 11.
[74] For 1997 numbers, see RoR 1997, p. 64. Note the incorrect numbers on p. vi. For 2001 and 2004 figures, see Kanyarukiga et al. 2006, p. 34; UNDP 2007c, p. 23. For 2008 figures, see Bridgeland, Wulsin, and McNaught 2009, p. 10. See also RoR 2007a, p. 21. On provincial disparities, see Obura 2005, p. 23.
[75] UNESCO 2009.
[76] Bridgeland, Wulsin, and McNaught 2009, p. 11; RoR 2010a, p. 4.
[77] UNDP 2007c, p. 24; RoR 2010a, pp. 4, 17, 20.
[78] UNESCO 2009.
[79] For more "challenges remaining for a fee-free system of education," see Obura 2005, pp. 55–56.
[80] Author's interview, female Tutsi, Kigali, January 27, 2006.

[Parents need to pay] school fees, uniforms, exercise books, pens, PTA [Parent-Teacher Association] money. Schools ask for contributions for guards' salaries, for windows. So, actually, going to school is really expensive. Some schools absolutely insist on uniforms. It is about 5,000 francs [about US$10] for a uniform and books.[81]

Indeed, 92 percent of primary-aged Rwandan children from the richest quintile enroll in primary school, in comparison to 79 percent of those in the poorest quintile.[82] Moreover, actual attendance is probably much lower than the enrollment would suggest. The most recent government estimates put dropout rates at 15–27 percent and repetition rates at 15–30 percent.[83] While access is much improved, and the gap in school enrollment rates between richest and poorest has decreased since 2000, experts agree that targeting the most marginal populations is a significant challenge.

While free access to school is nationally mandated, in practice local government and school officials hold much power in determining who gets access to schools. In 2009, one parent I met in a rural community lamented that he could not pay the 300 franc (about US$0.55) fee required to pay the cooks for the World Health Organisation-run school feeding program and that his son was consequently not allowed to sit the school exams.

In sum, despite the challenging post-genocide context, the government of Rwanda has done a good job at improving access to primary education. Nonetheless, the exclusion of the poorest may create new categories of resentment and discrimination. This is especially true, as I illustrate in the discussion of scholarships that follows, if Hutu remain the poorest. Moreover, as I will show shortly, whether horizontal equity is a genuine goal of the Kagame government is highly questionable.

Promotion Past Primary School

Interviewees also noted a great improvement in equality of access to secondary school in comparison with past periods and maintained that access is now generally based on merit:

When we correct [the exams], we write the number of the child, without even writing the child's name. We correct without knowing his name, and after, we put the list [of those that passed] without even knowing the name.[84]

It is really positive. Because the person is appreciated by merit, not only her origin. Although there is the problem of rich/poor. But promotion is only based on success. And that is really encouraging for all sides.[85]

[81] Author's interview, NGO representative, eastern Rwanda, March 9, 2006.
[82] RoR 2007a, p. 21.
[83] Bridgeland, Wulsin, and McNaught 2009, p. 17; RoR 2010a, p. 4.
[84] Author's interview, male Tutsi, Kigali, January 23, 2006.
[85] Author's interview, male Tutsi, Kigali, January 20, 2006.

Now, if a parent comes from a place, to come and beg a minister to allow his child to go to school, it's no longer the case [that this works]. We mark exams, and it is the national council [that] sends you to the schools you are supposed to go to. The minister does not have the right now to allocate schools like before.[86]

This development could improve horizontal equity. As Christopher Gibson and Michael Woolcock write, empowerment is a "process of revising the routines by which more and less powerful groups interact."[87]

Yet, the number of secondary school spots remains far below demand; recent government figures put secondary NER at 10 percent nationally and 7.9 percent in rural areas, with a gross enrollment rate (GER) only slightly higher than 15 percent.[88] These are very low rates, even by Sub-Saharan African standards where average secondary school GER hovers around 30 percent. With the new commitment to a nine-year basic education, Rwanda's lower secondary GER is near 35 percent (2009), although the upper secondary figures remain much lower. Unsurprisingly, one's level of education is correlated with employment status in Rwanda; 87.7 percent of primary school graduates call themselves farmers, whereas only 19.1 percent of secondary school graduates do.[89] The government further reports that Rwandans who complete upper secondary earn on average double that of those who complete only lower secondary school.[90] This makes secondary school positions particularly sought after.[91]

A number of Rwandans also mentioned that there are now more tertiary opportunities than there were in the past, although this is a comment of the elite, because even secondary school is beyond the reach of the vast majority. The tertiary NER in Rwanda is 3.2 percent (2003), on the low side of the Sub-Saharan African average of 5 percent. The 2003 Rwandan census revealed that only 0.5 percent of the Rwandan population holds tertiary education degrees, in comparison with an average of 4 percent in Africa.[92]

Poverty again emerged as an important barrier to equitable access to education. For example, figures from the 2005–2006 school year show that secondary school enrollment among children from the richest quintile was ten times higher (26 percent) than among children from the poorest quintile

---

[86] Author's interview, Ministry of Education, Kigali, February 2, 2006.
[87] Gibson and Woolcock 2008, p. 2.
[88] The enrollment rates in the next two paragraphs are derived from Kanyarukiga et al. 2006, p. 25; RoR 2000, p. 25; Obura 2005, p. 25; RoR 1997, pp. vii, 124; RoR 2007a, p. 23; UNESCO 2009; RoR 2010a.
[89] RoR 2007b, p. 19.
[90] RoR 2010a, p. 27.
[91] For fascinating insight into the perspective of poor youth, aged eighteen to thirty-five, with only primary school education, on a variety of issues related to youth and adulthood, including education, see Sommers 2012. Sommers finds that, like the group that I interviewed, these youth generally hold post-primary education in very high regard, but, in contrast, sadly have often given up the hope of achieving it.
[92] RoR 2007a, p. 23.

(2.6 percent).[93] As has been the case throughout Rwanda's history, class plays an important role in accessing opportunities and the state. Class also relates to who one knows. Recent personal communications attest, despite movement toward merit-based decision making, to the ongoing importance of connections in access to education and especially jobs.

Financial access to schooling also intersects with ethnicity. Many interviewees discussed how scholarships for genocide survivors, under the *Fonds d'Assistance aux Rescapés du Génocide* (Genocide Survivors Support and Assistance Fund, or FARG), render secondary school access inequitable. While many also recognized the importance of access to schooling for genocide survivors, Rwandan youth representatives at the National Summit for Children and Young People raised FARG as one of the most pressing obstacles to unity and reconciliation, and many of my interviewees concurred.[94] Created in 1998, FARG is a program for needy survivors to help offset school fees (especially at the secondary level), as well as the costs of health care and housing. Approximately 5 percent of the national budget is directed toward FARG and 75 percent of FARG funds have been spent on education. Since its inception, FARG has supported 53,000 secondary school students and more than 3,000 university students.[95]

A central issue regarding this funding is that recipients of FARG are equated with Tutsi. Rwandans of diverse backgrounds agreed that Tutsi are the principal beneficiaries:

> So, for example, excuse me for using the correct word, if we take a Hutu child, he is not involved [in FARG]. But, since the government is paying for someone who was touched [by genocide] yet his family is not capable of paying for his school fees, he is jealous, because he sees another, a Tutsi, and the government is paying for him. It makes that one start saying, "oh so FARG is for Tutsi children." He doesn't connect it to those that lost people.[96]

> I am a child alone in the world. No father, no mother, no brothers, no sisters. I am alone. I am not able to be helped by the FARG because it is for children with Tutsi fathers and Tutsi mothers. But me, my mother was Tutsi, my father no.[97]

> If I have no parents because of the war, the other has no parents because of genocide, he [the former] should also be helped, but the Hutu is not helped.[98]

In order to receive funds, one must be officially recognized by the government as a "genocide survivor," which requires signatures from local officials and

[93] Ibid.
[94] Personal notes from attendance, January 2006.
[95] Buckley-Zistel 2006, p. 139; Edwin Musoni, "Has FARG achieved its mission?" *The New Times*, April 16, 2012; Survivors Fund (SURF) 2012.
[96] Author's interview, male Tutsi, southern Rwanda, February 14(B), 2006.
[97] Author's interview, female of mixed ethnicity, northern Rwanda, April 3(D), 2006. On FARG and children of mixed ethnic background, see Burnet 2009.
[98] Author's interview, female Hutu, northern Rwanda, April 3(E), 2006.

witnesses, again granting local authorities important gate-keeping power.[99] In law, *rescapé* is defined as "persons that escaped genocide and massacres perpetrated in Rwanda between October 1 1990 and December 31 1994," and the fund is intended for the very "needy, especially orphans, widows and the handicapped."[100] The definition is not reserved solely for Tutsi, although the acronym refers only to genocide survivors. Moreover, I met no Hutu recipients of FARG, Rwandan experts with whom I spoke were not aware of any Hutu beneficiaries, and some researchers have used FARG receivers as a proxy for Tutsi.

In addition, FARG often provokes jealousy because recipients are readily identified by their classmates and singled out for advantages. Lyndsay McLean Hilker even reports that FARG recipients hold special identity cards that have virtually replaced pre-genocide Tutsi identity cards.[101] In my interviews, the common mode of distribution, in which recipients are called to the front of the class to be given books and pens, was identified as particularly problematic, as it heightens both awareness of beneficiaries and jealousy:

> In class we say, "FARG children, go out to get books, uniforms, pens and notebooks." It is communicated at school. All of the FARG children leave, and the Hutu and kids with parents in prison are left.[102]

> In reality, we have to help children from the genocide that don't have parents, or at least help them cure their trauma. But the way the help comes, it is not really a good way to help them. When we call [FARG survivor] students to the front of the class, right in front of the other students, the children that are still sitting start to become very jealous. Jealous.[103]

Despite ethnicity being officially banned in an effort at recategorization, these practices hide ethnic categories just below the surface. The policy of ethnic unity actually reinforces ethnic divisions. Many Rwandans felt that FARG sends a message of survivor (read: Tutsi) worthiness over other Rwandans.

In my interviews, much contention centered around the fact that many Rwandans, and especially Hutu, are equally in need, yet are not eligible for FARG. While a scholarship from the Ministry of Local Affairs (MINALOC) is available to all Rwandans, many Hutu lamented that it allocates substantially fewer funds than FARG. As my interviewees expressed:

> We need to pay for the child survivors of genocide. But there are also others [in need] because our country is among the poorest in the world. There are many children who are not survivors of genocide but who really suffer, that have really difficult conditions.... MINALOC helps poor children, but they don't help them like they do survivors. That is a problem. For example, here in our school, there are a lot of survivors who come from the city, who have good lives, who have

[99] Burnet 2009, pp. 93–94.
[100] Rombouts 2004, p. 372.
[101] McLean Hilker 2011, p. 275.
[102] Author's interview, female Hutu, Kigali, March 10(A), 2006.
[103] Author's interview, male Tutsi, Kigali, January 30, 2006.

mothers that work for example. While there are other children [not survivors] who live in the countryside who live miserably.[104]

There are orphans of genocide, AIDS orphans, even those whose mothers were raped during the genocide and are dying now. But some are saying how can they help the ones [former] and leave the others [latter]? They tell us "if we're not from the genocide, we're not orphans."[105]

These quotes speak to the concern that Tutsi genocide survivors are ranked far above other Rwandans, even those Hutu that have survived violence. Teachers said that some children – likely out of jealousy and a sense of inequality – accuse survivors of faking or exaggerating trauma so that their FARG funding is continued.

Some maintain that FARG funding is also inconsistent with funding to other important sectors. As previously noted, FARG represents about 5 percent of the Rwandan government budget. While the budgetary amount is relatively small, only approximately 4 percent of the population receives FARG support. In contrast, just 3 percent of the government budget is dedicated to agriculture, which sustains about 80 percent of the Rwandan population, especially rural Hutu.[106]

Additionally, some interviewees charged the government with misdistribution of FARG funds to old caseload refugees, or through bribery,[107] consolidating Tutsi that were in and outside of Rwanda at the time of the genocide into a single "survivor" group. As one man put it, "The government is trying to make a right, but people are hiding it, and they [the government] put in people [to FARG] who are not orphans, who are not genocide survivors."[108] There appear to have been some improvements in the management of FARG over recent years, although a recent report finds "ghost students" illegally benefiting from FARG and other types of inconsistencies between fund intentions and outcomes.[109]

Moving forward, the government expects the number of FARG recipients to increase in the short term, then decrease as survivors pass through the education system.[110] There is some mention of FARG being streamed into broader social protection programming, and reallocating university scholarships to support basic education, although details are scant.[111] At present, FARG fosters horizontal inequalities between dichotomous and collectivized survivor and perpetrator groups.

---

[104] Author's interview, male mixed ethnicity, southern Rwanda, February 14(A), 2006.
[105] Author's interview, female Tutsi, Kigali, April 8(A), 2006. The same concerns were raised by participants in NURC's national consultations. The government replied that FARG as a way of "discriminating Rwandan people" is "groundless indeed." See RoR 2002d, pp. 7, 16.
[106] UNDP 2007c, p. 11.
[107] See also Burnet 2009, p. 219 and pp. 93–94.
[108] Author's interview, male Tutsi, Kigali, February 8(B), 2006.
[109] Edwin Musoni, "Has FARG achieved its mission?" *The New Times*, April 16, 2012.
[110] SURF 2012.
[111] RoR 2011a; RoR 2011b, p. 20.

Another issue of access to secondary school relates to the quality and geographic distribution of schooling and to opportunities for patronage. Students can be sent all over Rwanda for secondary school. As a teacher explained, "a child from Kigali [in the center of the country], we send him to Cyangugu, right near the Congo."[112] Students who receive the highest grades on their exams are given priority in choosing secondary schools and usually prefer schools closest to their homes. This seems fair, but as one NGO worker explained,

> If you have a good score on the exam, it is very likely that you were from a good public school. If you pass, with a worse score, they will send you to a secondary school anywhere in the country. This results in lots of school fees and travel costs. The poorer schools have worse teachers, students do worse, and get sent to geographically poor schools, and because the poor can't afford it, those places become available for allocation by the state.[113]

Here, as in past chapters, class and ethnicity become intricately intertwined and the state plays an important role in the allocation of educational resources. The RPF tends to provide state services, like education, to certain kinds of people, especially Tutsi RPF loyalists.

Likewise, many interviewees noted that tertiary education in Rwanda and scholarships for overseas education are dominated by Tutsi. In the research for his 1997 book, Prunier estimated that 95 percent of academic staff and 80 percent of students at the National University of Rwanda were Tutsi. Reyntjens also estimated that more than 80 percent of students were Tutsi, and several of my interview participants expressed concern about Tutsi dominance in tertiary education and other positions of power in the country.[114] Though current estimates are unavailable, I often heard similar assertions from Hutu interviewees. Indeed, the charges remain serious enough to warrant President Kagame's devoting a significant amount of time to denying them in his Opening Remarks at the 2006 Development Partners Meeting.[115] In 2009, I met with several Hutu university students who did not feel they had been disadvantaged, but it is difficult to know the proportions of Hutu and Tutsi students in schools with any certainty since, in line with the banning of ethnicity, such records are no longer kept. Such charges are worrisome, whether they are true or merely perception among Rwandans.

Overall, the educational pie is growing. Some consider this a peace dividend because they see their needs being met. Peter Coleman and colleagues review theory and research on personal satisfaction and argue "that the rate of progress in achieving one's goals is more important than is the magnitude of the discrepancy between one's current state and the desired states of affairs."[116]

---

[112] Author's interview, male Tutsi, Kigali, January 23, 2006.

[113] Author's interview, NGO representative, eastern Rwanda, March 9, 2006.

[114] Prunier 1997, p. 188. See also McLean Hilker's (2011) description of her interviews for an experience similar to mine.

[115] Author's personal communication with an attendee.

[116] Coleman et al. 2008.

Nonetheless, access to higher levels of schooling is not keeping pace with primary education, and most Rwandans will not get the salaried jobs to which they aspire. My sense is that the pie will not grow fast enough for distributional issues not to matter. Indeed, at higher levels of schooling, preference (and perception of preference) for Tutsi survivors in funding secondary school and university is creating a "moral hierarchy" along ethnic lines.[117] Some are identified and collectivized with the new category of survivors (Tutsi) and others feel stigmatized as perpetrators (Hutu). This may recreate a sense of horizontal inequality reminiscent of what Hutu felt in the years leading up to the intergroup violence and revolution at the end of the colonial era. Although ethnic blindness sounds fair, important inequalities are hiding behind the government's ban on ethnicity, and in practice, imperfect implementation of the ethnicity ban by the government threatens once again to align these inequalities along ethnic lines.

Reintroducing History Teaching

The content of post-genocide education also needs to be examined. As discussed earlier, Rwanda's government suspended history teaching from schools in 1994. While the moratorium has never been formally revoked, some important efforts have been made to reintroduce history into schools, raising a multitude of questions and much controversy.

Most of the Rwandans with whom I spoke agreed that history needs to be formally reintroduced into Rwanda's schools systemwide, although their opinions varied as to how to do so. Some said that they did not want the conflictual elements of their country's history taught to their children: "I want to wait until we will write a history that does not divide people. The primordial objective is to bring people together."[118] Nonetheless, those who shared this view disagreed on what should be left out, with opinions varying roughly along ethnic lines.

However, most of my interviewees, who hailed from varying regions and ethnic groups, felt that omitting details, euphemizing, or tempering the truth was dangerous: "I am not in favor of the suppression of history teaching. If our history is atrocious, it is our history. We still need to teach it."[119] Interestingly, the reason given both for not talking about the past at all and for talking about potentially inflammatory elements of the past was the desire to prevent a recurrence of conflict. A much higher proportion of those in the first group were poor and less educated, compared to those in the second group.

Nevertheless, both groups generally affirmed that Rwanda's national history should be rewritten as *one* "true" history. As one woman suggested, "My idea is that we find a group of researchers that we put together, that they study the

---

[117] See Pottier 2002, p. 126.
[118] Author's interview, male Tutsi, Kigali, March 11, 2006.
[119] Author's interview, female Tutsi, Kigali, February 6(A), 2006.

real history of the country. Even if it takes years, we'll teach the history that is true."[120] The Kigali-based *Institute for Research and Dialogue on Peace* similarly found that a great number of Rwandans desire an "objective and true history," and Anna Obura's interviews revealed that children felt that "school can and should give unbiased and objective explanations on social relations and on the history of Rwanda."[121] During a teacher training exercise, Freedman and colleagues found a similar desire for the presentation of hard historical facts.[122] Nevertheless, the divergent transcripts and high level of societal distrust suggest that arriving at an agreed-on narrative, be it inclusive or exclusive of certain events, will be very difficult.

A number of committees have been convened since the genocide to develop national-level history curricula for Rwandan schools. Four recent initiatives – two at the primary and two at the secondary levels – have reintroduced select history into Rwandan classrooms. Given that little, and in some cases nothing, has been written on these initiatives, I provide quite a lot of detail about them in the subsections that follow. Readers interested in more of an overview may wish to proceed directly to the section entitled "History Teaching and Peacebuilding."

A Primary School Guide to Civic Education

First, in 2004, with funding from UNICEF, Rwanda introduced a primary-level civics textbook, *A Guide to Civic Education*. This text, available in French and English, includes several historical modules currently being taught in Rwanda's schools and foreshadows how more general history texts and curriculum are likely to develop. The units on "National Unity in Rwanda" and "Genocide and Reconciliation" are telling. They assert the existence of national unity in Rwanda prior to colonialism, and that divisions in Rwanda were part of a colonial divide-and-rule strategy. The units overview "the institutionalization of lies and crime," "loss of cultural identity," "mismanagement of resources," "ethnic ideology," and "social inequality" during the colonial period and after independence. In explaining the "Rwandan genocide" – a more inclusive label than "genocide of the Tutsi", which is the dominant language in the newer social studies texts – the text dates the first manifestations of hate, injustice, and divisions to the "massacre of Tutsi of 1959." It also mentions the 1963 and 1973 killings of Tutsi. The text discusses the development of the *interahamwe* by the government of the Second Republic with a mission to murder Tutsi, to pillage and burn their homes, and to massacre their families as RPF spies. It contends that the genocide of 1994, in which "more than one million Tutsi and moderate Hutu" were massacred in 90 days, had been meticulously planned for a long time. The text reviews some of the torturous killing methods. It says

---

[120] Author's interview, female Tutsi, Kigali, January 29(A), 2006.
[121] Institut de Recherche et de Dialogue pour la Paix 2004, p. 16.
[122] Freedman et al. 2008, p. 678.

that genocide was the work of military and paramilitary groups, politicians, and the media. The authors mention that Hutu judged as traitors for hiding Tutsi were forced to kill them or were themselves killed. It describes the consequences of genocide, asserts "empathy with refugee problems," and promotes "unity and reconciliation."[123] This text also introduces other genocides around the world: the Armenian genocide and "the genocide of the Jews and Roma." In 2009, the text was still in use in a Kigali school that I visited, and a representative from the National Curriculum Development Center emphasized that it contains important lessons. On the other hand, some teachers are put off by the delicateness of teaching history and the politics of this narrative. One teacher from Southern province told me in 2008 that "everybody is so uncomfortable, so they're staying away from it. It sits in the principal's office and is not used."[124]

Primary Social Studies

The second initiative involves a series of Primary Social Studies books with pupil and teacher's editions, printed in 2006 by Macmillan Rwanda.[125] The texts for primary grades one through three are in Kinyarwanda and those from grades four to six are available in Kinyarwanda and English. Of the four history initiatives reviewed, the social studies texts include the most explicit and comprehensive historical narrative, introduced in grades four to six and most detailed in the sixth grade text.

Beginning with the precolonial period, the sixth grade student book advises students that "[i]t is important to remember that there were no tribes in Rwanda. People from every social group belonged to the same clans.... They shared the same religion and culture. They intermarried with each other. They spoke the same language.... Social classes or groups in early Rwanda depended on a person's occupation (the kind of work they did)." The students are taught that the Belgians "divided people into three groups: Tutsi, Hutu and Twa, and gave them identity cards." Students are also taught about *ubuhake* clientship in grades four through six, explained as "voluntary and benefit[ing] both patrons and clients." This is a starkly different narrative than the "arrival of the populations" taught pre-genocide.

Sixth grade students are also taught about the move toward independence with quite different emphases than the narrative of the revolution reviewed in the preceding chapter. The text explains how "in 1952 the Belgians set up the first elected councils to try to give more power to the Hutu." It praises the king, who is said to have been worried about ethnic division and "asked that the terms 'Mututsi', 'Muhutu' and 'Mutwa' be removed from documents" and

[123] Baranyizigiye et al. 2004, pp. 29–38.
[124] Personal communication.
[125] The material for the next four paragraphs comes from Bamusanire et al. 2006a, 2006b, 2006c, 2006d, 2006f. See especially Bamusanire et al. 2006d, pp. 28–30, 40–68.

"said that all citizens should see themselves as Rwandans." The text goes on to teach students that Kayibanda "thought that the Hutu as a group should have more power and a fairer share of the wealth of Rwanda," and that Kayibanda "saw the monarchy as a continuation of Tutsi dominance in Rwanda." In explaining the transition to independence and Kayibanda's presidency, the text states that "since Hutu voted for their own people, this increased the number of Hutu who were elected," and that "the people of Rwanda did what the government wanted. They voted for a republic." Ordinary Rwandans' agency is continually denied. Similar to the civics book discussed earlier, the text dates the beginning of "Hutu massacres of Tutsi" to this period. The texts teach students about the "racist" policies of the First and Second Republics.

The 1994 genocide is explained in a fashion similar to its treatment in the *A Guide to Civic Education* civics text, although in more detail. It lists the causes of the genocide as racial divisions and injustice caused by the colonialists (and accepted by the population) and bad leadership and governance in independent Rwanda. It describes the genocide as "a time when members of one group of Rwandans set out to kill all the members of another group," but then uses ethnic language. It notes that the shooting down of Habyarimana's plane "acted as a signal to the Hutu militias. They began to kill all the Tutsis they could find, as well as Hutu moderates who did not follow the government's extreme policies." The social studies lesson also reviews the consequences of the genocide much as the civics text did. The two initiatives further resemble each other in their uses of distance as a technique to teach about genocide; the sixth grade text introduces the genocides of the Herero, Armenians, and Jews.

The text contrasts the bad governance of the past to "the RPF [who] wanted to bring national unity to Rwanda and establish real democracy again." Moreover, once the RPF became the government, the text explains that it "wanted to help Rwandans to discover the unity they had once had, before the Europeans came. They wanted to provide justice for everyone."

These social studies texts can be purchased in bookstores in Kigali. Some of the schools that I visited had them, but many primary schools do not own these texts. In those cases, I was simply told that teachers deal with teaching history on their own.

Materials for a History Curriculum for Secondary Schools

At the secondary level, in 2006, the University of California at Berkeley's Human Rights Center, along with the Rwandan National Curriculum Development Center, scholars from the National University of Rwanda, and a U.S. NGO called *Facing History and Ourselves* collaboratively created a pedagogical guide for teaching history in Rwanda's secondary schools.[126] *Facing History* specializes in teaching methods for controversial history in divided societies. Its

---

[126] This section is based on personal communications with participants, as well as Freedman et al. 2008; RoR 2006b; Weinstein, Freedman, and Hughson 2007.

approach encourages reflection, dialogue, an emphasis on agency and multiple points of view, and engaging critical learners.

The exercise to create materials for teaching history was meant to model a collaborative process by involving multiple stakeholders in the production of history. This included meetings among the Rwandan and U.S. partners listed earlier, as well as Rwandan Hutu, Tutsi, and Twa, Rwandans living abroad, and rural and urban Rwandans. In contrast to the objective of the previous two initiatives, which posit one history that aims to whitewash divergent narratives, the meetings involved developing a process through which contested stories could be addressed in a political climate used to teaching history as propaganda. Over the course of the project, the National Curriculum Development Center labeled what they were doing "creating materials for a history curriculum," yet the international contributors sometimes faced fears that they were trying to "colonize history curriculum."[127]

The resultant materials are broken down into modules with diverse research presented such that teachers and students can engage in conversation and critical analysis about four periods of Rwanda's history: the precolonial period, colonialism (1897–1962), postcolonial Rwanda (1962–1990), and later postcolonial Rwanda (1990–1994). The guide also presents one theme for each of the periods, with the precolonial period examining "clans," the colonialism section concentrating on "the Mortehan reform" that refers to the colonial era political, economic and sociocultural reforms discussed in Chapter 2, the postcolonial section titled "Regional and Ethnic Segregation," and the later postcolonial section called "Education Policy and Genocide Ideology."

Although their final product is neither a textbook nor a curriculum, and was destined only for Rwanda's secondary schools, the guide served as a significant starting point for the reintroduction of history to Rwandan schoolchildren without focusing on a single narrative. The creators paired the guide's launch with training for 250 high school history teachers in Rwanda. The idea was that Rwandans would use the process as a model, secure additional funding, and continue the process to build cases and elaborate on the ones that the project had started. Today, its progress has been halted by the government.

National Curriculum Development Center Secondary School History Guidelines

For its part, the National Curriculum Development Center set curricular guidelines in 2008 for history teaching for the first three years of secondary school (ordinary level, now included as part of basic education) and in 2010 for the second three years, called advanced or upper secondary school level.[128] Key goals of this curriculum are "to make the citizen know the Rwandese value and universal of peace, the respect of personal rights, gender equality, of democracy,

---

[127] Author's personal communication.

[128] RoR 2008; RoR 2010b. Quotes throughout this section stem from the lower secondary school curriculum, and are largely replicated in the upper secondary school document.

of justice, of solidarity and of good governance," to "work with the critical spirit," "to live with the world without ethnic, religious distinction or other forms of discrimination and of exclusion that led to genocide of Tutsi in 1994," and "to promote the culture of peace, tolerance and of reconciliation and the love of the homeland."

The curricular guidelines are presented in three columns: "specific objectives," "contents," and "teaching/learning activities." There is no detailed historical narrative, and teachers are thus given significant responsibility and leeway. For example, under the objective of "Social, Political and Economic dependence of pre-colonial Rwanda," "ubuhake, ubukonde and uburetwa" are listed as objectives and the activity suggests, "With the help of different documents read an extract of text concerning ubuhake, ubukonde and uburetwa and help the learners to understand the importance of two institutions in socio-politico and economic relations among the Rwandese." The activity for the contents of "Belgian Military Occupation 1916–1926" is to "start a conversation with learners criticising the reform enterprises of the Belgian colonisers." Some contents are even vaguer, such as the lesson title "unusual things that Happened in 1959."

The section entitled "The war of 1990–1994 and the genocide of Tutsi" is scheduled to receive the most class time in comparison to other periods of Rwandan history. Guidelines are similar to the type discussed earlier: without much detail, it only lists different causes of genocide such as the press and the hardening of dictatorship, the roles of different actors internationally and domestically, key events such as the Arusha Accords and "the phase of execution [sic] extermination of Tutsi and Hutu opposition to the Genocide ideology," terminology such as "genocide," and general topics such as the "political, economic, social and cultural" consequences of genocide, and "Efforts of the Government of National Unity." The documents themselves are replete with English spelling and grammatical errors.

History Teaching and Peacebuilding

These four educational initiatives represent serious steps away from the post-genocide moratorium on history teaching and make strides toward pedagogical innovation as well. All four initiatives recognize "active learning" and "participation" in theory and through suggested pedagogical activities. The secondary curriculum guidelines state that "in the process of teaching, the teacher will develop into his learners the spirit of critical thinking and to arouse learners' need for continuous perfection."[129] One practical example suggests that students "[a]sk … parents or other members of [their] family whether they think national reconciliation is beginning to happen. Listen to what they have to say about the problems we still have."[130]

[129] Ibid., p. 73.
[130] Bamusanire et al. 2006e, p. 65.

Teachers and experts frequently raised the importance of critical thinking rather than the conformity and blind obedience they sometimes attribute to the past, and students confirmed that they are sometimes encouraged to ask questions in class:

> Today the consensus is starting to come on how to teach. "Here are the facts, here is what happened, and here are the diverse interpretations that people make. Can we talk about this?"[131]

> It was easy to manipulate a poor man by promising him property, or an illiterate person, each in the sense that it's not knowing how to read and write, but also not knowing about what is happening in national life. But educate them so that they can have a critical mind. Because if you look at the Holocaust, I imagine the Germans were educated, so even educated people can be manipulated but probably if you have critical analysis, if you can critically analyze events, if someone tells you this, you will think twice. You will ask, "but what is his interest? Or high [government] interest? What do I get from that?"[132]

The second quote, in particular, highlights the realization that just any education is not enough to prevent conflict. The various initiatives explicitly aim to improve critical thinking and highlight the importance of children being able to question what they are taught.[133] These statements indicate that the development of critical thinking skills – a psychocultural factor underlying sustainable peace – is at least receiving lip service.

Moreover, nearly all of the peacebuilding concepts introduced in this book's theoretical framework are explicitly recognized in at least some of the curricular initiatives. For example, the importance of combating inequality – or "horizontal equity" – is emphasized in the social studies textbooks: "If large numbers of people are treated unequally, they may join together and be violent."[134] Teachers are instructed that an important way of working toward equality is through equitable education and treatment of pupils.[135] Overcoming feelings of superiority is also explicitly mentioned. A sample social studies question for students in the fifth grade asks: "Why is it dangerous if one group of people think they are better than others?"[136] There is also an emphasis on the importance of interdependence and mutual support. Nonconsultative decision making is rejected: "New projects and ideas are a cause of disharmony in communities throughout the world, if they are not properly discussed or if they are imposed without agreement."[137] These are positive, pro-peacebuilding developments. Nonetheless, such written texts, divorced from implementation

---

[131] Author's interview, Rwandan researcher, Kigali, February 6, 2006.
[132] Author's interview, National Unity and Reconciliation Commission, Kigali, March 29, 2006.
[133] See, for example, Bamusanire et al. 2006b, pp. 1–2.
[134] See also Bamusanire et al. 2006a, p. 105; 2006b, p. 3; 2006c, p. 90.
[135] Bamusanire et al. 2006d, p. 93.
[136] Ibid., p. 98.
[137] Ibid., p. 56.

and context, do not necessarily contribute to peace; they must be supplemented with a teaching program that encourages students to think critically about what is written in their textbooks.

One History in Rwanda: History Content and Pedagogy

There is a stark difference between this open rhetoric and the reality of a singular univocal narrative. The RPF shows clear disdain for "ordinary Rwandans," and this, alongside its preoccupation with maintaining power, is clear in its education policies.[138] While the aforementioned approaches seem to encourage open dialogue, in reality such critical thinking is not permitted outside the bounds of the government-approved narrative. The primary school initiatives marginalize some viewpoints and present an oversimplified "correct" narrative. The National Curriculum Development Center secondary school guidelines, while sparse enough to permit the possibility of different narratives, also reflect government discourse. In general, there have been harsh government responses to divergent versions of history.[139] The Ministry of Education Web site includes among its goals that "future populations will learn the *true* history of Rwanda."[140] In this sense, as in the past, the history curriculum is a reflector of dominant government narratives from which deviation is not permitted. Most educators believe that this sort of teaching runs counter to meaningful peacebuilding.

Even the initiative spearheaded by UC Berkeley, while differing significantly from the other initiatives and offering the prospect of a more open approach to history, can be interpreted as quite consistent with governmental discourse. For example, the choice of themes seems curious and may have been shaped by the public transcript. The particular periodization of the past, with the colonial period as the pivotal moment, also reflects the centrality of the colonial period to the RPF's narrative, and thus is in line with the Kagame government's position.

In late 2007, the government ran assemblies in many Rwandan secondary schools to explain, as one ex-patriot teacher told me, "what could and could not be said." Similar issues were discussed, among other things, during a three-and-a-half-week mandatory training for secondary school teachers. Held in April 2008, the event was described to me as a "drill camp including physical training and lots of workshops." According to several ex-patriot teachers, Rwandan students and teachers were very guarded about the content of these meetings, which as non-Rwandans they were not invited to attend, and no student that they asked found them to be useful. "There was no frank exchange" in the assemblies, one teacher recounted. "It is impossible."[141]

---

[138] On disdain for ordinary Rwandans, see Ansoms 2009b.

[139] See, for instance, Charles Mugabo, "Do Not Distort Rwanda's History," *The New Times*, August 30, 2007; Charles Mugabo, "If All Could Emulate Archbishop Emmanuel Kolini," *The New Times*, September 30, 2007; Charles Mugabo, "Rusesabagina's Ill-Conceived Agenda," *The New Times*, September 26, 2007.

[140] RoR 2003a, p. 4.

[141] Author's personal communication.

In fact, the legitimacy of post-genocide curriculum arose in interviews as a recurrent concern. As one man expressed his concerns:

So now they say that the past history is false. So they've hired people to remake history. But what's to say that the current researchers are not attached to the government and current politics? There's a question! I don't know if ever this government leaves if another won't just as quickly suppress it [their new version of history].[142]

Timothy Longman and Théonèste Rutagengwa likewise found that 49.2 percent of interviewees agreed or strongly agreed that "whoever is in power rewrites Rwandan history to serve their own interests." Only 21.7 percent disagreed or strongly disagreed.[143] The 2010 opposition hopeful, and Hutu, Victoire Ingabire's campaign platform, pasted on the social networking site Facebook, included initiating "a non-political commission in charge of rewriting and interpretation of the actual history of Rwanda."[144]

The details of historical representations are contentious and how genocide is represented is particularly delicate. Victims and survivors deserve respect and acknowledgment. Recognizing and commemorating victims and crimes are crucial steps in reconciliation and part of a transitional justice process. They are important to counter denial. Learning about the causes and consequences of genocide may also be important for its future prevention.[145]

However, many Hutu with whom I spoke felt excluded from mourning and fear further delegitimization by being left out of the history curriculum as well. One Rwandan Hutu woman complained that "the other history that we must teach" must do more than limit discussion to Tutsi genocide victims and survivors. "For example, I lost three quarters of my family during the war.... But we [Hutu] don't have any right to say that we lost people."[146] Indeed, the history initiatives make no mention of the RPF's crimes, thus excluding the experiences of many Rwandans who suffered at their hands during the war preceding the genocide, during the genocide, and since. The government is, in Van Evera's terminology, conducting "chauvinistic mythmaking" by glorifying the Tutsi in-group, highlighting its victimization, and whitewashing its faults. It also devalues the Hutu out-group: several Hutu Rwandans explained that by failing to recognize their pain and to acknowledge their mourning, the limited content of the current curricula makes it difficult for them to relate to and embrace the suffering of Tutsi Rwandans. This stigmatization and devaluation of Hutu suffering could serve as a psychocultural factor underlying future intergroup conflict.

---

[142] Author's interview, male Hutu, Kigali, March 22(C), 2006.
[143] Longman and Rutagengwa 2004, p. 170.
[144] Facebook, "Victoire Ingabire Umuhoza," http://www.facebook.com/pages/Victoire-Ingabire-Umuhoza-for-President/109504816547?v=info.
[145] Staub, Pearlman, and Miller 2003, pp. 287, 290.
[146] Author's interview, female Hutu, northern Rwanda, March 21(C), 2006.

A second example of the exclusion engendered by the dominant singular narrative concerns precolonial history. In the mainstream narrative, illustrated in the civics and social studies texts, the precolonial period is presented as a harmonious golden age, ruptured by the divide-and-rule strategies of the colonial powers. This is factually incorrect, as we saw in Chapter 2; there were a number of sociopolitical divisions in precolonial Rwanda, including Hutu and Tutsi, that were hardened, but not created, by colonial rule. In what Suzanne Buckley-Zistel calls a "chosen amnesia," past conflicts between Hutu and Tutsi "are eclipsed from the discourse."[147] Freedman and colleagues also note that the government's stress on the importance of clans vis-à-vis lineages and regions and its presentation of precolonial Rwanda as a nation-state are all inconsistent with available historical records.[148]

While an emphasis on inclusion is often to be praised, the way history is beginning to be introduced into schools involves great exclusion and coercion. This is, to borrow Ross's term, a "paradox of inclusiveness."[149] Despite critical thinking being widely embraced in theory, the narrative emerging from the civics initiative is streamlining history and "Rwandanness" into a simple, singular, homogenizing narrative. The process through which the history curriculum is being generated also lacks genuine dialogue and consensus, leading Rwandans to experience censorship and self-censorship. The Rwandan government is founding history on selective episodes that exclude many Rwandans, and it is failing to address and challenge the social cleavages and exclusion that have characterized Rwanda's past. Indeed, even though the narrative is different, the reductionist view of history and tendency toward top-down teaching are reminiscent of the pre-genocide situation. Teachers recounted frustration at the constraints, especially among Hutu students.[150] Exclusion of some Rwandans is provoking horizontal inequalities below the surface that could help lay the foundations for future violent interethnic conflict.

Given the salience and importance of the multiple, and often contradictory, narratives that emerged in my interviews, building a nuanced history into curriculum seems imperative. But the question of how to arrive at a nuanced narrative in Rwanda is even more complicated than in other divided societies, such as Northern Ireland or the former Yugoslavia. A common idea is to bring the multiple sides to the table for debate, as the *Facing History* initiative attempted to do within the constraints imposed by the current government's narrative; Mamdani suggests that interpretations should be allowed to "compete in the marketplace of ideas."[151] Given the practice of self-censorship in which most Rwandans engage, it is unlikely that many people would participate openly

---

[147] Buckley-Zistel 2006, p. 131.
[148] Freedman et al. 2008, pp. 676–677.
[149] Ross 2007, p. 318.
[150] Author's personal communication.
[151] Mamdani 2001, pp. 278–279.

in such a process. Because ethnic identification is outlawed, Hutu and Tutsi versions of history cannot be discussed in a public forum prior to important political reform. A multiplicity of historical narratives also comes up against a justice system based on one dominant account of history.

As reviewed in Chapter 1, scholars working on history in divided societies suggest that narratives can help foster reconciliation when they encourage critical analysis and learning about each side's framings, create alternative narratives including points of convergence, foster mutual affinity between groups and stories of past cooperation, frame narratives in more nuanced ways, encourage cross-cutting ties, and promote common views of the future. As Elizabeth Cole and Judy Barsalou write, "even when one party to the conflict clearly is more responsible for promoting or creating the structural conditions that led to violence, history education can make a positive contribution by acknowledging that all parties participated in the violence and pointing out the relative roles of different groups."[152] As noted earlier, this should not devolve into obfuscation or denial; *tout comprendre* need not be *tout pardonner*. Yet, the historical narratives taught in schools are not living up to their potential to make a positive difference in Rwanda and appear moreover to be bolstering ethnic divisions through forced ethnic unity and silence.

History and Ethnicity

An especially difficult subject in history is the question of ethnicity. The Rwandan government favors recategorization of identity as a collective Rwandanness, with the subtext that ethnicities do not exist, or at the very least do not matter. Interview participants often prefaced their views on ethnicity with "we are told that," or "our government says that," hinting that their genuine opinion may differ from the government line. "The government gave the order to put Rwandans together," explained one individual.[153] Legitimations for "Rwandanness" include that ethnicities were a fabrication of colonialists and thus untrue or that one cannot tell a Hutu from a Tutsi. The most educated interviewees explained that Hutu, Tutsi, and Twa are not "ethnicities," but may be other types of categories.

Findings have to be put into the context that interview participants, and especially students, believed that they could be jailed for simply *saying* their ethnicity:

> But if you speak of that [ethnicity], they put you in jail. Yep. If they catch you, you have to go directly to jail.... So today you hide that, because if they hear you say it, they can punish you.[154]

> But you shouldn't talk about ethnicity. If you speak of that, they put you in prison!

[152] Cole and Barsalou 2006, p. 4.
[153] Author's interview, male Tutsi, Kigali, March 11, 2006.
[154] Author's interview, female Tutsi, southern Rwanda, February 14(C), 2006.

Author: I would like some precision. You think they'll put you in jail if you do what?

If you speak of your ethnicity.

Author: How did you learn that?

They teach it in class and it's talked about on the radio.

Author: Is it just not good to say it, or they can put you in jail?

In jail! It is really bad to talk about that because war will restart again.[155]

It appears that these understandings are coming, at least in part, from schools. Teachers too are fearful about any discussion of ethnicity, and there is great disagreement as to whether the issue of ethnicity should be taught in schools.[156] Government officials denied that people could be jailed for merely mentioning ethnicity. Yet, the new social studies texts define and equate ethnic "division" with "categorization,"[157] and Rwandans had widely heard about schools being closed and teachers imprisoned for the vague offense of divisionism.[158] Experts concur that the government "has created a phobia of speaking about ethnicity."[159]

Students who had been schooled in the post-genocide period were frequently of the understanding that ethnicity caused the genocide. One declared, "If we keep teaching and talking about [ethnicity], there will be another genocide; another war can be born."[160] Another explained that people should not talk about ethnicity "because it is bad and it will bring war and is bad for the development of the country."[161] Most youth could also state other causes for violence, including ignorance, misunderstanding, and bad leadership, but they still tended to equate the existence of ethnicity with violent conflict.

Meanwhile, ethnicities are not disappearing in Rwanda.[162] While, of course, the years since the genocide comprise a relatively short time in which to judge identity change, the same interviewees that claimed that ethnicity did not exist readily pointed to Hutu and Tutsi in their classrooms and in the street:

It's that there are physical traits upon which you can say that this one is Hutu and that one is Tutsi. For example, when one has a big nose. Me, for example, you can easily tell than I am Hutu because I do not have very refined traits, but a poor, unhappy Tutsi risks appearing to be a poor Hutu. It's very difficult today. But, despite everything, children can usually tell from first sight, yes, he is this, she is that [ethnicity].[163]

---

[155] Author's interview, female Hutu, northern Rwanda, April 1, 2006.

[156] Freedman et al. 2008, p. 679.

[157] Bamusanire et al. 2006f, p. 43.

[158] See also Bonny Mukombozi, "School in Genocide Ideology Scandal," *The New Times*, August 31, 2007; Sarah Mumvaneza, "Imprison That Teacher," *The New Times*, September 1, 2007.

[159] Author's interview, education administrator, northern Rwanda, March 17, 2006.

[160] Author's interview, female Hutu, northern Rwanda, March 22(A), 2006.

[161] Author's interview, female Hutu, northern Rwanda, April 3(C), 2006.

[162] For a similar analysis based on interviews with urban youth, see McLean Hilker 2009.

[163] Author's interview, male Hutu, Kigali, February 6(B), 2006.

You ask if you have a father, "no," you know it's a Tutsi. If you see scars, surely you know. Or someone says they don't have a father, nor a mother, no sisters, and they tell you their whole story. Where they were, what they saw, like that. You get ideas and it [ethnicity] comes out very easily.[164]

Do you think that one with an imprisoned father isn't known as a Hutu? That a child that is paid by FARG isn't recognized as a survivor?[165]

Others explained that different ethnicities are "a fact," and a good number made clear that ethnicities cannot be erased:

That is the policy [that ethnicities do not exist], but the daily reality is that we know that ethnicity cannot be erased like that, all in one shot. It still exists in our hearts. Everyone knows who is there and when you are sitting there and you see a Hutu, you know it is a Hutu. There are conversations you can't have in the presence of a Hutu. There are conversations that Hutu can't have in the presence of a Tutsi.[166]

The Rwandan government's ban on ethnicity is an example of conflict avoidance, making students fear ethnicity rather than deal with it.

There are many reasons to believe that in Rwanda, the recategorization approach to an all-inclusive and conforming "Rwandanness," at least in the top-down way it is currently deployed, is unlikely to be successful. First, the "Rwandanness" policy is reaching unity without reconciliation by commanding individuals to unite. There is a difference, as many of my interviewees pointed out, between parroting unity and reconciliation and living it. As one man summarized, "We say that we have reconciliation and unity, we sing it in the radios, in the *ingandos*, everywhere, and in the radio we hear this, but in practice it is lacking. That's the problem."[167] Genuine reconciliation cannot be coerced. Denying ethnicity may merely be suppressing the difficult intergroup dialogue that Rwandans require to work through reconciliation to peacebuilding.

Second, identities matter. Social Identity and Self-Categorization Theories tell us that Rwandans are likely to find meaning in identity groups, which may be even stronger after the experience of violence. Arguments based on the nonexistence of ethnic groups are of little use because it is not their objective existence, but the fact that people believe in them, that matters. This is not to say that other categories do not and have not mattered in Rwanda – class and region, for instance, have been important categories throughout Rwandan history. Yet ethnicity has played an important part too. By forbidding ethnicity, the government is driving it underground and actually may be making it more intriguing to Rwandan youth.

Third, even though ethnicity is constructed, it is not infinitely malleable. As Staven Majstorovic explains, myth and memory impose constraints on identity

[164] Author's interview, female Hutu, northern Rwanda, April 1, 2006.
[165] Author's interview, female Hutu, southern Rwanda, March 15(C), 2006.
[166] Author's interview, female Tutsi, Kigali, February 8(G), 2006.
[167] Author's interview, male Hutu, Kigali, April 5(B), 2006.

transformation. "Identity is not produced upon a blank slate, and ethnic groups do not suffer from historical Alzheimer's disease. There is historical clay that needs to be reshaped, and the shape of the clay in a previous epoch is a constraining factor to the political elites in a subsequent historical juncture."[168] As Joseph Moreau argues in the context of the United States, while forgetting is central to the reconstruction of identity and history, "[r]epressing truths about subjects central to a country's identity, as slavery and racism are to the United States, makes it impossible to construct a version of the national past that doesn't collapse under its contradictions."[169] This is all the more true, as in Rwanda, when ethnic violence has caused immense death and suffering and ethnic differences can thus not easily be wished away.

Fourth, the emphasis on youth's ability to achieve the recategorization model goals, although understandably hopeful, is overly optimistic. It is commonly acknowledged that "chosen traumas" are easily absorbed by the children of a group and passed on through generations, even to those who did not experience them firsthand. For example, when a Serb village librarian was interviewed regarding a recent conflict in his town, "in his explanation of what happened the day before, he went back to 1943 at least."[170] That this will be done for generations to come with the Rwandan genocide is not unlikely. Even constructivists recognize that ethnicity can become resistant to wholesale change.

Fifth, the goals of peacebuilding and the maintenance of power for the Kagame regime are likely to be contradictory. The government of Rwanda calls its goal "unity and reconciliation," but this is a tricky assertion. There may be no alternative to emphasizing peace and a broader Rwandan identity, and denying difference, in a state in which a group of select Tutsi hold, and wish to maintain, disproportionate power. Lemarchand calls ethnic amnesia a "rational choice" in order to maintain ethnic hegemony.[171] Imposed ethnic amnesia may help the government maintain power for now, but will not necessarily bring sustainable peace. Moreover, the Rwandan government's strategy is full of potentially destructive contradictions. The Kagame government simultaneously espouses that reconciliation is underway and that ethnicity no longer matters, while it also bases its rule on the notion that Tutsi status as victims of the genocide grant it the moral high ground and right to make decisions. The hypocrisy of maintaining both positions is evident in the feelings of deprivation engendered by such practices as a singular narrative of Hutu perpetrators and Tutsi victims and the distribution of educational scholarships.

It is worth inquiring whether other social peacebuilding strategies might work better than attempting to force group erasure. Some Rwandans argued

---

[168] Majstorovic 1997, p. 173.
[169] Moreau 2003, pp. 337–338.
[170] Quoted in Davies 2004, p. 81.
[171] These comments are in reference to Burundi, but are equally applicable to Rwanda. Lemarchand 1994, pp. 30–32.

that people can at the same time embrace Rwandanness and maintain different ethnicities, so long as ethnic groups are not used as a basis for discrimination. As one Rwandan put it, "We need to explain that there are differences, and that these differences should make the country's richness, because each ethnicity has something to bring to this country."[172] A hybrid identity strategy, for example, would involve positive and simultaneous appreciation of Hutu and Tutsi – which has never been truly achieved in Rwanda – and a host of other categories. Rwandans themselves could enjoy the freedom to determine their constantly transforming identities, loyalties, and priorities from among the many groups to which they already simultaneously belong. Such a strategy might overcome a number of the conflict-conducive pitfalls of the current recategorization approach. If Rwandans' experiences consistently show them that ethnicity is not a politically important category, they may themselves eventually choose a bottom-up recategorization to Rwandanness.

In short, however, the current approach to ethnicity, including how it is being addressed in the history curriculum, hides inequalities. Such an approach prevents reconciliation and is therefore unlikely to build sustainable peace.

Pedagogy, Language, and Classroom Practices

Pedagogy, language, and classroom practices are additional ways in which schooling underlies conflict or peace, and teachers are at the center of these practices. The decimation of teachers in 1994 prompted important challenges for installing a post-genocide teaching force and for pedagogy. Many teachers have since returned, some Rwandans that were long-time exiles have been added to the teaching cadre, and there are at least eleven pedagogical institutes conducting teacher training for new and unqualified or underqualified teachers.[173] As George Njoroge comments, "teachers are among those accused of committing genocide in Rwanda in 1994," and so they now need new kinds of training in order to become positive agents of change in post-genocide Rwanda.[174]

Teachers face an enormous task and a number of obstacles. Njoroge describes some innovative techniques being implemented at the Kigali Institute of Education (KIE), Rwanda's most elite teacher training institution, to "reconstruct the teacher's psyche."[175] Several experienced teachers with whom I spoke mentioned much more basic post-genocide pedagogical training that has been made available to all. It is a challenge, however, even for those receiving the most innovative instruction, that teachers are being trained in an increasingly repressive context at odds with some of the values that they may be learning, such as openness to talking about the past,

---

[172] Author's interview, male Hutu, Kigali, April 8(B), 2006.
[173] RoR 2002b, p. 9.
[174] Njoroge 2007, p.215.
[175] Ibid.

which Njoroge notes is encouraged at KIE.[176] As a result of this atmosphere, teachers interviewed by Freedman and colleagues also explained a fear of discussing conflicts in class.[177] At least one NGO program promoting "active pedagogy" was shut down by the government, despite its success at reaching program goals.[178] As such, the importance of the mainstream historical narrative is amplified by schools.

The introduction of other genocides in both the civics and social studies curricula may be a good analytical thinking tool and a way to broach topics that may otherwise be too difficult to discuss. Such "distancing" techniques, used in Rwanda and elsewhere, are discussed further in Chapter 5.

Language is also central to the experience of schooling. As I have shown in previous chapters, the politics of language have been important in education in Rwanda. Aptitude in the language of state power – French during the colonial period and two Republics and English today – is of great consequence, and students raised the improvement of language training as one of their key priorities. The current English-language policy causes many challenges in the classroom. At the primary school level today, a majority of classes are supposed to be taught in English, despite most teachers' difficulty with the language. Rwandan teachers currently attend night classes to learn English while teaching it during the day. According to some reports, the total of teacher training in English amounts to just twenty days.[179] As a result, the overall quality of education is declining significantly. Most students that I met in 2009 had extremely low or even no English-language comprehension. I found some optimism, and a lot of resignation, on the part of teachers regarding the recent change to English. Already overworked and underpaid, largely French-speaking teachers feel that they are losing out in the transition. For some, the English-language policy is subtly removing teachers who were in Rwanda before the genocide from the classroom.

Indeed, the move to English is top-down, compulsory, and has important political effects. Beth Samuelson and Sarah Freedman report that in one case, refusal to teach in English was interpreted as evidence of "genocidal ideology."[180] They further note that the English-language policy is beyond critique because "political dissidents who lived in Rwanda before the genocide are likely to be Francophone and are effectively silenced by the switch to English."[181] As one teacher told a Canadian magazine, the switch to English language is like "telling me to keep quiet. It's stopping me from talking."[182]

---

[176] Ibid.
[177] Freedman et al. 2008, p. 665.
[178] Alidou, Gasibirege, and Muyango 2007.
[179] Helen Vesperini, "Rwanda Teachers Struggle to follow Switch to English," *Agence France-Presse*, February 19, 2010.
[180] Samuelson and Freedman, 2010, p. 199.
[181] Samuelson and Freedman 2010, p. 196.
[182] Halejriis 2010.

Yet, certain groups can benefit from this change. Tutsi with English-language backgrounds from Uganda, as well as those Rwandans of the upper class who can access private schools, are likely to learn more quickly and have better access to general education, as well as English, the language of opportunity. Only 1.9 percent to 5 percent of Rwanda's population speaks English and almost all of those are returnees.[183] Hutu in general, and Tutsi without family experience in Anglophone countries, are likely to learn English of a lower quality and more slowly and are likely to miss out on other topics too because they are ostensibly taught in English. Language policies are producing new horizontal inequalities that intersect with background. Samuelson and Freedman describe English and French speakers as rival political elites.[184]

Language has become a very sensitive political issue at risk of dividing the society into Anglophone and Francophone Rwandans. Njoroge warns that "[t]he English and French languages become new labelling tools among Rwandans perpetuating the 'US' versus 'THEM' dichotomy."[185] For example, a student council election at the tertiary-level Kigali Institute for Science and Technology was plagued by Anglophone-Francophone conflict.[186] Njoroge found that teacher-learners at the Kigali Institute for Education, where he conducted his research, define themselves not as Rwandan but as Francophones and Anglophones. Recent personal communications suggest that French-speaking Hutu and Tutsi may be finding some common ground in a joint experience of marginalization.

At the same time, many raised the disjuncture in the country between English and French speakers and were concerned that this divide could replace or be superimposed on the Hutu-Tutsi cleavage, thereby replicating "historical language divides related to power and ethnicity."[187] Njoroge reports that each identity is invested with collectivized characteristics, such as the stereotype that French-speaking students work harder than English-speaking ones.[188] I heard this among Hutu interviewees, with the implication that Anglophone Tutsi students need not work hard because everything in Rwanda will be handed to them on a plate. The language policy promotes collectivized and stigmatized groups, which could underlie future conflict.

Beside access and what is being taught, informal classroom relations give insight into the peace and/or conflict role of schooling. Despite students' varying experiences, most Rwandans said there were no problems between classmates in primary schools today, although problems between diverse students were common immediately after the war. Indeed, the quality of relations

---

[183] Samuelson and Freedman 2010, p. 195.
[184] Ibid., p. 196.
[185] Njoroge 2007, p. 222 (emphasis in the original).
[186] See Innocent Gahigana, "Phone Wrangles Stall Kist Guild Race," *The New Times*, June 25, 2007.
[187] Rutayisire 2004, p. 13.
[188] Njoroge 2007.

between students of different backgrounds appears to fluctuate, as in previous periods, with the wider political context. A number of Rwandans noted that genocide mourning week and *gacaca* trials heighten tensions in classrooms and in schoolyards.

Moreover, interethnic conflict may be on the rise in secondary schools. My conversations with Rwandan students and teachers in 2006 suggested subtle intergroup tension, such as the survivor/non-survivor status dynamics surrounding FARG. A parliamentary report on genocide ideology in schools released shortly thereafter, however, claims that survivors are openly ridiculed and harassed. Some pamphlets are alleged to include violent messages such as: "Tutsi are snakes, we are fed up with them, and we will kill them."[189] At a school in southern Rwanda, ranked as being one of the worst schools in terms of "genocide ideology," ex-patriot teachers reported finding graffiti in the bathrooms, presumably written by Hutu, to the effect that "Tutsi are favored" and "You're treated too well. You'll see, it will change. You'll suffer like us." They also noted that they have seen messages, presumably written by Tutsi, to the effect that "we'll get more now that we're in power."[190] I heard stories about a female Hutu student in southern Rwanda who was sent to jail for asking a question about survivors that could (or could not) have been interpreted in a disrespectful way, and one about a teacher imprisoned for conjugating the verb "to insult" in a way that phonetically sounded like he was saying something about Tutsi. These teachers allege that only Hutu are sent to jail on genocide ideology charges.[191] Schools are reflecting, and possibly amplifying, tensions in wider society. These trends need to be addressed if schools are to avoid contributing to conflict and become sites of peacebuilding.

Conclusion: The Peace and Conflict Role of Schooling Today

The findings presented throughout this chapter suggest that the peace and conflict impact of post-genocide schooling is mixed and that on the whole, it warrants concern. On one hand, some positive strides toward peacebuilding have been taken, especially in terms of increased access to basic education and classroom practices at the primary level that do not differentiate Rwandans. On the other hand, Rwanda's education system reflects and amplifies an exclusivist state. Ethnic trends in access to post-primary education are worrisome

---

[189] "Rwanda: Use All Diplomatic Means to Curb Genocide Ideology," *The New Times*, December 18, 2007; "Rwanda 'Still Teaching Genocide'," *BBC News*, January 17, 2008; James Buyinza, "Rwanda: Damning Revelations," *The New Times*, December 12, 2007; James Buyinza, "Rwanda: MPs Grill Education Ministers," *The New Times*, December 19, 2007; Geoffrey Mutagoma, "Genocide Hatred Lingers in Rwanda Schools," *BBC News*, February 19, 2008; Florence Mutesi and James Buyinza, "Rwanda: Shocked MPs Condemn Genocide Ideology in Secondary Schools," *The New Times*, December 13, 2007.

[190] Author's personal communication.

[191] Author's personal communication.

and mirror past trends in how they differentiate, collective, and stigmatize Rwandans with new identities (survivor, perpetrator) that parallel their former ethnic groups. Tensions between groups of Hutu and Tutsi students are also rising in some schools. Language policies are at risk of dividing Rwandans as well. In terms of content and pedagogy, a single, homogenizing narrative is taught in schools, promoting conformity and dangerously excluding the experiences of many Rwandans. Embracing the rhetoric of critical thinking will do little if only a singular narrative is taught. On balance, even though there have been significant successes in the educational sector, there is reason to be wary about the peace and conflict impact of post-genocide education.

I have sketched a rather critical picture of Rwanda in this chapter. Some would contend that my analysis is too critical. In examining processes of peace-building, which are long-term endeavors, the period since 1994 is a relatively short amount of time in which to judge progress. However, there are dangerous parallels with both pre-genocide and colonial periods that need to be addressed if Rwanda's schools are to help the country move toward a more constructive and peaceful future.

5

Education for Peacebuilding

Rwanda in Comparative Perspective

Contrary to the predominantly positive view of education in both literature and practice, a central contention of this book is that education in Rwanda contributed to multiple episodes of violent intergroup conflict. At the same time, Rwanda's education system did not do many of the things that promote peacebuilding: building horizontal equity, shaping inclusive identity strategies, promoting reconciliation, and developing critical thinking skills. Designing education such that at a minimum it does not contribute to underlying conflict – what humanitarians call a "do no harm" approach – and such that, at a maximum, it actively contributes to peace is a challenge around the world. Because there was limited evidence of the positive role of Rwandan education, the findings of this book do not give us answers to "what works" for peacebuilding. They do, however, help us ask the right questions.

As a result, this chapter poses four key questions: How can education be structured to promote horizontal equity between groups? How can teachers tackle history in the aftermath of conflict? How can schools address identity to build peace after identity-based conflict? What is the role of international actors in these post-conflict educational dilemmas? I examine how my study of Rwanda speaks to each of these questions, as well as the additional questions my findings raise. I also consider what we can learn about these challenges from the experience of other societies. I draw primarily on post-conflict settings because they are likely to have the most to teach to and learn from Rwanda and because the peace education literature recognizes particular challenges in regions of intractable conflict.[1] But the same questions apply to education the world over, to different degrees. In some ways, this chapter raises more questions than it answers, and in doing so, it lays out a research agenda for education and peacebuilding.

[1] Kuppermitz and Salomon 2005; Salomon 2002.

How Can Education Be Structured to Promote Horizontal Equity between Groups?

In Rwanda and elsewhere, horizontal inequalities developed through differing levels of access to schooling have been an important foundation of conflict. For example, the 2000 Arusha Peace and Reconciliation Agreement to end the conflict in Burundi specifically names unequal access to education along ethnic lines as "a cause of violence and insecurity."[2] As a result, many countries have tried to address horizontal inequalities in education. In Burundi, the agreement explicitly appeals for equitable allocation of schools and educational equipment for all Burundians. This is similar to the current approach, at least rhetorically, in Rwanda. Does horizontal equity only require an "equal playing field" where each student can enter school and then succeed or fail on his/her own merit? This is, in itself, very difficult to achieve. In Rwanda, intentional and unintentional inequalities link just below the surface of post-primary education.

In some contexts, desegregation is a first step. One way that Rwandan schools fostered horizontal inequality was through its segregation and streaming practices in the early parts of colonial rule. This process has been even stronger in other cases, such as Northern Ireland, where de facto segregation in schools along religious/identity lines dates to even before the 1921 partition of Ireland.[3] There was a distinction in Northern Ireland between "state controlled" schools, which have historically received full funding, and less well-funded "voluntary schools," which retained more management autonomy and included most Catholic schools. Funding for the two types of schools gradually increased since the 1930s, especially with antidiscrimination laws in the 1970s, but reached parity only in the 1990s. These discrepancies in resource allocation produced important horizontal inequalities. In brief, throughout most of the twentieth century, Catholics had unemployment rates almost twice as high as Protestants, their incomes were generally lower, and they had worse access to housing. In the late 1980s, the Standing Advisory Commission on Human Rights (SACHR) reported that different levels of educational achievements between students leaving Protestant and Catholic schools led to occupational and economic inequalities later in life. Moreover, the SACHR attributed the inequalities between the two groups, at least in educational quality and employment patterns, to different funding patterns for Catholic and Protestant schools. These inequalities reflected and amplified essentialized intergroup differences and power relations in Northern Ireland.

The findings are similar in South Africa, where schooling is said to have helped entrench and justify apartheid and to have fostered horizontal inequality via unequal access to quality education.[4] Schooling for whites was free and

[2] Quoted in Dupuy 2008.
[3] This paragraph draws on Dunn and Morgan 1999; Gallagher 1998; Hayes, McAllister, and Dowds 2007; Smith 2001.
[4] Christie 2009.

obligatory until the age of fifteen, and enrollment rates were comparable to the world's most developed countries, whereas schooling was optional for people of other races. Per capita funding for a white child was twelve times that for a black child.

As a result, a first potential strategy for improving horizontal equity, where applicable, is desegregation, which can reduce social-structural grievances and improve psychocultural perceptions. Approximately 6 percent of students in Northern Ireland now attend integrated schools, with many studies referenced in Chapter 1 showing positive results on horizontal equity and intergroup relations. In post-apartheid South Africa, as in Rwanda and Burundi, opening school doors to all students has been a key goal for post-apartheid governments working toward a more equitable society and on building positive relationships among citizens. Studies have found that South Africa's now desegregated school system has increased contact among individuals of different racial groups inside and outside schools and improved students' attitudes toward other groups.[5] Yet, achieving a sense of horizontal equity by desegregating schools is very difficult. In South Africa, because educational inequality was so high, merely equalizing the playing field at the point of entry may be inadequate. As one scholar notes, "Leaving peace, equity, and justice to chance ... inevitably opened possibilities of not only continuing existing inequalities but also of increasing them."[6]

Indeed, horizontal equity may demand more to address historic injustices. A number of countries hoping to mitigate conflict have thus gone further to promote horizontal equity – implementing preferential policies of different kinds, such as the quotas in Rwanda during the two republics. However, the results of these policies are mixed in their ability to produce positive intergroup relations. For example, the 2001 peace agreement for Macedonia and the 1997 peace agreement for Bangladesh, rather than vaguely calling for equality in access, include affirmative action programs and scholarships to help remedy past inequalities and appear to have had some success at ameliorating intergroup relations.[7] Similarly, in Malaysia, systematic affirmative action, including educational quotas and targets, helped improve the position of the Bumiputera vis-à-vis ethnic Chinese and to dispel tensions between groups.[8] Yet, in Sri Lanka, policies to reverse colonial era advantages for Tamils, including educational quotas and Sinhalese language policies, fostered sharp societal change, created new inequalities, and are considered to have contributed to Tamil rebellion.[9] Likewise, in Rwanda, the ethnic and regional quota system implemented during the two Republics did not attenuate intergroup inequality. Indeed, ethnic

---

[5] Holtman et al. 2005.
[6] Christie 2009, p. 82.
[7] Dupuy 2008.
[8] Stewart 2002, p. 20.
[9] Ibid.

and regional quotas under Presidents Kayibanda and Habyarimana, as well as jealousy over scholarships for genocide survivors under President Kagame, likely increased intergroup conflict. Researchers caution in particular about change that is zero-sum. As Tony Jackson writes of education in Burundi, improving the situation for one group at the cost of the other "would provoke a backlash that could easily re-ignite conflict."[10]

Horowitz's assertion that "it is too soon for a definitive evaluation of preferential policies, but it is not too soon for skepticism regarding their impact" remains true today and is further strengthened by my findings in Rwanda.[11] More comparative work is needed to understand the impact of post-conflict preferential policies, particularly in education. The case of Rwanda suggests that particular variables of interest include the types of preferential policies (quotas, targets, scholarships, etc.), the magnitude of the preferences, the sensitivity of the selection process, the identifiability of the beneficiaries, and the extent of support to beneficiaries. The links between preferential policies and social mobility, especially higher education and job prospects, also seem particularly important for future research.[12]

Indeed, strategies for promoting horizontal equity open a host of research questions. What happens when equity, however defined, and building sustainable peace come into contradiction, as they sometimes do when preferential policies are implemented? What are the other options when the educational pie is of limited size? What wider issues are related to school access? For instance, denial of access to language skills, through either exclusion from schools or segregation, was an additional channel for promoting horizontal inequalities in Rwanda. What about equitable access to jobs? We still need a better understanding of how and why specific public policies best contribute to horizontal equity in post-conflict contexts under different historical and political circumstances. Education policies matter on their own and also cannot be divorced from other policy areas.

How Can Schools Address History in the Aftermath of Conflict?

The preceding three chapters, which described Rwanda from the colonial period to today, showed that alongside the structure of education, the content of education – and especially how history is taught – has potentially destructive implications for intergroup relations. Teaching history is thus a particularly contentious issue. This is true far beyond Rwanda. At around the same time as Rwanda was placing a moratorium on history teaching post-genocide, so-called history wars were ongoing around the world. In the United States, legislators battled about history curriculum standards and such issues as which

---

[10] Jackson 2000, pp. 3–4.
[11] Horowitz 1985, p. 676.
[12] Weisskopf 2004.

historical figures to include.[13] In Afghanistan, anonymous secret letters were delivered to school officials threatening violence to those who dared change the school curriculum.[14] In post-war Lebanon, the creation of new textbooks involved more than six years of discussion and compromise, ultimately ending in suspended distribution in objection to a lesson in the third grade textbook about the nature of the 636 AD Arab conquest.[15]

Given the difficulty and political sensitivity of determining what history to teach, some post-conflict countries have experimented with historical silence. German policy makers did not integrate the Holocaust into school curriculum until nearly twenty years after the end of World War II.[16] In Cambodia, where the legitimacy of the post-genocide regime was tied to narratives about past violence, the Vietnamese-backed People's Republic of Kampuchea put the genocide and other Khmer Rouge crimes front and center in curriculum. Later, following UN-backed elections in 1993, most of the references to the Khmer Rouge period were removed from schools in favor of silence, a reconciliation discourse, and the reintegration of some Khmer Rouge officials.[17] In 2002, some historical material was introduced to ninth and twelfth grades, but it was vague and limited in scope.[18] Is there a case to be made for avoiding these controversial issues? Summarizing the need for better research on teaching history, Davies notes: "After a conflict, in my experience, there is a general downplaying of the causes and results of violence in the interest of promoting and maintaining 'harmony.' Yet we need to know whether this silence does indeed foster harmony or whether it simply leaves the learner open to other influences."[19] Further development of comparative research, including cases that have experimented with short- and long-term silence, would be exceptionally useful.

My analysis of Rwanda questions whether reconciliation is possible without teaching history. Silence on certain topics and perspectives may obstruct peacebuilding, as it has in Rwanda. Likewise, one scholar of Cambodia concludes that "the absent or limited education since the peace agreement has culminated in sustained myths, unanswered questions and denial in Cambodian youth," which presents challenges for Cambodia's future.[20] Hughes and Donnelly came to similar conclusions in their comparison of integrated education in Northern Ireland and bilingual/binational education in select schools in Israel. The schools that they studied in Israel tackle divisions and discuss them. In contrast, the schools they researched in Northern Ireland avoid divisive issues,

[13] Moreau 2003, p. 10.
[14] Jones 2009, p. 117.
[15] Frayha 2004.
[16] Education For All Global Monitoring Report team 2011, p. 243.
[17] Hinton 2008; Munyas 2008.
[18] Munyas 2008.
[19] Davies 2005, p. 54.
[20] Munyas 2008, p. 428.

and teachers and parents endeavor to make the school a "neutral" space.[21] Teachers and parents interviewed in Northern Ireland were much less positive about the effectiveness of integrated schools than those interviewed in Israel. The research suggests that the Israeli approach of embracing the diversity and nuance of contrasting narratives may facilitate new learning about the out-group and challenge negative stereotypes. In comparison to the schools they studied in Israel, Hughes and Donnelly believed that the schools in Northern Ireland generate less tolerant and more prejudiced individuals.[22]

My findings in Rwanda, as well as the aforementioned examples from Northern Ireland and Israel, suggest history teaching that fosters critical thinking, debate, and individual agency has a better chance of helping build peace than rote memorization of any singular historical narrative. But while it might be reassuring to have a well-tested recipe book, it is impossible to determine what exactly a history curriculum or textbook should say. The same narratives can be used for multiple, and even contradictory, purposes. In Rwanda, in the colonial period, the Hamitic hypothesis that Tutsi were from Ethiopia was used to justify Tutsi superiority. In the post-independence period, however, the same story was used to exclude Tutsi as foreigners. In Israel and Palestine, for example, people that are described by one side as martyrs are often terrorists to the other. In the United States, the voyage of Christopher Columbus is traditionally celebrated as the "discovery" of America, but the same event is considered by a growing group as the beginning of genocide against Native Americans. In this sense, historical narratives are akin to Ann Swidler's cultural "tool kit ... which people may use in varying configurations."[23] One can only really discover in hindsight how a particular frame will be deployed, and much depends on "memory entrepreneurs."[24]

Nonetheless, NGOs have piloted many innovative initiatives to replace conflict-conducive history teaching. For instance, in Israel, Jewish children are traditionally taught a negative view of Arabs in their mainstream textbooks. A study of 124 textbooks on grammar, literature, history, geography, and citizenship shows how "Jews are industrious, brave and determined, and able to improve the land," in contrast to Arabs, who "are incapable, unproductive, and apathetic, as well as sick, dirty, noisy, colored, easily inflamed, hostile, deviant, cruel, immoral, unfair, and bloodthirsty."[25] History is presented to youth as zero-sum; positives for Jewish Israelis are negatives for Arabs, and vice versa. In a creative effort to overcome negative collectivization and stigmatization and to build reciprocity and a shared view of the future, the Peace Research Institute in the Middle East (PRIME) initiated a multiyear exercise to develop

---

[21] Hughes and Donnelly 2007, p. 127.
[22] Ibid., p. 131.
[23] Swidler 1986, p. 273.
[24] Jelin 2003; Payne 2001.
[25] Starrett and Doumato 2007.

parallel historical narratives from Israeli and Palestinian perspectives.[26] In the early 2000s, in the midst of violent conflict, the project engaged teachers in the production of the material and translated it into Hebrew and Arabic. The texts were then tested, with mostly positive receptions, in the Palestinian and Israeli classrooms of the teachers that helped produce them. A blank space was intended to be placed between the two written narratives so that teachers and students could work toward building bridges and bringing the versions closer together.[27] The project leaders plan to further nuance the material by developing multiple narratives on each side. The overall impact of the initiative, however, was limited. Because peace processes have failed and tensions remain high, the project team tried to keep this work "under the radar" of Israeli and Palestinian education authorities. Wider implementation and a rigorous impact evaluation are thus still pending. A reminder of the entrenchment of education systems in political structures came in 2004 when the right-wing Israeli education minister threatened disciplinary actions for teachers that used the booklets in their classrooms.

While the difference in types of conflict is notable, similar initiatives have been attempted elsewhere. In Canada, after the 1995 referendum in Québec, when Québécois voted to remain a part of Canada by the slimmest of margins, the Institute for Research on Public Policy published *Si je me souviens bien/As I Recall* (also to be found under the title of *As I Recall/Si je me souviens bien*).[28] This initiative examines thirty-four events in Canadian history from different perspectives, such as those of francophone and anglophone Canadians and the federal and Québec governments. According to the book's editors, "divergent assessments of historical events stir up powerful emotions and exacerbate current political tensions ... this collection seeks to bridge the divide not by finding common ground, but by bringing to light the distinctive perspectives of each side."[29] The book was a best-seller at a major book chain in Québec during the year of its release and, thanks to a grant from the Institute for Research on Public Policy, was distributed to all high schools across the country. While the book was generally very well received and was the subject of a number of public meetings and debates, it was sometimes criticized for privileging a Québécois perspective. This is perhaps an inescapable critique, notes one of the book's researchers, when an equal space is granted to interpretations of the minority alongside those of the majority.[30] Some schools in the United Kingdom have developed similar pedagogical exercises to examine the purpose

[26] The information on this initiative comes from Bar-On and Adwan 2006; Joanna Chen, "To Get on the Same Page," *Newsweek*, August 13, 2007.

[27] Pingel 2008, p. 189.

[28] Meisel 1999.

[29] Shira Herzog, "Once Upon a Time ... In Israel and Palestine," *The Globe and Mail*, October 1, 2005.

[30] Author's personal communication.

of history through parallel narratives, and this initiative has spread to other parts of Europe, North America, and South America, as well as Taiwan.[31]

Impact assessments of these programs should be at the top of a research agenda and would do much to move forward the field of peacebuilding education. Note, however, that the described initiatives are generally piloted by NGOs, not by the national governments in charge of "ordinary education." In addition, most of these programs take place at the local level rather than the national level that has been the subject of this book. In theory, these innovative programs could be scaled up if research provided firmer evidence of their positive impact on peacebuilding. As in Rwanda, however, national politicians are often not ready to approve multi-perspective initiatives after conflict.[32] My research in Rwanda confirmed that even creative initiatives can be significantly limited – but not entirely negated – by a closed political context.

One innovation to address conflict in ordinary classrooms is through "distancing techniques," which, in this context, refers to strategies in post-conflict contexts that introduce other conflicts in a way so as to indirectly raise important issues facing the society in question. According to a study in Rwanda, when trainers integrated the discussion of other genocides into their train-the-trainer program (among other issues like trauma and basic needs), participants' trauma symptoms were reduced and "orientation toward the other" scores increased.[33] Another study found similar results: when grade twelve Jewish-Israeli students were taught about conflict in Northern Ireland, they were subsequently better able to imagine things from the point of view of Palestinians than students who had not participated in learning about Northern Ireland.[34] Such strategies are a central tenet of ongoing training by *Facing History and Ourselves*, the NGO that worked to develop curricular material in Rwanda.[35] For distancing techniques to be effective, the environment must be open enough to permit learning transfers. Even so, it appears that some issues need to be discussed more directly.

Moreover, the success of any curricular innovation depends on teachers. Teaching in ways that encourage critical thinking and embrace complexity is difficult. This is all the more true in political contexts, such as in Rwanda, Bosnia, and Northern Ireland, where teachers often fear engaging with political issues, or have themselves been socialized to accept highly exclusive narratives. *Facing History and Ourselves* also operates in the United States, Israel, Ireland, and South Africa to help teachers gain the skills to teach nuanced, controversial, and complex history. Their pedagogical techniques have been very positively evaluated in many studies on such things as raising analytical

[31] Lee 2004.
[32] Pingel 2008.
[33] Staub et al. 2005.
[34] Lustig in Kuppermitz and Salomon 2005, p. 296.
[35] Freedman et al. 2008, pp. 682–683.

skills, awareness of prejudice and discrimination, and tolerance for others with different views.[36] Unfortunately, teachers in Rwanda and beyond are already seriously overburdened and class sizes are currently so large that implementation may be particularly challenging. Further research of this type is required to continue to build a strong evidence base of the impact of different history teaching techniques in various settings.

Additionally, a scoping exercise to specify the aims of education in a given context, and history teaching in particular, is warranted. Even if the goal of education is peacebuilding, which we have seen is not always or exclusively the case – some governments use education to maintain power, as in Rwanda, or to justify violence, as in Nazi Germany – specifics may differ. The goal of history teaching can be social cohesion, promoting democracy, peace and reconciliation, tolerance, national identity, state-building, and/or civic consciousness.[37] History teaching can also play a role in commemoration, acknowledgment, and truth telling.[38] What happens when these goals contradict each other? What should be the balance "between factual accuracy and the inculcation of patriotic pride"?[39] Students also have their own goals. In Rwanda, students and teachers generally expect schools to answer key historical questions, and this has been the case in other contexts as well.[40] However, students also have practical goals, such as learning material to pass an exam and getting a good job. In some instances, these practical goals may be important for peacebuilding insofar as they are able to contribute to a more equitable and economically stable society. Future research needs better to acknowledge and classify the discrepant goals of history teaching in diverse political settings.

How Can Schools Address Identity to Build Peace after Identity-Based Conflict?

Just as history teaching is highly contested, so too are approaches to ethnicity. In the aftermath of the Rwandan genocide, the government chose to make public identification by ethnicity illegal, making the state officially – if not always in practice – ethnically blind. In my analysis, however, ignoring and actively repressing identity has worked against peacebuilding. Some might counter that acknowledging and valuing diversity problematically entrenches differences. These kinds of contestations over how to address identity reach far beyond Rwanda. For example, one of the key debates in writing the curriculum in post-conflict Lebanon regarded the distinctiveness of Lebanese identity in relation to regional Arab identity. Important arguments over

---

[36] See, for example, Barr 2010.
[37] See Barsalou 2005.
[38] Cole 2007a.
[39] Starrett and Doumato 2007, p. 9; see also Torsti and Ahonen 2009, p. 223.
[40] Davies 2005.

terminology – "plural society" versus "diversified society" – also arose.[41] In the United States, revision of national curricular history standards included heated debate that turned references to American "peoples" into American "people."[42]

How should schools address ethnicity in pursuit of peacebuilding after ethnic violence? Education, as a vehicle for socialization and construction of goals and norms, is particularly important in attempts to transform identities. This is also tied to the content of education: how history is taught affects how people view themselves and each other, which in turn can affect their understanding of, and openness toward, other historical narratives. There have been numerous educational initiatives aiming to transform conflict-conducive essentialized and stigmatized groups into more inclusive identities. Approaches, introduced in Chapter 1, include decategorization from groups to individuals, recategorization of previous groups into one group, and positive valuation of group differences. Each has strengths and weaknesses, and relative success will depend on context.

Decategorization, for example, has been attempted through contact workshops, such as the *Seeds of Peace* camp, which brings hundreds of Israeli and Palestinian teenagers together face to face.[43] By doing so, participants may find a mismatch between their existing stereotypes and the other campers that they meet and thus come to see and relate to each other as individuals.[44] In strategies like the *Seeds of Peace* experience, participants may, however, have difficulty generalizing the positive characteristics that they see in individuals from the other group to other individuals from that group whom they have not met, unless they perceive the individual participants as representatives of the whole.[45] Decategorization might also succeed through programs that emphasize the variation of opinions among in-group members and some similarities between in-group and out-group opinions.[46] Furthermore, *Seeds of Peace* is an NGO: similar decategorization approaches in an ordinary school setting may first require successful desegregation.

A second approach to building more inclusive identities is recategorization. Around the world, recategorization has often occurred through assimilation. This is especially true of post-independence African countries that focused on commonalities and national unity in an effort to combat colonial era divide-and-rule strategies.[47] The burden has often been placed on one group to conform to the values and lifestyle of a dominant group and this strategy often institutionalizes power differentials between different groups.

[41] Frayha 2004, p. 181.
[42] Moreau 2003, p. 25.
[43] Wallach 2000.
[44] Fiske and Neuberg 1990.
[45] Johnson and Hewstone 1992.
[46] Korostelina 2007, p. 202.
[47] Dei et al. 2006, pp. 118–119.

An alternative that may be more conducive to peace is to recategorize groups to a common identity at a higher level of abstraction than previous groups. This is mainly achieved by developing common superordinate goals.[48] Some point to Muzafer Sherif's Robber's Cave experiment, where boys at camp were divided into two groups, engaged in competitive activities that produced intergroup antagonism, and were then brought to cooperate and share through common superordinate goals.[49] This is roughly the strategy that the Rwandan government pursues today, where the common goal is development. Yet, the fact that neither the boys in the Robber's Cave experiment nor Hutu and Tutsi in Rwanda have fully given up their original identity groups is indicative of the difficulties in achieving full recategorization. Furthermore, if trust cannot be established, common goals may increase conflict rather than decrease it, and prevent recategorization. Rwanda's experience also illustrates how inclusive recategorization cannot simply be commanded from the top down. Moreover, recategorization to a higher identity will unlikely succeed amid contradictory societal conditions that keep ethnic identities meaningful but illegal because it prevents the open dialogue necessary to build trust, reciprocity, and under-standing between groups.

A third approach to building inclusive identity is positive valuation of group distinctiveness. Strategies to achieve such positive valuation include parallel narratives, where history is presented side by side from different points of view, as discussed previously.[50] It might also include celebrations of multiculturalism and diversity. Multiculturalism addresses some of the weaknesses of the afore-mentioned approaches but is subject to critiques of its own: the positive valua-tion of group distinctiveness may essentialize and reify groups.

Therefore, the best approach may be a *dual identity model*, which combines recategorization with positive valuation of group differences. This fosters a common superordinate identity while preserving subgroup identities. Rwanda's current situation, in which many people have expressed dissatisfaction with the state's effort to ban their original identities, suggests that a dual identity model may be good way forward.

Researchers have the task of applying experiments and normative assertions to in-depth cases studies, as in this book's study of Rwanda, to better understand the conditions under which different education-based identity strategies best contribute to peace. A next step will then be to develop stronger comparative research. For instance, one could usefully contrast Rwanda's recategorization, or unity in homogeneity strategy, with Bosnia's current educational emphasis on separate identities.[51] When the 1995 Dayton Accords put an end to three years

---

[48] Gaertner et al. 2000a; Gaertner et al. 2000b.
[49] Sherif 1967.
[50] See also "Museum of Free Derry." Available at: www.museumoffreederry.org/introduction. html.
[51] See Perry 2003; Stabback 2004.

of violence that pitted Bosnian Croats, Serbs, and Bosniaks against each other and left more than 100,000 people dead, education was left off the agenda. Rather than trying to change the locus of one's identification, Bosnian policy encourages continued identification with one's own ethnic group by dividing responsibility for education between thirteen administrations – the two entities (a Croat-Muslim Federation and a predominantly Serb Republika Srpska), ten cantons with varying majority populations, and the small protectorate of Brcko. Three parallel school systems were developed during the war for the three "constituent peoples," and the children of these different groups are still not generally taught together today. While there are some common lessons, the three groups follow separate curricula and learn about different histories, languages, and cultures. Although the Bosnian strategy differs from that of Rwanda by taking the importance of groups seriously and by assuming they are more enduring than they are erasable, it also prioritizes diversity at the cost of unity, fostering separation and alienation of groups. Furthermore, unlike the Rwandan approach, which denies diversity, the Bosnian strategy must present diversity as a social value to avoid the dangers of essentialization and stigmatization; in contrast to a true multicultural perspective, it fails to do this. In each group – Bosniak, Croat, and Serb – the "we" is exclusive of the others. Even this cursory comparison suggests that a middle-ground approach, a hybrid strategy that simultaneously recognizes both group distinctiveness and includes all groups at a higher level of abstraction, might better contribute toward peacebuilding than the strategies currently being deployed in Rwanda and Bosnia.

What Is the Role of International Actors in These Post-Conflict Educational Dilemmas?

A final issue in terms of post-conflict education relates to the question of outside aid groups and foreign governments. What is the role of the international community vis-à-vis national governments and local communities? Peacebuilding theory suggests that outsiders may have an important role to play, but that the bulk of tasks must remain in the hands of locals, whatever that may mean in practice. The Rwandan grade five social studies textbook similarly teaches students that "[i]nternational organisations can also play their part in building peace in Rwanda but they must listen to what the citizens of our country say."[52] One example of international/national collaboration, often deemed successful, relates to U.S. efforts in post-war Germany to employ indirect influence in the education system, rather than attempting direct control. This approach has been judged important for the relationship between the Allies and the new German government, as well as for German national development, although Americans did not achieve all of their educational goals.[53]

[52] Bamusanire et al. 2006c, p. 56.
[53] Tent 1982.

Some argue, however, that because education affects more than just the local and national levels, there should be an international organization able to provide professional guidelines and standards for curricula.[54] A variety of agencies have made steps in this direction. Both the United Nations (UNESCO) and its precursor, the League of Nations, have long been involved in facilitating inter-state textbook reform, but not intrastate standards.[55] The George Eckert Institute for International Textbook Research provides a reference center for the study of social studies textbooks and supports international comparative analysis.[56] The Inter-Agency Network for Education in Emergencies presents minimum standards for education in states emerging from disasters or violent conflicts, and promotes cooperation between different agents, but does not speak directly to those thorniest political and educational issues discussed in this chapter.[57]

There is a delicate balance to be struck between different actors involved in education. On one hand, as I argue in the next chapter, international support and financial assistance are much needed. Furthermore, it is important that the international community speak up when education systems and governments are not serving their citizens well. On the other hand, national governments and local citizens are best situated to make meaningful educational choices and changes to work toward a sustainable peace.

What happens when various actors' goals are contradictory? Chapter 2 recounted opposition to the transition from missionary to national leadership in schools as Rwanda went through independence, and Chapter 4 noted some of the tensions in present-day Rwanda between the educational recommendations of at least one international collaborative history project and the preferences of the national government. Tensions such as these are common. In Bosnia since 1995, international forces have dominated educational reform and have oftentimes met with significant local resistance.[58] Similarly, in Kosovo, the UN mission initiated major educational reform in 1999 and has largely marginalized Kosovar educators.[59] The UNESCO International Bureau of Education warns about international aid agencies and donors acting as "new missionaries" in the educational reform process, potentially tarnishing their legitimacy. World Bank funding, for instance, is sometimes packaged as "educational reform," but is little more than disguised structural adjustment.[60] Different actors in the international community have additionally used bilateral education aid to support their own linguistic or religious agendas.[61]

---

[54] Heyneman 2003, pp. 35–37. For a similar suggestion, see Van Evera 1994, p. 37.
[55] Pingel 2008.
[56] Georg Eckert Institute for International Textbook Research, http://www.gei.de/en/georg-eckert-institute-for-international-textbook-research.html.
[57] Inter-Agency Network for Education in Emergencies 2004.
[58] Cilliers 2006, p. 185.
[59] Sommers and Buckland 2005, pp. 38–39.
[60] Smith and Vaux 2003, p. 35; UNESCO 2003a, p. 12.
[61] Brock-Utne and Holmarsdottir 2004, p. 80; Frayha 2004.

In many cases, politics determines where aid to education is directed, and "hearts and minds" strategies have long been a key part of this determination. For example, the international community presently dedicates much effort to moderating extremist religious ideologies through education.[62] In the next chapter, I discuss the related securitization of education.

Moving research forward, political scientists, as well as education scholars, could usefully investigate the dilemmas of international involvement in education. For example, what is the difference between peacebuilding and stabilization strategies as they relate to education interventions and international interventions more broadly?[63]

Conclusion

The potential role of education in violent intergroup conflict is neither only a Rwandan nor an African problem, but extends to other continents, cultures, and levels of socioeconomic development. The challenges that Rwanda faces in terms of harnessing education for peacebuilding are no more unique. Findings from previous chapters, as well as the discussion here, affirm that an "add education and stir" approach is inadequate for peacebuilding.[64] The tough questions on specific educational strategies, raised in this chapter, move us a long way from simplistic accounts, in the rebel recruitment literature for instance, of education being a merely binary variable and of peace as being fostered straightforwardly through increased educational access.

This chapter has laid out a number of specific questions that researchers could take up to move forward the peacebuilding education agenda. In addition to academic studies, strong impact evaluations by governmental and nongovernmental organizations could have much to contribute. Given that education is often a microcosm of society, these questions are not only relevant for education scholars and practitioners. They are also entry points into crucial issues in peacebuilding more broadly, such as transitional justice, historical memory, sovereignty, and power sharing. As such, cross-disciplinary dialogue between peace and conflict studies, international studies, and education, of the type initiated in this book, would usefully advance these various fields.

---

[62] Nicholas Kristof, "It Takes a School, Not Missiles " *The New York Times*, July 13, 2008; Mortenson 2009; Mortenson and Relin 2006.

[63] Burde et al. 2011.

[64] Bush and Saltarelli 2000, p. v.

Conclusion

Most of time scholars, as well as governments, international organizations, and aid agencies, work on the presumption that education is a "good thing." This positive view of education carries over into the peace and conflict arena as well: education is considered an important tool of conflict prevention and post-conflict peacebuilding. These presumptions, however, need to be investigated and contextualized; they have resulted in our overlooking the ways in which education can contribute to conflict and under-specifying the ways in which education can contribute to peace. Accordingly, this book discussed how schooling can underlie violent interethnic conflict by creating a permissive environment for it. In doing so, it also suggested how education may alternatively avoid promoting destructive social-structural and psychocultural processes and help build sustainable peace. This reframing places education among a growing number of previously unquestioned issues that are now being reassessed through peace and conflict lenses, from community-driven development interventions, to decentralization, to international observer missions.[1]

Surprisingly, given the inherently political nature of education, political scientists and education scholars interact relatively rarely. This book's arguments, however, required moving across and beyond these disciplinary boundaries. For political scientists interested in conflict, this book drew attention to the oft-ignored issue of schooling. For education specialists, it helped theorize education's roles at the group and societal levels, which have been under-explored in comparison to the individual and institutional levels of analysis. In addition, whereas most education studies examine either the content of schooling (i.e., history lessons, classroom practices) or its structure (i.e., access, segregation), the trend in conflict studies toward linking micro and macro levels encouraged

[1] A few examples are Geschière 2009; Hutchison 2009; King, Samii, and Snilstveit 2010.

focus on both elements and their interaction.[2] This book helped bridge the gap between these two disciplines and direct lines of questioning for further research.

It also pressed scholars of both Rwanda and peace and conflict to critically examine their usual assumptions. Education has been important for intergroup relations and for the reproduction and transformation of identities, but these facts have not been examined in any depth by most experts. In regards to Rwanda, my findings lie in contrast to some international accounts, as well as the accounts of many Rwandans themselves, who blame intergroup conflict in Rwanda on "ignorance."[3] Similarly, the broader and simpler argument that a *lack* of schooling contributes to conflict proved to be somewhat more complicated. The facts on the ground demand a reexamination in scholarly literature of traditional views toward education. As this book showed, education is not a one-size-fits-all cure for conflict-ridden countries and any type of education is not necessarily a "good thing."

I showed that current explanations for intergroup conflict in Rwanda rely on a societal foundation that is often assumed yet inadequately explained. I contended that such leading accounts of violent conflict rely on a foundation of underlying factors and showed that these factors – including horizontal inequalities and categorized, collectivized, and stigmatized groups – manifested through ordinary schooling. In this way, education provided this foundational material upon which proximate causes could take effect, for example, by providing a basis on which ethnic entrepreneurs could mobilize the population to violence. These social-structural and psychocultural factors also provided ordinary citizens with an outlet through which to channel their despair. As such, recognizing the role that schooling played helps us better understand the foundation for intergroup conflicts in Rwanda. I also argued that, despite limited evidence in Rwanda, schooling could contrarily contribute to peacebuilding by promoting horizontal equity, embracing identity strategies that recognize hybridity and complexity, working toward reconciliation by building reciprocity and a shared future, and developing critical thinking skills.

The argument was not that education is a smoking gun; education is neither necessary nor sufficient for either violent conflict or sustainable peace. Instead, its relationship to both is through more complex means of causation that can change in different contexts. Education is a reflector, amplifier, signal, and causal contributor to group-level processes. Different elements of education can work together or be at cross-purposes. Moreover, children's experiences of schooling interact with their experiences in the family, the community, and other institutions, as well as with broader social, economic, political, and environmental forces. Indeed, my argument suggests that we would do well to learn from complexity theorists who embrace multicausality, nonlinearity, and

---

[2] Kalyvas 2006; King 2004.
[3] See, for example, Zorbas 2009, pp. 131–133.

feedback loops, and the fact that many different causal paths can lead to the same outcome.[4]

Nonetheless, I ultimately found that by fostering social-structural and psychocultural processes, schooling contributed to the foundation on which violent conflict became possible in both the colonial period (1919–1962) and during the two Republics (1962–1994). The picture is mixed in the post-genocide period (1994– present): schools make some contributions to peacebuilding, but some of the educational factors that underlay interethnic conflict in the past remain evident, albeit often in new guises.

Policy Implications

A number of practical implications follow from this book's arguments. While the importance of education in the Global South has been recognized as a human right and a key to economic progress, it must also be recognized as linked to both peace and conflict around the world. This is especially important given the high proportion of the population made up by children in the Global South, and is compounded by the increasing emphasis on universal primary education.[5] With almost 43 percent of Rwanda's population under the age of fourteen and school enrollment rates rising, the education system is likely to become an even larger influence on the general population in the future. Similar trends hold throughout Sub-Saharan Africa, where 43 percent of the population is under fifteen years old, and extend to many other parts of the world such as Pakistan (35 percent), Afghanistan (46 percent), and East Timor (42 percent).[6] Given that more than half of out-of-school youth currently live in conflict-affected fragile states[7] and that school enrollment rates are steadily increasing, more and more children in states most prone to violence are likely to find themselves affected by the content and structure of schooling. It is thus crucial to design schooling in ways that do not contribute to conflict, and, whenever possible, that help build peace. In this vein, I make a number of recommendations for policy and practice around the world, as well as for Rwanda in particular.

Global Policy and Practice

First, based on this book's argument that certain kinds of education produce mechanisms recognized as underlying conflict, the content and structure of schooling should be more systematically included as an indicator for early warning lists and conflict risk assessments. While education appears in a few such documents, the major aid donors' conflict assessment tools rarely include

---

[4] See, for example, Gell-Mann 1997; Jervis 1997; Rosenau 1997.

[5] UNDP 2007a; UNESCO 2000.

[6] Population Reference Bureau 2012.

[7] Dolan 2007.

education.[8] Education that displays the negative mechanisms discussed in this book can be seen as an early warning sign of possible impending violence. As discussed throughout, education is a reflector of changes that have already occurred in political circles, as well as an amplifier of those changes.

Evidence of conflict-conducive school structure is easiest to identify in discriminatory and exclusive school institutions and practices. For example, under the Nazi regime, the structure of schools rapidly changed to be more unequal and radicalized along Jewish/Aryan lines. In April 1933, legislation limited the number of non-Aryans to be admitted to high schools to 1.5 percent.[9] Later that same month, all Jewish civil servants, including teachers, were discharged, and remaining teachers were instructed to join a Nazi combatants' organization, to attend school in uniform when possible, and to live in camps. Near the end of 1937, Hebrew teaching in secondary schools was banned and by March 1938, all levels of Jewish religious instruction were prohibited. In November 1938, the system was completely segregated by a total ban on Jews in public schools. This kind of deterioration in the structure of schooling should be a warning sign to the international community of likely future conflict. Similarly, in Yugoslavia, the education system became further decentralized and nationally politicized as the economic and political context worsened in the late 1980s and early 1990s. Nationalist politicians of the three main groups – Serbs, Croats, and Bosniaks – reformed curriculum. Each group was presented as distinct and collectivized. Each side's history was presented as one of victimhood – of "suffering, of deprivation and endangering, caused always by the other nation" – thereby stigmatizing other groups.[10] This transformation of education demonstrates education's role as a reflector of wider society and highlights its potential to be an early warning sign of impending violence.

While pinpointing educational content that tends toward violence along ethnic lines is difficult, it is not impossible. For example, exclusive and mutually incompatible narratives can provide evidence of the categorization, collectivization, and stigmatization of groups that can underlie intergroup conflict. Conversely, mass changes to remove offensive sections in textbooks, such as in post–World War II England and Germany, may offer signs that positive change is in the air.

Second, thinking about education as a peace and conflict issue opens the possibility for schooling to be tackled through a "whole-of-government" approach. The Organisation for Economic Co-operation and Development's (OECD) Development Assistance Committee (DAC) has argued that "successful development in a fragile environment depends, at least in part, on well-

---

[8] Bird 2009; Harff and Gurr 1998; Leaning 2002.

[9] This refers to high schools leading to university. Note that only approximately 1% of the German population was Jewish. As in Rwanda, quotas may have been hard felt, sending an important message, without necessarily being numerically unrepresentative.

[10] Hopken 1996, p. 117; see also Perry 2003, p. 22.

sequenced and coherent progress across the political, security, economic and administrative domains" and that "[w]orking effectively across these domains requires donor countries to adopt a 'whole-of-government' approach."[11] Canada, for example, has attempted a whole-of-government, or 3-D (defense, diplomacy, and development), strategy in its peacebuilding and reconstruction work in Afghanistan since 2005. The United States' Africa Command, Africom, worked with the State Department to implement a 3-D approach in a number of African nations. The United Kingdom has created a specialized agency, now called the Stabilisation Unit, to implement its "whole-of-government" plan. Whole-of-government efforts are also being attempted in the Global South by countries such as Australia, France, Germany, and Sweden, yet they have had limited effect and are assessed by the International Peace Academy as "at best a work in progress."[12]

Because education is simultaneously important for conflict prevention, human rights, and development, as has been discussed in the case of Rwanda, education could be a *sector* of coordinated effort for the "whole-of-government." That is, multiple government departments should better coordinate their efforts toward education. Indeed, lack of coordination has been cited as a hindrance to the impact of education assistance; a Brookings Institute report argues that U.S. government education aid is "punching below its weight" in conflict-affected and fragile states partially as a result of fragmented policies.[13] The Inter-Agency Network for Education in Emergencies could be increasingly used to coordinate international efforts.[14] Thinking about education as a "node," densely linked to a network of policy issues such as development, human rights, and security, could also potentially galvanize political interest and funding for education.

Nonetheless, whole-of-government practices should be broached with caution, so that peacebuilding and/or development initiatives do not become subsumed by a security agenda. While it may be useful to think about education as an unconventional security issue, the interests and priorities of foreign governments and agencies should never surpass the primary intended beneficiaries of educational reform – children and other citizens on the ground in the neediest countries. Furthermore, if education is perceived by those on the ground as part of a hearts-and-minds campaign, education could be rejected, or schools, children, and teachers could be put at increased risk. Moreover, in suggesting a whole-of-government approach, I do not wish to divert attention or money away from education as a human right and development concern to focus entirely on security. Nonetheless, employing a whole-of-government approach to education could bring much needed attention to the relationship

---

[11] OECD 2006.
[12] Patrick and Brown 2007, p. 128.
[13] Winthrop 2010.
[14] Ibid.

between education, peace, and conflict, and serve as a model on how to apply the whole-of-government method to other matters.

Third, it makes sense in many cases that educational issues be included in peace agreements. In her review of peace agreements between 1989 and 2005, Kendra Dupuy found that 55 percent of all peace agreements refer to education and about 70 percent of full agreements (rather than partial agreements such as ceasefires) mention education. She also discovered that some agreements directly address the challenges laid out in this book. For example, the 2000 Arusha Peace and Reconciliation Agreement for Burundi asserts that "one of the causes of violence and insecurity in Burundi … is a discriminatory system which did not offer equal educational access to all Burundian youths from all ethnic groups," and calls for horizontal equity in access to education. In the peace agreements to end identity-based conflicts in Chiapas Mexico, Guatemala, and the Philippines, identity issues are directly addressed through assertions for more pluralistic curricula that incorporate different points of view and values.[15] While progress toward peace agreement goals may be slow – for example only about 6 percent of Northern Ireland's schools are integrated, despite the fact that the 1998 Good Friday Agreement calls for "initiatives to facilitate and encourage integrated schooling" – making a place for education in peace accords symbolizes its importance to both citizens and international actors alike.[16] Progress that is too slow, however, can have the opposite effect: it may lead to disappointment and indicate that schooling is not a priority.

As we have seen throughout this book, implementing post-conflict education is a major challenge, so a peace accord that clearly lays out responsibility, and even the first steps to implementation, may help advance this difficult agenda. In Afghanistan, education was only an "add on" to the peace- and state-building processes. This led to some major educational errors in the first post-Taliban years, such as a large campaign to reprint conflict-conducive textbooks.[17] These mistakes might have been mitigated if education had been taken up earlier and more comprehensively. Similarly, the Dayton Peace Accords in Bosnia, despite being extremely broad in reach, mentioned education only in an annex on human rights and fundamental freedoms. As noted in the preceding chapter, thirteen distinct educational administrations reinforce and perpetuate ethnically divisive politics in Bosnia today. Yet educational administration and education for peace could have been better addressed as part of the peace agreements. Making a place for education in peace agreements may also help ensure the issue is addressed early and attracts international funding, thereby making the most of the peacebuilding potential of education.

Fourth, rather than simply relying on youth to be subjects to education reforms, young people could be invaluable contributors in the process of

[15] Dupuy 2008.
[16] Nolan 2009.
[17] Spink 2005.

school change.[18] Article thirteen of the United Nations' Convention on the Rights of the Child gives children the right to have a say in matters affecting their lives. This book similarly endeavored to give a voice to students, teachers, and parents rather than talking for them. It shows that these constituencies have important opinions and that their support will be key to the success of educational changes. Initiatives such as Rwanda's National Summit for Children and Young People, which annually brings together policy makers and selected children from across the country, demonstrate the potential of youth to meaningfully voice their opinions on peace, even though the authoritarian context reined in this potential.[19] Young people have also been involved in peacebuilding in the South African and Sierra Leonean Truth Commissions, although there too, participation was limited.[20] These types of initiatives should be pursued more frequently in Rwanda and around the world to welcome a broader range of perspectives and to meaningfully engage youth.

Fifth, the Millennium Development Goal, which strives to "ensure that all boys and girls complete a full course of primary schooling,"[21] has attracted much-deserved attention to the importance of primary education. This book argued that alongside universal primary education, access to higher levels of schooling matters for conflict and peacebuilding. In Rwanda, the competition for promotion past primary school has been fierce and has often played out along ethnic lines. Currently, only about 30 percent of children in the least-developed countries go to secondary school.[22] In post-conflict states in particular, there is an imbalance in education aid toward supporting basic education.[23] While the importance of primary education in affecting the overall system is clear, data from World Bank projects show that 43 percent of education-related lending to conflict-affected countries goes to primary, while only 8 percent is earmarked for secondary.[24] The experience of Rwanda illustrates the importance of widening access to secondary school and to employment. Tellingly, the concern of "education but no jobs" was also highlighted in the 2011 *Education for All* (EFA) *Global Monitoring Report* in a section called "education failures can fuel armed conflict."[25]

In addition, the Millennium Development Goals have produced a global focus on quantity. While quantity may be good for economic progress and human rights, the peace and conflict impact of this development is less certain.

[18] Hart 2006.
[19] For more on this initiative, see Pells 2011.
[20] Morill 2004, p. 34; author's personal communications.
[21] UN, "Millennium Development Goals." Available at: http://www.un.org/millenniumgoals/bkgd.shtml.
[22] UNICEF 2009, p. 26, statistical tables.
[23] World Bank 2005, p. xix.
[24] Ibid., pp. 63–64.
[25] Education For All Global Monitoring Report team 2011, p. 165.

Many countries have seen dramatic increases in net enrollment rates, with little attention paid to educational quality.[26] Both the structure and content of education matter for mitigating conflict. Improving access to education will have a positive but limited impact on peacebuilding if, as in Rwanda today, it is not accompanied by changes in the quality of education. In Rwanda's case, this includes, for example, making space for different groups to feel included in the historical narrative.

Sixth, this book calls for sustained national and international commitment to education. Some educational changes can make an impact quite quickly, but to attain the broader peacebuilding goals of socioeconomic transformation and socio-psychological reconciliation, the peacebuilding process must be extended in time. Meaningful social change is best evaluated in terms of decades or even generations.[27]

These commitments need be not only rhetorical, but financial: educational reform is costly and financing educational change is especially challenging for countries emerging from conflict. For example, in 1994, two-thirds of Rwanda's teachers were not qualified and 65 percent of school structures were physically damaged. In post-war Mozambique, 40 percent of schools were destroyed.[28] In Iraq, it is estimated that rebuilding and upgrading primary, secondary, and tertiary education institutions will cost between US$6 billion and US$12 billion.[29] Educational reform requires a significant financial commitment, for teacher training programs, to (re)build physical infrastructure, and to improve quality.

When there are so many other priorities in competition with education, it may be difficult to commit and sustain both international and national government funding at adequate levels to make peacebuilding gains. There is a annual US$9 billion gap between the current funding and the amount required by the basic education Millennium Development Goal. Only two of twenty-eight countries have met their 2005 G8 commitments to education, and just 18 percent of the global aid that does exist goes to conflict-affected and fragile states, even though those are arguably the most in need.[30] Other priorities often trump education. According to the *EFA Global Monitoring Report*, if international donors transferred six days of military spending to basic education budgets, they could likely close the international financing gap for Education for All goals.[31] In Afghanistan, it would cost the United States the same amount to start twenty schools as it does to keep one American soldier on the ground for one year.[32] Many of the world's poorest countries, including those in or emerging from conflict, make the same

---

[26] Bleck and Guindo 2010; Duflo, Dupas, and Kremer 2009.

[27] Lederach 1997.

[28] Smith and Vaux 2003.

[29] Emma Clark, "Iraq Rebuilding 'Could Cost $90bn'," *BBC News*, July 23, 2003.

[30] Dolan 2007, p. 18.

[31] Education For All Global Monitoring Report team 2011, p. 16.

[32] Nicholas Kristof, "1 Soldier or 20 Schools?," *The New York Times*, July 28, 2010.

domestic military-over-education trade-offs, spending far more on the military than basic education.[33]

Sustaining long-term educational funding for current recipients and expanding aid to those in need will be difficult. For the time being, most U.S. educational funding for conflict-affected states goes to Iraq, and in terms of official development assistance, Iraq receives almost as much aid as all of Sub-Saharan Africa. Nonetheless, it is hard to say where attention will be drawn in the future. The volatility in aid makes long-term planning, essential for education, especially difficult.[34] It is also particularly difficult to mobilize funding for higher levels of education, despite its importance.[35] Sustained financial commitments to education around the world are needed.

Policy in Rwanda

Finally, the analysis in the foregoing chapters also allows me to put forth some practical lessons for education in Rwanda for both Rwandan and international policy makers. Equalizing access to schools for all groups is important for peacebuilding. Important progress has been made at the primary level. Clearing up remaining inequalities in secondary school scholarship distribution should be at the top of the to-do list; according to some interviewees, the *Fonds d'Assistance aux Rescapés du Génocide* (FARG) scholarships for genocide survivors are still sometimes awarded to Tutsi who were not in Rwanda at the time of the genocide, or to "ghost students." It is also necessary to improve distribution methods so that they avoid highlighting and singling out survivors, and efforts should be made to fund scholarships for needy groups other than survivors. These changes would reduce the survivor-perpetrator dichotomy and moral hierarchy, at least as developed by schools, and help build horizontal equity and an inclusive moral community.

Another issue to address is the English-language policy. While a quick roll-over to English-language teaching is praised by many in hopes that is will lead to increased social mobility, current capacity is nowhere near sufficient to make this policy a reality. In the interim, it may be doing more damage than good. Teachers, in particular, feel overburdened and underprepared. English-language skills are currently so low that the overall quality of education is declining significantly from already low past levels. This is widening the educational chasm between the privileged, who can access private schools, and the rest. In addition, language, ethnicity, and class often intersect in Rwanda, with richer Tutsi being the most competent in English. The English-language policy thereby potentially contributes to the reproduction of horizontal inequalities between former ethnic groups. It makes sense to slow down and phase in the transition to English to allow teachers better training, to provide students with

---

[33] Education For All Global Monitoring Report team 2011, p. 15.
[34] Dolan 2007, p. 53; Education For All Global Monitoring Report team 2011, pp. 172–175.
[35] World Bank 2005, p. 64.

better-quality instruction, and to reduce inequalities. International support for quality English education – teacher training and didactic material – could also help lessen horizontal inequalities. Supporting high-quality Kinyarwanda education, throughout and beyond the transition, may also help unite Rwandans around their common language.

Changes in history teaching are also required. My findings in Rwanda show that most students, teachers, and parents want schools to address the causes and consequences of violence. Findings also indicate that promoting conformity via a univocal narrative that excludes the experiences of much of the population, especially Hutu, is problematic for peacebuilding. It appears that promoting critical thinking, for example by embracing conflicting narratives with an effort to draw out nuances and similarities, may be more fruitful. Moving from a rhetoric of critical thinking to a reality of embracing it requires supporting teachers in developing their confidence and pedagogical skills[36] as well as allowing them the political space to do this work. The exclusion of Hutu narratives of loss from public space is an important grievance among some segments of the population, which must be addressed to support sustainable peace.

On the issue of ethnicity, my research in Rwanda suggests that endeavoring to recategorize Rwandans as solely Rwandan, without ethnic identities, while the lived experience maintains ethnicity's importance is driving those ethnicities underground and promoting fear, rather than erasing them. Peacebuilders may do better to find other strategies, at least for the time being, that help Rwandans make space for multiple simultaneous and complex identities, including ethnic identities and a broader all-inclusive Rwandanness. As Rwandans themselves come to see that ethnicity does not matter, they may embrace recategorization. Today, however, the suppression of ethnic identities and teaching Rwandanness are unlikely to make an impact while memories of violence along ethnic lines are so fresh and while ethnicity is still perceived to be a source of discrimination throughout the country. These recommendations are interconnected; for example, progress on equitable access to education may help decrease the salience of ethnic categories.

All policy recommendations are a careful balance between theory and the pragmatic situation on the ground. The reality of packed classrooms and underequipped teachers and schools – one that became vivid when I was in charge of a class of sixty third-graders for just fifteen minutes! – must be kept in mind when elaborating educational proposals.

Moreover, the feasibility of all of these policy recommendations is embedded in the political context. Advocating more critical thinking in schools and more space for diverse perspectives in history narratives will come face to face with the reality of an increasingly repressive authoritarian government. Some may wonder if the cost of security in Rwanda today is repression and power asymmetry. But this strategy is certainly not without consequences that may well backfire.

[36] Cole and Barsalou 2006.

For its part, the international community is doing a continued disservice to Rwandans by maintaining silence about, and so often praising, the Rwandan government in the face of the authoritarianism and human rights abuses. As discussed in Chapter 4, this silence may stem from guilt at not having intervened during the genocide. However, international researchers and practitioners are in a special position of privilege. Rwandans often told me things like, "I can't say some things, but you maybe can." This is a responsibility to be taken seriously.

These recommendations will also need modification with time and frequent reassessment. All of the Rwandans with whom I spoke were of an age to have lived through and remember the genocide. Less than twenty years have passed since. Subsequent generations, which are more detached from direct experiences of violence, may require matters to be treated in different ways. Germans, for example, have recognized the need to adapt education as generations grow further and further away from the experience of direct perpetrators and victims of the Holocaust; similarly, second- and third-generation victims of the Rwandan genocide will have different experiences and educational needs than its original victims.

Final Thoughts

Schools have been understudied by those interested in conflict and peacebuilding, and their potential to underlie conflict, in particular, has been neglected. This book consequently asked scholars, policy makers, and practitioners to consider schooling through peace and conflict lenses. In the case of Rwanda, it showed that insight into education's multiple roles is vital to understanding the etiology of ethnic conflict and to using education as a tool to move toward a more peaceful future. There is an African proverb that "the best time to plant a tree is twenty years ago. The second-best time is now." It is high time that we better understand education, to make sure that schooling does not contribute to conflict, and, whenever possible, to harness education for sustainable peace.

Appendix: The Interview Sample

In seeking interview participants who could speak to each temporal period, I tried to vary ethnicity, gender, rural/urban, socioeconomic background, and region in which primary school was attended. In the end, my interviewees were fairly evenly split between Hutu and Tutsi, men and women, and region in which they attended primary school. I over-sampled among Tutsi to ensure that I gathered a wide range of opinions across ethnic cleavages.

Because trust is so low among the general population in Rwanda, I used a multiple snowball sampling technique, involving simultaneous and evolving networks, whereby my interviewees and other contacts recommended me to other people, thus vouching for my basic trustworthiness. All of those sharing their reflections as past students had completed primary school in Rwanda but had not necessarily continued their studies. During the genocide, the youngest interviewees had been four years old, while the eldest were seniors. Interviewees played a variety of roles in the genocide and had been in many different places in 1994.

I interviewed people who could speak to each of the three periods in which I was interested. For instance, I was fortunate to find seventeen interview participants of an age to offer personal experience from the colonial education system. This included twelve Rwandans who had been students and/or teachers during the colonial period and who were in their late sixties, seventies, or eighties at the time of the interviews, as well as a group of older Rwandans who comprised a Rwandan historical society. I also conducted fieldwork in Belgium, locating three former colonial *administrateurs du territoire*, serving from 1946 to 1961, from 1948 to 1961, and from 1951 to 1961, respectively. I furthermore spoke with two Belgian missionaries with direct involvement in the Rwandan colonial education system; these two men collectively offered twenty years of experience in colonial Rwanda and more than one hundred years of on-the-ground experience in the country.

TABLE A.1: *Interviewees by Ethnicity and Gender*

Gender	Ethnicity					
	Hutu	Mixed	Tutsi	Unidentified	Belgian	Total
Female	16	2	17	3	0	38
Male	17	1	10	4	5	37
Total	33	3	27	7	5	75
N = 75						

TABLE A.2: *Interviewees by Region and Gender*

Gender	Region			
	Kigali	North	South	Total
Female	15	11	12	38
Male	8	15	9	32
Total	23	26	21	70
N = 70				

Region refers to the location in which the interviewee attended or taught primary school. While many interviewees attended secondary schools in other regions, the focus here is on primary schooling as it provides a clearer picture of where the subject, and his or her family, are from. Interviewees who both attended and taught at Rwandan primary schools, but in different regions, are categorized by the location at which they were students. The tables that categorize interviewees by region do not include the five Belgian interviewees.

TABLE A.3: *Interviewees by Ethnicity and Region*

Region	Ethnicity				
	Hutu	Mixed	Tutsi	Unidentified	Total
Kigali	4	0	16	3	23
North	21	2	2	1	26
South	8	1	9	3	21
Total	33	3	27	7	70
N = 70					

Region refers to the location in which the interviewee attended or taught primary school. While many interviewees attended secondary schools in other regions, the focus here is on primary schooling as it provides a clearer picture of where the subject, and his or her family, is from. Interviewees who both attended and taught at Rwandan primary schools, but in different regions, are categorized by the location at which they were students. The tables that categorize interviewees by region do not include the five Belgian interviewees.

I interviewed forty-four Rwandans who had been primary school students and/or teachers under the First and/or Second Republics (1962–1994) and who represented a good cross-section of Rwandan society. I additionally spoke with forty-three Rwandans about their experiences as students and/or teachers in post-genocide primary schools. Because I spoke to some people about their experiences with multiple periods, I count them in each of these periods. I met with one woman, for instance, still a school administrator in Kigali, who had been a student in colonial Rwanda, had become a teacher just prior to independence, and who had been teaching ever since. She, and others like her, offered particularly insightful long-range views.

TABLE A.4: *Participants by Period and Ethnicity*

Ethnicity	Period			
	Colonial	1962–1994	1994–2009	Total
Hutu	7	24	20	51
Mixed	0	1	2	3
Tutsi	5	16	16	37
Unidentified	0	3	5	8
Belgian	5	0	0	5
Total	17	44	43	104
N = 75				

Period refers to when the interviewee was involved with Rwandan primary education, either as a student or a teacher. Some interviewees were involved with Rwandan primary education in multiple periods. Interviewees whose experiences fit in more than one period are counted in each relevant column, which explains why the resulting total is greater than the seventy-five interviewees.

TABLE A.5: *Participants by Period and Gender*

Gender	Period			
	Colonial	1962–1994	1994–2009	Total
Female	6	24	25	55
Male	11	20	18	49
Total	17	44	43	104
N = 75				

Period refers to when the interviewee was involved with Rwandan primary education, either as a student or a teacher. Some interviewees were involved with Rwandan primary education in multiple periods. Interviewees whose experiences fit in more than one period are counted in each relevant column, which explains why the resulting total is greater than the seventy-five interviewees.

Works Cited

Aelvoet, Walter. 1962. "Rwanda et Burundi." *Vivante Afrique*, 218: 45–46, 51–53.

Aguilar, Pilar, and Gonzalo Retamal. 1998. *Rapid Educational Response in Complex Emergencies: A Discussion Document*. Geneva: UNESCO/IBE.

Ali, Taisier, and Robert O. Matthews, eds. 1999. *Civil Wars in Africa: Roots and Resolution*. Montreal: McGill-Queens University Press.

    2004. *Durable Peace: Challenges for Peacebuilding in Africa*. Toronto: University of Toronto Press.

Alidou, Hassana, Simon Gasibirege, and Joseph Muyango. 2007. *Training in Active Pedagogy to Reinforce Peace Education at Schools: Peace Education Project, Rwanda 2003–2007 Evaluation Report*. Bonn: Capacity Building International.

Allen, Tim, and John Eade. 2000. "The New Politics of Identity" in *Poverty and Development into the 21st Century*, eds. Tim Allen and Alan Thomas (pp. 485–508). Oxford: Oxford University Press.

Allport, Gordon W. 1958. *The Nature of Prejudice*. Garden City, NY: Doubleday Anchor Books.

Amnesty International. 2007. *Amnesty International Report 2007: Rwanda*. Amnesty International.

    2009. *Amnesty International Report 2009: Rwanda*. Amnesty International.

Anderson, Benedict. 2003. *Imagined Communities: Reflections on the Origin and Spread of Nationalism*. New York: Verso.

Ansoms, An. 2009a. "Faces of Rural Poverty in Contemporary Rwanda: Linking Livelihood Profiles and Institutional Processes." PhD diss., University of Antwerp, Antwerp.

    2009b. "Re-Engineering Rural Society: The Visions and Ambitions of the Rwandan Elite." *African Affairs*, 108(431): 289–340.

Apple, Michael W. 1979. *Ideology and Curriculum*. London: Routledge & Kegan Paul.

Avery, Patricia G., David W. Johnson, Roger T. Johnson, and James M. Mitchell. 1999. "Teaching an Understanding of War and Peace through Structured Academic Controversies" in *How Children Understand War and Peace: A Call for International Peace Education*, eds. Amiram Raviv, Louis Oppenheimer, and Daniel Bar-Tal (pp. 261–277). San Francisco: Jossey-Bass.

Avery, Patricia G., John L. Sullivan, and Sandra L. Wood. 1997. "Teaching for Tolerance of Diverse Beliefs." *Theory into Practice*, 36(1): 32–38.

Azar, Fabiola, Étienne Mullet, and Geneviève Vinsonneau. 1999. "The Propensity to Forgive: Findings from Lebanon." *Journal of Peace Research*, 36(2): 169–181.

Bamusanire, Emmanuel, Joseph Byiringiro, Augustine Munyakazi, and Johnson Ntagaramba. 2006a. *Primary Social Studies 4: Pupil's Book*. Kigali: Macmillan Rwanda.

2006b. *Primary Social Studies 4: Teacher's Book*. Kigali: Macmillan Rwanda.

2006c. *Primary Social Studies 5: Pupil's Book*. Kigali: Macmillan Rwanda.

2006d. *Primary Social Studies 5: Teacher's Book*. Kigali: Macmillan Rwanda.

2006e. *Primary Social Studies 6: Pupil's Book*. Kigali: Macmillan Rwanda.

2006f. *Primary Social Studies 6: Teacher's Book*. Kigali: Macmillan Rwanda.

Bar-On, Dan, and Sami Adwan. 2006. "The Prime Shared History Project" in *Educating toward a Culture of Peace*, ed. Yaacov Iram (pp. 309–323). Charlotte, NC: Information Age Publishing.

Bar-Tal, Daniel. 1998. "The Rocky Road toward Peace: Beliefs on Conflict in Israeli Textbooks." *Journal of Peace Research*, 35(6): 723–742.

Bar-Tal, Daniel, and Yigal Rosen. 2009. "Peace Education in Societies Involved in Intractable Conflicts: Direct and Indirect Models." *Review of Educational Research*, 79(2): 557–575.

Baranyizigiye, Jeanne d'Arc, John Rutayisire, Méschac Bizimana, Clémentine Gafiligi, Marie Kankindi, and Yassini Maniraguha. 2004. *A Guide to Civic Education: Life Skills for Rwanda Primary Schools, Upper Primary Level – P4 – P5 – P6*. Kigali: National Curriculum Development Centre.

Barnett, Michael. 1999. "Culture, Strategy, and Foreign Policy Change: Israel's Road to Oslo." *European Journal of International Relations*, 5(1): 5–36.

2003. *Eyewitness to a Genocide: The United Nations and Rwanda*. Ithaca, NY: Cornell University Press.

Barr, Dennis. 2010. *Evaluation Research Summary*. Facing History and Ourselves. Available at http://www.facinghistory.org/sites/facinghistory.org/files/Evaluation%20Research%20Summary.pdf, last modified November 9, 2009.

Barsalou, Judy. 2005. "Unite or Divide? The Challenges of Teaching History in Societies Emerging from Violent Conflict," paper presented at the USIP Grant Program Roundtable, United States Institute of Peace, November 21, Washington, DC.

Barton, Keith C., and Alan McCully. 2003. "History Teaching and the Perpetuation of Memories: The Northern Ireland Experience" in *The Role of Memory in Ethnic Conflict*, eds. Ed Cairns and Micheal D. Roe (pp. 107–124). New York: Palgrave Macmillan.

Bertrand, Janet, ed. 2006. *Early Learning for Every Child Today (ELECT): A Framework for Ontario Early Childhood Settings*. Toronto: Best Start Expert Panel.

Bickmore, Kathy. 1999. "Teaching Conflict and Conflict Resolution in School: (Extra-) Curricular Considerations" in *How Children Understand War and Peace: A Call for International Peace Education*, eds. Amiram Raviv, Louis Oppenheimer, and Daniel Bar-Tal (pp. 233–259). San Francisco: Jossey-Bass Publishers.

2005. "Foundations of Peacebuilding and Discursive Peacekeeping: Infusion and Exclusion of Conflict in Canadian Public School Curricula." *Journal of Peace Education*, 2(2): 161–181.

2008. "Peace and Conflict Education" in *The Sage Handbook of Education for Citizenship and Democracy*, eds. James Arthur, Ian Davies, and Carole Hahn (pp. 438–454). London: Sage.

Bigirumwami, Aloy. 1958. "Les Problèmes Sociaux et Ethniques au Rwanda." *Témoignages Chrétiens (édition belge)*, 5(9).

Bird, Lindsay. 2003. *Post Conflict Education: A Review of the CfBT Experience*. Reading: Centre for British Teachers (CfBT) Research & Development.

2009. "Promoting Resilience: Developing Capacity within Education Systems Affected by Conflict" in *Think Piece Prepared for the Education for All Global Monitoring Report 2011*. Paris: UNESCO.

Biton, Yifat, and Gavriel Salomon. 2006. "Peace in the Eyes of Israeli and Palestinian Youths: Effects of Collective Narratives and Peace Education Program." *Journal of Peace Research*, 43(2): 167–180.

Blackburn, Gilmer W. 1985. *Education in the Third Reich: A Study of Race and History in Nazi Textbooks*. Albany: State University of New York Press.

Bleck, Jaimie, and Boubacar Mody Guindo. 2010. "Education for All, Education for Whom? A Cautionary Tale from Mali." Paper presented at International Studies Association Conference, February 17–20, New Orleans, LA.

Blum, Andrew. 2010. *Improving Peacebuilding Evaluation: A Whole-of-Field Approach*. Washington DC: United States Institute of Peace Press.

Borchgrevink, Kaja. 2008. "Book Note: The Madrassah Challenge: Militancy and Religious Education in Pakistan." *Journal of Peace Research*, 45(6): 853.

Bowles, Samuel, and Herbert Gintis. 1976. *Schooling in Capitalist America: Educational Reform and the Contradictions of Economic Life*. New York: Basic Books.

Brewer, Marilynn B. 1999. "The Psychology of Prejudice: Ingroup Love or Outgroup Hate?" *Journal of Social Issues*, 55(3): 429–444.

2000. "Superordinate Goals versus Superordinate Identity as Bases of Intergroup Cooperation" in *Social Identity Processes*, eds. Dora Capozza and Rupert Brown (pp. 117–132). London: SAGE Publications.

Bridgeland, John, Stu Wulsin, and Mary McNaught. 2009. *Rebuilding Rwanda: From Genocide to Prosperity through Education*. Washington, DC: Civic Enterprises.

Brock-Utne, Birgit, and Halla B. Holmarsdottir. 2004. "Language Policies and Practices in Tanzania and South Africa: Problems and Challenges." *International Journal of Educational Development*, 24(1): 67–83.

Brown, Graham K., and Arnim Langer. 2010. "Horizontal Inequalities and Conflict: A Critical Review and Research Agenda." *Conflict, Security & Development*, 10(1): 27–55.

Brown, Michael E. 1996. "The Causes and Regional Dimensions of Internal Conflict" in *The International Dimensions of Internal Conflict*, ed. Michael E. Brown (pp. 571–601). Cambridge, MA: MIT Press.

1996. "Introduction" in *The International Dimensions of Internal Conflict*, ed. Michael E. Brown (pp. 1–31). Cambridge, MA: MIT Press.

Brown, Roger. 1986. *Social Psychology: The Second Edition*. New York: Free Press.

Brown, Rupert. 2000. "Social Identity Theory: Past Achievements, Current Problems, and Future Challenges." *European Journal of Social Psychology*, 30(6): 745–778.

Buckley-Zistel, Susanne. 2006. "Remembering to Forget: Chosen Amnesia as a Strategy for Local Coexistence in Post-Genocide Rwanda." *Africa*, 76(2): 131–150.

Burde, Dana, Amy Kapit-Spitalny, Rachel Wahl, and Ozen Guven. 2010. *Education in Emergencies: A Literature Review of What Works, What Does Not, and Why.* Oslo: Norwegian Agency for Development Cooperation.

   2011. *Education and Conflict Mitigation: What the Aid Workers Say.* Washington, DC: USAID.

Burnet, Jennie E. 2009. "Whose Genocide? Whose Truth? Representations of Victim and Perpetrator in Rwanda" in *Genocide : Truth, Memory, and Representation,* eds. Alexander Laban Hinton and Kevin Lewis O'Neill (pp. 80–110). Durham, NC: Duke University Press.

   2012. *Genocide Lives in Us: Women, Memory and Silence in Rwanda.* Madison: University of Wisconsin Press.

Bush, Kenneth D., and Diana Saltarelli. 2000. *The Two Faces of Education in Ethnic Conflict: Towards a Peacebuilding Education for Children.* Florence: UNICEF Innocenti Research Centre.

Byrne, Sean. 2000. "Conflict and Children: Integrated Education in the Segregated Society of Northern Ireland" in *Social Conflicts and Collective Identities,* eds. Patrick G. Coy and Lynne M. Woehrle (pp. 91–112). Lanham, MD: Rowman & Littlefield.

Capozza, Dora, and Rupert Brown. 2000. *Social Identity Processes.* London: SAGE Publications.

Cederman, Lars-Erik, Nils B. Weidmann, and Kristian Skrede Gleditsch. 2010. "Horizontal Inequalities and Ethno-Nationalist Civil War: A Global Comparison." *American Political Science Review,* 105(3): 478–495.

Central Intelligence Agency (CIA). 2012. "The World Fact Book." Available at https://www.cia.gov/library/publications/the-world-factbook/index.html

Centre for Conflict Management. 2002. "Peuplement Du Rwanda: Enjeux Et Perspectives" in *Cahiers du Centre de Gestion des Conflits.* Butare: Centre for Conflict Management, National University of Rwanda.

Chrétien, Jean-Pierre. 2003. *The Great Lakes of Africa: Two Thousand Years of History.* Translated by Scott Straus. New York: Zone Books.

Christie, Pam. 2009. "Peace, Reconciliation, and Justice: Delivering the Miracle in Post-Apartheid Education" in *Peace Education in Conflict and Post-Conflict Societies: Comparative Perspectives,* eds. Claire McGlynn, Michalinos Zembylas, Zvi Bekerman, and Tony Gallagher (pp. 75–88). New York: Palgrave Macmillan.

Cilliers, Jaco. 2006. "Transforming Post-Accord Education Systems: Local Reflections from Bosnia-Herzegovina" in *Troublemakers or Peacemakers? Youth and Post-Accord Peace Building,* ed. Siobhán McEvoy-Levy (pp. 173–194). South Bend, IN: University of Notre Dame Press.

Clark-Kazak, Christina. 2011. "Politicizing Age: Where are the Children in International Studies?" Paper presented at the International Studies Association Conference, March 16–19, Montreal.

Classe, Leon. Undated. *Instructions Pastorales: 1922–1932.* Kabgayi: Vicariat apostolique.

   1935. "Un Pays De Trois Races." *Grands Lacs* 51e année (5–6 numéro spécial): 135–139.

Clifford, Paul. 2006. "Peacebuilding in Sierra Leone." *Committee for Conflict Transformation Report (CCTS) Review,* 26: 1–3.

Cole, Elizabeth A. 2007a. "Reconciliation and History Education" in *Teaching the Violent Past: History Education and Reconciliation,* ed. Elizabeth A. Cole (pp. 1–30). New York: Rowman and Littlefield.

2007b. "Transitional Justice and the Reform of History Education." *International Journal of Transitional Justice*, 1(1): 115–137.

Cole, Elizabeth A., and Judy Barsalou. 2006. "Unite or Divide? The Challenges of Teaching History in Societies Emerging from Violent Conflict". Washington, DC: United States Institute for Peace.

Coleman, Peter T., Robin R. Vallacher, Andrzej Nowak, and Lan Bui-Wrzosinska. 2008. "Rethinking Intractable Conflict: The Perspective of Dynamical Systems." *American Psychology*, 65(4): 262–278.

Colletta, Nat J., and Michelle L. Cullen. 2000. *Violent Conflict and the Transformation of Social Capital: Lessons from Cambodia, Rwanda, Guatemala, and Somalia.* Washington, DC: The World Bank.

Colletta, Nat J., Teck Ghee Lim, and Anita Kelles-Viitanen, eds. 2001. *Social Cohesion and Conflict Prevention in Asia: Managing Diversity through Development.* Washington, DC: The World Bank.

Collier, Paul, and Anke Hoeffler. 2004. "Greed and Grievance in Civil War." *Oxford Economic Papers*, 56(4): 563–595.

Coloroso, Barbara. 2007. *Extraordinary Evil: A Brief History of Genocide.* Toronto: Penguin Group.

Crisp, Richard J., and Miles Hewstone. 2000. "Multiple Categorization and Social Identity" in *Social Identity Processes*, eds. Dora Capozza and Rupert Brown (pp. 149–166). London: SAGE Publications.

Crisp, Richard J., and Miles Hewstone eds. 2006. *Multiple Social Categorization: Processes, Models and Applications.* New York: Psychology Press.

Crokaert, Paul. 1931. *Rapport présenté par le Gouvernement Belge au Conseil de la Société des Nations au Sujet de l'Administration du Ruanda-Urundi pendant l'Année 1930.* Brussels: Établissements Émile Bruylant.

Dallaire, Romeo. 2003. *Shake Hands with the Devil: The Failure of Humanity in Rwanda.* Toronto: Vintage Canada.

Dance, E. H. 1960. *History the Betrayer: A Study in Bias.* London: Hutchinson.

Davies, Lynn. 2004. *Education and Conflict: Complexity and Chaos.* London: RoutledgeFalmer.

2005. "Evaluating the Link between Conflict and Education." *Journal of Peacebuilding & Development*, 2(2): 42–58.

2006. "Understanding the Education-War Interface." *Forced Migration Review*, 13: 13.

de Lacger, Louis. 1939. *Ruanda: Le Ruanda Ancien.* Paris: Grands Lacs.

de Lame, Danielle. 2005. *A Hill among a Thousand: Transformations and Ruptures in Rural Rwanda.* Translated by Helen Arnold. Madison: University of Wisconsin Press.

Dei, George J. Sefa, Alireza Asgharzadeh, Sharon Eblaghie Bahador, and Riyad Ahmed Shahjahan. 2006. *Schooling and Difference in Africa: Democratic Challenges in a Contemporary Context.* Toronto: University of Toronto Press.

Des Forges, Alison. 1995. "The Ideology of Genocide." *Issue: A Journal of Opinion*, 23(2): 44–47.

1999. *Leave None to Tell the Story.* New York: Human Rights Watch.

Deutscher, Irwin. 2002. *Accommodating Diversity: National Policies That Prevent Ethnic Conflict.* Lanham, MD: Lexington Books.

Devine-Wright, Patrick. 2003. "A Theoretical Overview of Memory and Conflict" in *The Role of Memory in Ethnic Conflict*, eds. Ed Cairns and Michael D. Roe (pp. 9–33). Houndmills, Basingstoke, Hampshire and New York: Palgrave Macmillan.

Diamond, Jared. 2005. *Collapse: How Societies Choose to Fail or Succeed*. New York: Penguin Group.

Dolan, Janice. 2007. *Last in Line, Last in School: How Donors Are Failing Children in Conflict-Affected Fragile States*. London: Save the Children International.

Dovidio, John F., Samuel L. Gaertner, Gordon Hodson, Blake M. Riek, Kelly M. Johnson, and Missy Houlette. 2006. "Recategorization and Crossed Categorization: The Implications of Group Salience and Representations for Reducing Bias" in *Multiple Social Categorization: Processes, Models and Applications*, eds. Richard J. Crisp and Miles Hewstone (pp. 65–89). New York: Psychology Press.

Dubuisson-Brouha, M., E. Natalis, and J. Paulus. 1958. *Le Problème de l'Enseignement dans le Ruanda-Urundi: Rapport d'une Mission d'Étude*. Liège: Fondation de l'Université de Liège pour les Recherches Scientifiques au Congo Belge et au Ruanda-Urundi.

Duflo, Esther, Pascaline Dupas, and Michael Kremer. 2009. *Additional Resources versus Organizational Changes in Education: Experimental Evidence from Kenya*. Cambridge, MA: Abdul Latif Jameel – Poverty Action Lab.

Dunn, Seamus, and Valerie Morgan. 1999. "A Fraught Path: Education as a Basis for Developing Improved Community Relations in Northern Ireland." *Oxford Review of Education*, 25(1/2): 141–153.

Dupuy, Kendra E. 2008. "Education in Peace Agreements: 1989–2005." *Conflict Resolution Quarterly*, 26(2): 149–166.

Education for All Global Monitoring Report team. 2004. "Education for All: The Quality Imperative" in *EFA Global Monitoring Reports*. Paris: UNESCO.

2011. "The Hidden Crisis: Armed Conflict and Education" in *EFA Global Monitoring Reports*. Paris: UNESCO.

Eller, Jack David. 1999. *From Culture to Ethnicity to Conflict: An Anthropological Perspective on International Ethnic Conflict*. Ann Arbor: University of Michigan Press.

Eltringham, Nigel. 2004. *Accounting for Horror: Post-Genocide Debates in Rwanda*. London: Pluto Press.

Erny, Pierre. 1994. *Rwanda 1994: Clés pour Comprendre le Calvaire d'un Peuple*. Paris: L'Harmattan.

2001. *L'École Coloniale au Rwanda (1900–1962)*. Paris: L'Harmattan.

Eyoh, Dickson. 1999. "Community, Citizenship and the Politics of Ethnicity in Post-Colonial Africa" in *Sacred Spaces and Public Quarrels*, eds. Paul Zeleza and Ezekiel Kalipeni (pp. 37–54). Trenton, NJ: Africa World Press.

Facebook Inc. 2013. "Victoire Ingabire Umuhoza's Facebook Page." Available at : http://www.facebook.com/pages/Victoire-Ingabire-Umuhoza-for President/109504816547? v=info. Accessed January 5, 2013.

Fearon, James D., and David D. Laitin. 2003. "Ethnicity, Insurgency, and Civil War." *The American Political Science Review*, 97(1): 75–90.

Fein, Helen. 1993. "Accounting for Genocide after 1945: Theories and Some Findings." *International Journal on Group Rights*, 1: 88–92.

Festinger, Leon. 1959. *A Theory of Cognitive Dissonance*. Palo Alto, CA: Stanford University Press.

Fiske, Susan T., and Steven C. Neuberg. 1990. "A Continuum Model of Impression Formation: From Category-Based to Individuating Processes as a Function of Information, Motivation, and Attention" in *Advances in Experimental Social Psychology*, ed. Mark P. Zanna (pp. 1–74). San Diego, CA: Academic.

Frayha, Nemer. 2004. "Developing Curriculum as a Means to Bridging National Divisions in Lebanon" in *Education, Conflict and Social Cohesion*, eds. Sobhi Tawil and Alexandra Harley (pp. 159–205). Paris: UNESCO-IBE.

Freedman, Sarah Warshauer, Harvey M. Weinstein, Karen Murphy, and Timothy Longman. 2008. "Teaching History after Identity-Based Conflicts: The Rwanda Experience." *Comparative Education Review*, 52(4): 663–690.

Freedom House International. 2006. *Freedom in the World: Country Report: Rwanda*. Washington, DC: Freedom House International.

Fujii, Lee Ann. 2009. *Killing Neighbors: Webs of Violence in Rwanda*. Ithaca, NY: Cornell University Press.

Fukuda-Parr, Sakiko, Maximillian Ashwill, Elizabeth Chiappa, and Carol Messineo. 2008. "The Conflict-Development Nexus: A Survey of Armed Conflicts in Sub-Saharan Africa 1980–2005." *Journal of Peacebuilding and Development*, 4(1): 6–22.

Fuller, Bruce. 1990. *Growing Up Modern: The Western State Builds Third-World Schools*. New York: Routledge.

Gaertner, Samuel L., John F. Dovidio, Brenda S. Banker, Missy Houllette, Kelly M. Johnson, and Elizabeth A. McGlynn. 2000a. "Reducing Intergroup Conflict: From Superordinate Goals to Decategorization, Recategorization, and Mutual Differentiation." *Group Dynamics: Theory, Research, and Practice*, 4(1): 98–114.

Gaertner, Samuel L., John F. Dovidio, Jason A. Nier, Brenda B. Banker, Christine M. Ward, Melissa Houlette, and Stephanie Loux. 2000b. "The Common Ingroup Identity Model for Reducing Intergroup Bias: Progress and Challenges" in *Social Identity Processes*, eds. Dora Capozza and Rupert Brown (pp. 133–148). London: SAGE Publications.

Gaertner, Samuel L., Jeffrey Mann, Audrey Murrell, and John F. Dovidio. 1989. "Reducing Intergroup Bias: The Benefits of Recategorization." *Journal of Personality and Social Psychology*, 57(2): 239–249.

Gallagher, Anthony. 1998. "Religious Divisions in Schools in Northern Ireland." Paper presented at the British Education Research Association Annual Conference, August 27–30, Queen's University, Belfast.

Gasanabo, Jean-Damascène. 2004. "Mémoires et Histoire Scolaire: Le Cas du Rwanda de 1962 à 1994." PhD diss., Université de Genève.

Gehlbach, Hunter. 2004. "Social Perspective Taking: A Facilitating Aptitude for Conflict Resolution, Historical Empathy, and Social Studies Achievement." *Theory and Research in Social Education*, 32(1): 39–55.

Gell-Mann, Murray. 1997. "The Simple and the Complex" in *Complexity, Global Politics and National Security*, eds. David Alberts and Thomas Czerwinski (pp. 2–12). Washington, DC: National Defense University.

Gellner, Ernest. 1983. *Nations and Nationalism*. New York: Cornell University Press.

Geltman, Paul, and Eric Stover. 1997. "Genocide and the Plight of Rwanda's Children: Letter from Kigali." *Journal of the American Medical Association*, 277(4): 289–294.

Geschière, Peter. 2009. *The Perils of Belonging: Autochthony, Citizenship, and Exclusion in Africa & Europe*. Chicago: University of Chicago Press.

Gibson, Christopher, and Michael Woolcock. 2008. "Empowerment, Deliberative Development and Local Level Politics in Indonesia: Participatory Projects as a Source of Countervailing Power." *Studies in Comparative International Development*, 43(2): 151–180.

Gourevitch, Philip. 1998. *We Wish to Inform You That Tomorrow We Will Be Killed with Our Families*. New York: Picador USA.

2009. "The Life After: Fifteen Years after the Genocide in Rwanda, the Reconciliation Defies Expectations." *The New Yorker*, 85(12): 37–49.

Green, Andy, John Preston, and Jan Germen Janmaat. 2006. *Education, Equality and Social Cohesion: A Comparative Analysis*. New York: Palgrave Macmillan.

Gurr, Ted Robert. 1970. *Why Men Rebel*. Princeton, NJ: Princeton University Press.

Hanf, Theodor. 1974. *Education et Développement au Rwanda: Problèmes, Apories, Perspectives*. Materialien Zu Entwicklung Und Politik 7. Munchen: Weltforum Verlag.

Harber, Clive. 1996. "Educational Violence and Education for Peace in Africa." *Peabody Journal of Education*, 71(3): 151–169.

2004. *Schooling as Violence: How Schools Harm Pupils and Societies*. London and New York: RoutledgeFalmer.

Harff, Barbara, and Ted Robert Gurr. 1998. "Systematic Early Warning of Humanitarian Emergencies." *Journal of Peace Research*, 35(5): 551–579.

Hart, Jason. 2006. "Putting Children in the Picture." *Forced Migration Review*, July (Supplement): 9–10.

Hayes, Bernadette C., Ian McAllister, and Lizanne Dowds. 2006. "In Search of the Middle Ground: Integrated Education and Northern Ireland Politics." *Research Update: ARK Social and Political Archive*, 42: 1–4.

2007. "Integrated Education, Intergroup Relations, and Political Identities in Northern Ireland." *Social Problems*, 54(4): 454–482.

Heremans, Père Roger. 1971. *Introduction à l'Histoire du Rwanda*. Kigali: Éditions Rwandaises.

Hewstone, Miles, and Rupert Brown, eds. 1986. *Contact and Conflict in Intergroup Encounters*. New York: Basil Blackwell.

Hewstone, Miles, Rhiannon N. Turner, Jared B. Kenworthy, and Richard J. Crisp. 2006. "Multiple Social Categorization: Integrative Themes and Future Research Priorities" in *Multiple Social Categorization: Processes, Models and Applications*, eds. Richard J. Crisp and Miles Hewstone (pp. 271–310). New York: Psychology Press.

Heyneman, Stephen P. 2003. "Education, Social Cohesion and the Future Role of International Organizations." *Peabody Journal of Education*, 78(3): 25–38.

Hiebert, Maureen. 2008. "Theorizing Destruction: Reflections on the State of Comparative Genocide Theory." *Journal of Genocide Studies and Prevention*, 3(3): 309–339.

Hintjens, Helen M. 2001. "When Identity Becomes a Knife: Reflecting on the Genocide in Rwanda." *Ethnicities*, 1(1): 25–55.

Hinton, Alexander Laban. 2005. *Why Did They Kill? Cambodia in the Shadow of Genocide*. Berkeley: University of California Press.

2008. "Truth, Representation, and the Politics of Memory after the Cambodian Genocide" in *People of Virtue: Reconfiguring Religion, Power and Moral Order in Cambodia Today*, eds. Alexandra Kent and David Chandler (pp.62–81). Washington, DC: NAIS Press.

Hirsch, Herbert. 1995. *Genocide and the Politics of Memory: Studying Death to Preserve Life*. Chapel Hill: University of North Carolina Press.

Hoben, Susan J. 1989. *School, Work, and Equity: Educational Reform in Rwanda*. Boston: African Studies Center.

Holtman, Zelda, Johann Louw, Colin Tredoux, and Tara Carney. 2005. "Prejudice and Social Contact in South Africa: A Study of Integrated Schools Ten Years after Apartheid." *South African Journal of Psychology*, 35(3): 473–493.

Hopken, Wolfgang. 1996. "History Education and Yugoslav (Dis)-Integration" in *Oil on Fire? Textbooks, Ethnic Stereotypes and Violence in South-Eastern Europe*, ed. Wolfgang Hopken (pp. 99–124). Hannover: Verlag Hahnsche Buchhandlung.

Horowitz, Donald L. 1985. *Ethnic Groups in Conflict*. Berkeley: University of California Press.

Houlette, Melissa, Samuel L. Gaertner, Kelly M. Johnson, Brenda S. Banker, and Blake M. Riek. 2004. "Developing a More Inclusive Social Identity: An Elementary School Intervention." *Journal of Social Issues*, 60(1): 35–55.

Houser, Neil O. 1996. "Negotiating Dissonance and Safety for the Common Good: Social Education in the Elementary Classroom." *Theory and Research in Social Education*, 24(3): 294–313.

Hughes, Joanne, and Caitlin Donnelly. 2007. "Is the Policy Sufficient? An Exploration of Integrated Education in Northern Ireland and Bilingual/Binational Education in Israel" in *Addressing Ethnic Conflict through Peace Education: International Perspectives*, eds. Zvi Bekerman and Claire McGlynn (pp. 121–133). New York: Palgrave Macmillan.

Human Rights Watch (HRW). 2004. *Rwanda: Parliament Seeks to Abolish Rights Group*. New York: Human Rights Watch.

Humphreys, Macartan, and Jeremy Weinstein. 2008. "Who Fights? The Determinants of Participation in Civil War." *American Journal of Political Science*, 52(2): 436–455.

Hutchison, Sharon E. 2009. "Perilous Outcomes: International Monitoring and the Perpetuation of Violence in Sudan" in *Genocide: Truth, Memory, and Representation*, eds. Alexander Laban Hinton and Kevin Lewis O'Neill (pp. 54–79). Durham, NC: Duke University Press.

Ingelaere, Bert. 2009. *Do We Understand Life after Genocide? Centre and Periphery in the Knowledge Construction in/on Rwanda*. Antwerp: Institute of Development Policy and Management.

Inspection Générale de l'Enseignement. 1929. *Instructions pour les Inspecteurs Provinciaux Relatives aux Programmes à Suivre dans les Différentes Écoles et à leur Interpretation*.

Institut de Recherche et de Dialogue pour la Paix. 2005. *Histoire et Conflits au Rwanda*. Kigali: Institut de Recherche et de Dialogue pour la Paix.

Inter-Agency Network for Education in Emergencies. Undated. *Understanding Education's Role in Fragility: Synthesis of Four "Situational Analyses of Education and Fragility": Afghanistan, Bosnia-Herzegovina, Cambodia, Liberia – Policy Brief*. INEE.

2004. *Minimum Standards for Education in Emergencies, Chronic Crises and Early Reconstruction*. Paris: INEE & UNESCO.

Inter-Parliamentary Union. 2012. *Women in National Parliaments*. Inter-Parliamentary Union. http://www.ipu.org/wmn-e/classif.htm

Jackson, Tony. 2000. *Equal Access to Education: A Peace Imperative for Burundi*. London: International Alert.

Jefremovas, Villia. 1997. "Contested Identities: Power and the Fictions of Ethnicity, Ethnography and History in Rwanda." *Anthropologica*, 39(1/2): 91–104.

Jelin, Elizabeth. 2003. *State Repression and the Labors of Memory*. Minneapolis: University of Minnesota Press.

Jervis, Robert. 1977. *Perception and Misperception in International Politics.* Princeton, NJ: Princeton University Press.

1997. "Complex Systems: The Role of Interactions" in *Complexity, Global Politics and National Security,* eds. David Alberts and Thomas Czerwinski (pp. 20–31). Washington, DC: Department of National Defense.

Johnson, David W., and Roger T. Johnson. 1994. "Constructive Conflict in Schools." *Journal of Social Issues,* 50(1): 117–137.

Johnson, Lucy, and Miles Hewstone. 1992. "Cognitive Models of Stereotype Change: Subtyping and the Perceived Typicality of Disconfirming Group Members." *Journal of Experimental Social Psychology,* 28: 360–386.

Jones, Adele. 2009. "Curriculum and Civil Society in Afghanistan." *Harvard Educational Review,* 79(1): 113–122.

Jones, Bruce. 2001. *Peacemaking in Rwanda: The Dynamics of Failure.* London: Lynne Rienner.

Kagame, Alexis. 1958. *Histoire du Rwanda.* Leverville: Bibliothèque de l'Étoile.

Kalyvas, Stathis N. 2006. *The Logic of Violence in Civil War.* Cambridge and New York: Cambridge University Press.

Kanyarukiga, Sam, Esther van der Meer, Maria Paalman, Derek Poate, and Ted Schrader. 2006. *Evaluation of DFID Country Programmes: Country Study Rwanda 2000–2005.* London: Department for International Development.

Karangwa, Jean Bosco. 1988. "Study on the Realisation of UNESCO Guidelines. The Reformation of Primary Education in Rwanda." MA diss., Université Nationale du Rwanda, Ruhengeri.

Kaufman, Stuart. 2001. *Modern Hatreds: The Symbolic Politics of Ethnic War.* Ithaca, NY: Cornell University Press.

2006. "Escaping the Symbolic Politics Trap: Reconciliation Initiatives and Conflict Resolution in Ethnic Wars." *Journal of Peace Research,* 43(2): 201–218.

Kaufmann, Chaim. 1996. "Possible and Impossible Solutions to Ethnic Civil Wars." *International Security,* 20(4): 136–175.

Kawano-Chiu, Melanie. 2011. *Starting on the Same Page: A Lessons Report from the Peacebuilding Evaluation Project.* Washington, DC: Alliance for Peacebuilding.

Kelman, Herbert C. 1999. "Transforming the Relationship between Former Enemies: A Social-Psychological Analysis" in *After the Peace: Resistance and Reconciliation,* ed. Robert L. Rothstein (pp. 193–205). Boulder, CO: Lynne Rienner.

King, Charles. 2004. "Review: The Micropolitics of Social Violence." *World Politics,* 56(3): 431–455.

King, Elisabeth. 2009. "From Data Problems to Data Points: Challenges and Opportunities of Research in Postgenocide Rwanda." *African Studies Review,* 52(3): 127–148.

2010. "Memory Controversies in Post-Genocide Rwanda: Implications for Peacebuilding." *Journal of Genocide Studies and Prevention,* 5(3): 293–309.

King, Elisabeth, Cyrus Samii, and Birte Snilstveit. 2010. "Interventions to Promote Social Cohesion in Sub-Saharan Africa." *Journal of Development Effectiveness,* 2(3): 336–370.

Kinzer, Stephen. 2008. *A Thousand Hills: Rwanda's Rebirth and the Man Who Dreamed It.* Hoboken, NJ: Wiley, John and Sons.

Korostelina, Karina V. 2007. *Social Identity and Conflict: Structures, Dynamics, and Implications.* New York: Palgrave Macmillan.

Kuhn, Thomas. 1970. *The Structure of Scientific Revolutions*. Chicago: The University of Chicago Press.

Kumar, Krishna. 2001. *Prejudice and Pride: School Histories of the Freedom Struggle in India and Pakistan*. New Delhi: Penguin Books.

Kuppermitz, Haggai, and Gavriel Salomon. 2005. "Lessons to Be Learned from Research on Peace Education in the Context of Intractable Conflict." *Theory into Practice*, 44(4): 293–302.

Lai, Brian, and Clayton Thyne. 2007. "The Effect of Civil War on Education, 1980–97." *Journal of Peace Research*, 44(3): 277–292.

Lake, Anthony. 1993. "From Containment to Enlargement" *Dispatch Magazine*, 4(39).

Lake, David A., and Donald Rothchild. 1998. "Spreading Fear: The Genesis of Transnational Ethnic Conflict" in *The International Spread of Ethnic Conflict: Fear, Diffusion, and Escalation*, eds. David A. Lake and Donald Rothchild (pp. 3–32). Princeton, NJ: Princeton University Press.

Leaning, Jennifer. 2002. "Identifying Precursors" in *Will Genocide Ever End?*, eds. Carol Rittner, John K. Roth, and James M. Smith (pp. 117–122). St. Paul, MN: Aegis/Paragon House.

Lederach, John Paul. 1997. *Building Peace: Sustainable Reconciliation in Divided Societies*. Washington, DC: United States Institute of Peace Press.

Lee, Peter. 2004. "Understanding History" in *Theorizing Historical Consciousness*, ed. Peter Seixas (pp. 129–164). Toronto: University of Toronto Press.

Lema, Antoine. 1993. *Africa Divided: The Creation of 'Ethnic Groups'*. Lund: Lund University Press.

Lemarchand, René. 1970. *Rwanda and Burundi*. New York: Praeger Publishers.

1994. *Burundi: Ethnocide as Discourse and Practice*. Washington, DC: Woodrow Wilson Center Press.

Levine, Robert, and Donald Campbell, eds. 1972. *Ethnocentrism: Theories of Conflict, Ethnic Attitudes, and Group Behaviour*. New York: John Wiley.

Levy, Jack S. 2000. "Loss Aversion, Framing Effects, and International Conflict: Perspectives from Prospect Theory" in *Handbook of War Studies II*, ed. Manus I Midlarsky (pp. 193–221). Ann Arbor: University of Michigan Press.

Linden, Ian. 1999. *Christianisme et Pouvoirs au Rwanda (1900–1990)*. Translated by Paulette Gérard. Paris: Éditions Karthala.

Linden, Ian, and Jane Linden. 1977. *Church and Revolution in Rwanda*. Manchester: Manchester University Press.

Longman, Timothy. 2010. *Christianity and Genocide in Rwanda*. New York: Cambridge University Press.

Longman, Timothy, and Théonèste Rutagengwa. 2004. "Memory, Identity and Community in Rwanda" in *My Neighbor, My Enemy: Justice and Community in the Aftermath of Mass Atrocity*, eds. Eric Stover and Harvey M. Weinstein (pp. 162–182). Cambridge: Cambridge University Press.

Lootsma, Auke. 2012. "Rwanda: Gains Made against Poverty, a Lesson for Others." United Nations Development Program. Available at: http://www.rw.undp.org/content/rwanda/en/home/ourperspective/ourperspectivearticles/2012/10/15/rwanda-gains-made-against-poverty-a-lesson-for-others-/

Lund, Michael. 2003. *What Kind of Peace Is Being Built? Taking Stock of Post-Conflict Peacebuilding and Charting Future Directions*. Ottawa: International Development Research Centre.

Machel, Graça. 2001. *The Impact of War on Children: A Review of Progress since the 1996 United Nations Report on the Impact of Armed Conflict on Children.* London: C. Hurst & Company.

Majstorovic, Staven. 1997. "Ancient Hatreds or Elite Manipulation?: Memory and Politics in the Former Yugoslavia." *World Affairs*, 159(4): 170–182.

Malkki, Liisa. 1995. *Purity and Exile: Violence, Memory, and National Cosmology among Hutu Refugees in Tanzania.* Chicago: University of Chicago Press.

Mamdani, Mahmood. 1996. "From Conquest to Consent as the Basis of State Formation: Reflections on Rwanda." *New Left Review*, 1(216): 3–36.

    2001. *When Victims Become Killers: Colonialism, Nativism and the Genocide in Rwanda.* Kampala: Fountain Publishers.

    2004. *Good Muslim, Bad Muslim: America, the Cold War, and the Roots of Terror.* New York: Three Leaves Press.

Maney, Gregory M., Ibtisam Ibrahim, Gareth I. Higgins, and Hanna Herzog. 2006. "The Past's Promise: Lessons from Peace Processes in Northern Ireland and the Middle East." *Journal of Peace Research*, 43(2): 181–200.

Mann, Erika. 1938. *School for Barbarians.* New York: Modern Age Books.

Maquet, Jean Jacques. 1952. "Le Problème de la Domination Tutsi." *Zaire*, 4(10): 1011–1016.

Marshall, T. H. 1965. "Citizenship and Social Class" in *Class, Citizenship, and Social Development* (pp. 71–134). Garden City, NY: Anchor Books.

Matrai, Zsuzsa. 2002. "National Identity Conflicts and Civic Education: A Comparison of Five Countries" in *New Paradigms and Recurring Paradoxes in Education for Citizenship*, eds. Gita Steiner-Khamsi, Judith Torney-Purta, and John Schwille (pp. 85–104). Amsterdam: JAI/Elsevier Science.

Mbonimana, Gamaliel. 1978. "Christianisation Indirecte et Cristallisation des Clivages Ethniques au Rwanda (1925–1931)." PhD diss., Université Catholique de Louvain, Louvain-La-Neuve.

McCauley, Clark. 2002. "Head-First Versus Feet-First in Peace Education" in *Peace Education: The Concept, Principles, and Practices around the World*, eds. Gavriel Salomon and Baruch Nevo (pp. 247–258). London: Lawrence Erlbaum Associates.

McGlynn, Claire. 2009. "Negotiating Cultural Difference in Divided Societies: An Analysis of Approaches to Integrated Education in Northern Ireland" in *Peace Education in Conflict and Post-Conflict Societies: Comparative Perspectives*, eds. Claire McGlynn, Michalinos Zembylas, Zvi Bekerman, and Tony Gallgher (pp. 9–25). New York: Palgrave Macmillan.

McLean Hilker, Lyndsay. 2009. "Everyday Ethnicities: Identity and Reconciliation among Rwandan Youth." *Journal of Genocide Research*, 11(1): 81–100.

    2011. "The Role of Education in Driving Conflict and Building Peace: The Case of Rwanda." *Prospects*, 41(2): 267–282.

Meisel, John. 1999. *Si Je Me Souviens Bien/As I Recall.* Montreal: Institute for Research on Public Policy.

Merelman, Richard M. 1990. "The Role of Conflict in Children's Political Learning" in *Political Socialization, Citizenship Education, and Democracy*, ed. Orit Ichilov (pp. 47–65). New York: Teachers College Press.

Milligan, Jeffrey Ayala. 2003. "Teaching between the Cross and the Crescent Moon: Islamic Identity, Postcoloniality, and Public Education in the Southern Philippines." *Comparative Education Review*, 47(4): 468–492.

Ministère des Colonies. 1925. *Rapport sur l'Administration Belge du Ruanda-Urundi pendant l'Année 1925*. Brussels: Société des Nations.

Moreau, Joseph. 2003. *Schoolbook Nation: Conflicts over Textbooks from the Civil War to the Present*. Ann Arbor: University of Michigan Press.

Morill, Constance. 2004. "Reconciliation and the Gacaca: The Perceptions and Peace-Building Potential of Rwandan Youth Detainees." *The Online Journal of Peace and Conflict Resolution*, 6(1): 1–66.

Mortenson, Greg. 2009. *Stones into Schools: Promoting Peace with Books, Not Bombs, in Afghanistan and Pakistan*. New York: Viking.

Mortenson, Greg, and David Oliver Relin. 2006. *Three Cups of Tea: One Man's Mission to Promote Peace … One School at a Time*. New York: Penguin.

Muhimpundu, Félicité. 2002. *Education et Citoyenneté au Rwanda*. Paris: L'Harmattan.

Munyantwali, Eustache. 1991. "La Politique d'Équilibre dans l'Enseignement" in *Les Relations Interethniques au Rwanda à la Lumière de l'Agression d'Octobre 1990: Genèse, Soubassements et Perspectives*, eds. Francois-Xavier Bangamwabo, Maniragaba-Baributsa, Eustache Munyantwali, Jean Damascène Nduwayezu, Antoine Nyagahene, Emmanuel Rukiramakuba, Jean Gualbert Rumiya, and Laurien Uwizeyimana (pp. 300–307). Ruhengeri: Éditions Universitaires du Rwanda.

Munyas, Burcu. 2008. "Genocide in the Minds of Cambodian Youth: Transmitting (Hi) Stories of Genocide to Second and Third Generations in Cambodia." *Journal of Genocide Research*, 10(3): 413–439.

Musabimana, Jean Baptiste. Undated. *Le Coût de l'Efficacité et de l'Équité: l'Éducation au Rwanda*. Kigali.

Musolff, Andreas. 2007. "What Role Do Metaphors Play in Racial Prejudice? The Function of Antisemitic Imagery in Hitler's Mein Kampf." *Patterns of Prejudice*, 41(1): 21–43.

Ndura, Elavie. 2006. "Transcending the Majority Rights and Minority Protection Dichotomy through Multicultural Reflective Citizenship in the African Great Lakes Region." *Intercultural Education*, 17(2): 195–205.

Nevo, Baruch, and Iris Brem. 2002. "Peace Education Programs and the Evaluation of Their Effectiveness" in *Peace Education: The Concept, Principles, and Practices around the World*, eds. Gavriel Salomon and Baruch Nevo (pp. 271–282). London: Lawrence Erlbaum Associates.

Newbury, Catharine. 1980. "Ubureetwa and Thangata: Catalysts to Peasant Political Consciousness in Rwanda and Malawi." *Canadian Journal of African Studies*, 14(1): 97–111.

1983. "Colonialism, Ethnicity, and Rural Political Protest: Rwanda and Zanzibar in Comparative Perspective." *Comparative Politics*, 15(3): 253–280.

1988. *The Cohesion of Oppression*. New York: Columbia University Press.

1998. "Ethnicity and the Politics of History in Rwanda." *Africa Today*, 45(1): 7–24.

1992. "Rwanda: Recent Debates over Governance and Rural Development" in *Governance and Politics in Africa*, eds. Goran Hyden and Michael Bratton (pp. 193–219). Boulder, CO: Lynne Rienner.

Newbury, Catharine, and David Newbury. 1995. "Identity, Genocide and Reconstruction in Rwanda" in *Les Racines de la Violence dans la Région des Grands Lacs*. Brussels: European Parliament.

Ngendahimana, Aloys. 1981. "Study of the General Public's Participation in the Rwandan Education System 1900–1972: Contributing to Understanding the Evolution of the School System in Rwanda." MA diss., Institut Pédagogique National, Lyon.

Nicolai, Susan, and Carl Tripplehorn. 2003. *The Role of Education in Protecting Children in Conflict.* London: Humanitarian Practice Network.

Niyonzima, Maximilien, Grégoire Kayibanda, Claver Ndahayo, Isidore Nzeyimana, Calliope Mulindaha, Godefroy Sentama, Sylvestre Munyambonera, Joseph Sibomana, and Joseph Habyarimana. 1957. "Le Manifeste Des Bahutus" in *Rwanda Politique 1958–1960*, eds. F. Nkundabagenzi (pp. 20–30). Brussels: Centre de Recherche et d'Information Socio-Politique.

Njoroge, George K. 2007. "The Reconstruction of the Teacher's Psyche in Rwanda: The Theory and Practice of Peace Education at the Kigali Institute of Education" in *Addressing Ethnic Conflict through Peace Education: International Perspectives*, eds. by Zvi Bekerman and Claire McGlynn (pp. 215–229). New York: Palgrave Macmillan.

Nkomo, Mokubung, Carolyn McKinney, and Linda Chisholm. 2004. *Reflections on School Integration: Colloquium Proceedings.* Cape Town: HSRC Publishers.

No author. 1929. *Rapport Présenté par le Gouvernement Belge au Conseil de la Société des Nations.*

No author. 1966. *International Covenant on Economic, Social and Cultural Rights.* Office of the United Nations High Commissioner for Human Rights.

No author. 2004. "The Road out of Hell." *The Economist.* Available at: http://www.economist.com/node/2535789

Nolan, Paul. 2009. "From Conflict Society to Learning Society: Lessons from the Peace Process in Northern Ireland" in *Peace Education in Conflict and Post-Conflict Societies: Comparative Perspectives*, eds. Claire McGlynn, Michalinos Zembylas, Zvi Bekerman, and Tony Gallgher (pp. 59–74). New York: Palgrave Macmillan.

Novelli, Mario, and Mieke T.A. Lopes Cardozo. 2008. "Conflict, Education and the Global South: New Critical Directions." *International Journal of Educational Development*, 28(4): 473–488.

O'Malley, Brendan. 2010. *Education under Attack 2010.* Paris: UNESCO.

Obura, Anna. 2003. *Never Again. Educational Reconstruction in Rwanda.* Paris: International Institute for Education Planning.

   2004. *Peace, Reconciliation and Conflict Resolution: Framework Proposal – Rwanda (Proposal for DFID).* Kigali: UK Department for International Development.

   2005. *Planning a Systemic Response to the Needs of Orphans and Other Vulnerable Children in Rwanda: Draft Report.* Kigali: MINEDUC.

Organisation for Economic Co-operation and Development. 2006. "Whole of Government Approach to Fragile States" in *DAC Guidelines and Reference Series.* Paris: Organisation for Economic Cooperation and Development.

Oesterreich, Lesia. 1995. "Ages and Stages" in *Iowa Family Child Care Handbook*, eds. Lesia Oesterreich, Bess Gene Holt, and Shirley Karas (pp. 209–234). Ames: Iowa State University.

Østby, Gudrun. 2008. "Polarization, Horizontal Inequalities and Violent Civil Conflict." *Journal of Peace Research*, 45(2): 143–162.

Østby, Gudrun, Ragnhild Nordås, and Jan Ketil Rød. 2009. "Regional Inequalities and Civil Conflict in Sub-Saharan Africa." *International Studies Quarterly*, 53(2): 301–324.

Oyefusi, Aderoju. 2008. "Oil and the Probability of Rebel Participation among Youths in the Niger Delta of Nigeria." *Journal of Peace Research*, 45(4): 539–555.

Pagès, Père. 1930. *Un Royaume Hamite au Centre de l'Afrique.* Brussels: IRCB.

Paluck, Elizabeth Levy, and Donald P. Green. 2009a. "Deference, Dissent and Dispute Resolution: An Experimental Intervention Using Mass Media to Change Norms and Behavior in Rwanda." *American Political Science Review*, 103(4): 622–644.

2009b. "Prejudice Reduction: What Works? A Review and Assessment of Research and Practice." *Annual Review of Psychology*, 60: 339–367.

Patrick, Stewart, and Kaysie Brown. 2007. *Greater Than the Sum of Its Parts: Assessing 'Whole-of-Government' Approaches to Fragile States*. New York: International Peace Academy.

Paulson, Julia, ed. 2008. "Special Issue: The Two Faces of Education in Conflict." *Research in Comparative and International Education*, 3(1).

Payne, Rodger A. 2001. "Persuasion, Frames and Norm Construction." *European Journal of International Relations*, 7(1): 37–61.

Pells, Kirrily. 2011. "Building a Rwanda 'Fit for Children'" in *Remaking Rwanda: State Building and Human Rights after Mass Violence*, eds. Scott Straus and Lars Waldorf (pp. 79–86). Madison: University of Wisconsin Press.

Penal Reform International. 2004. "From Camp to Hill, the Reintegration of Released Prisoners" in *Research Report on the Gacaca*, 112. Kigali and Paris: Penal Reform International.

Perry, Valery. 2003. *Reading, Writing and Reconciliation: Educational Reform in Bosnia and Herzegovina*. Flensburg: European Centre for Minority Issues.

Pettigrew, Thomas F. 1998. "Intergroup Contact Theory." *Annual Review of Psychology*, 49: 65–85.

Pigozzi, Mary Joy. 1999. *Education in Emergencies and for Reconstruction: A Developmental Approach*. New York: UNICEF Education Section, Programme Division.

Pingel, Falk. 2008. "Can Truth Be Negotiated? History Textbook Revision as a Means to Reconciliation." *The Annals of the American Academy of Political and Social Science*, 617: 181–198.

Population Reference Bureau (PRB). 2012. *2012 World Population Data Sheet*. Washington, DC: Population Reference Bureau.

Posner, Daniel N. 2004. "The Political Salience of Cultural Difference: Why Chewas and Tumbukas Are Allies in Zambia and Adversaries in Malawi." *American Political Science Review*, 98(4): 529–545.

Pottier, Johan. 2002. *Re-Imagining Rwanda: Conflict, Survival and Disinformation in the Late Twentieth Century*. Cambridge: Cambridge University Press.

Prunier, Gérard. 1997. *The Rwanda Crisis: History of a Genocide 1959–1994*. London: C. Hurst and Company.

Reporters without Borders. 2009. "Rwanda." Available at: http://en.rsf.org/rwanda.html

Republic of Rwanda (RoR). Undated. *La Scolarisation Féminine*. Edited by Ministère Rwandais de la Santé Publique et des Affaires Sociales. Kigali: Direction de la Promotion Féminine.

1979a. "Discours d'Ouverture de son Excellence Monsieur le Ministre de l'Éducation Nationale, Militant Mutemberezi Pierre-Claver." *Education et Culture*, 4(Spéciale Réforme): 40–41.

1979b. "La Réforme Scolaire." *Education et Culture*, 4(Spécial Réforme): 46–50.

1983. *Amateka: Umwaka Wa 5*. Kigali: Ministère de l'Enseignement Primaire et Secondaire.

1985. *Amateka: Umwaka Wa 6.* Kigali: Ministère de l'Enseignement Primaire et Secondaire.

1986. *Des Disparités Ethniques et Régionales dans l'Enseignement Secondaire Rwandais.* Kigali: Ministère de l'Enseignement Primaire et Secondaire.

1987. *Histoire Du Rwanda, Iière Partie.* Kigali: Ministère de l'Enseignement Primaire et Secondaire, Direction Générale des Études et Recherches Pédagogiques.

1989. *Histoire Du Rwanda, IIième Partie.* Kigali: Ministère de l'Enseignement Primaire et Secondaire, Direction Générale des Études et Recherches Pédagogiques.

1991. *Travail Préparatoire à la Mise en Place d'un Programme de Prise en Charge des Frais de Scolarité des Enfants Issus de Familles Pauvres au Rwanda.* Kigali: Ministère du Plan.

1995. "Document Final Provisoire: Conférence sur la Politique et la Planification de l'Éducation au Rwanda" in *Conférence sur la Politique et la Planification de l'Éducation au Rwanda.* Kigali: Ministère de l'Enseignement Primaire et Secondaire & Ministère de l'Enseignement Supérieur, de la Recherche Scientifique et de la Culture.

1997. *Study of the Education Sector in Rwanda.* Kigali: Ministry of Education, UNESCO, and UNDP.

1998. *Consultation Sectorielle sur l'Éducation au Rwanda.* Kigali: Ministry of Education.

1999. *The Unity of Rwandans: Before the Colonial Period and under the Colonial Rule and under the First Republic.* Kigali: Office of the President of the Republic.

2000. *Rwanda Vision 2020.* Kigali: Ministry of Finance and Economic Planning.

2002a. *Curriculum in the Service of National Development.* Kigali: Ministry of Education, Science, Technology and Scientific Research.

2002b. *Education Sector Policy.* Kigali: Ministry of Education.

2002c. *Poverty Reduction Strategy Paper (PRSP).* Kigali: International Monetary Fund.

2002d. *Report on the Evaluation of National Unity and Reconciliation, 23 November 2001.* Kigali: National Unity and Reconciliation Commission.

2002e. *Results in Brief: The Rwanda 2002 Census of Population and Housing.* Kigali: National Census Service.

2003a. *Education Sector Policy.* Kigali: Ministry of Education.

2003b. *The Constitution of the Republic of Rwanda.*

2004a. *3rd National Summit Report on Unity and Reconciliation.* Kigali: National Unity and Reconciliation Commission.

2004b. *Children's Summit Report.* Kigali: National Unity and Reconciliation Commission.

2004c. *The Process of Decentralization and Democratization in Rwanda: Opinion Survey.* Kigali: National Unity and Reconciliation Commission.

2006a. *Rwanda Genocide Ideology and Strategies for Its Eradication.* Kigali: Senate of Rwanda.

2006b. *The Teaching of History of Rwanda: A Participatory Approach.* Kigali: National Curriculum Development Centre.

2006c. *The Teaching of History of Rwanda: A Participatory Approach (for Secondary Schools in Rwanda, a Reference Book for the Teacher).* Kigali: National Curriculum Development Centre.

2007a. *Economic Development and Poverty Reduction Strategy, 2008–2012.* Kigali: Ministry of Finance and Economic Planning.

2007b. *Social Cohesion in Rwanda: An Opinion Survey Results 2005–2007*. Kigali: National Unity and Reconciliation Commission.

2008. *History Program for Ordinary Level*. Kigali: National Curriculum Development Centre.

2010a. *Education Sector Strategic Plan: 2010–2015*. Kigali: Ministry of Education.

2010b. *History Program for Advanced Level Secondary School*. Kigali: National Curriculum Development Centre.

2011a. *National Social Protection Strategy*. Kigali: Ministry of Local Affairs.

2011b. *Strategic Plan for the Integrated Child Rights Policy in Rwanda*. Kigali: Ministry of Gender and Family Promotion.

2012. *The Evolution of Poverty in Rwanda 2000–2011: Results from Household Surveys (EICV)*. Kigali: National Institute of Statistics of Rwanda.

Reyntjens, Filip. 1996. "Rwanda: Genocide and Beyond." *Journal of Refugee Studies*, 9(3): 3–18.

2004. "Rwanda, Ten Years On: From Genocide to Dictatorship." *African Affairs*, 103(411): 177–210.

2006. "Post-1994 Politics in Rwanda: Problematising 'Liberation' and 'Democratisation'." *Third World Quarterly*, 27(6): 1103–1117.

Roberts-Schweitzer, Eluned, Vincent Greaney, and Kreszentia Duer. 2006. *Promoting Social Cohesion through Education*. Washington, DC: World Bank Publishers.

Rombouts, Heidy. 2004. *Victim Organisations and the Politics of Reparation: A Case Study on Rwanda*. Antwerp and Oxford: Intersentia.

Rosenau, James. 1997. "Many Damn Things Simultaneously: Complexity Theory and World Affairs" in *Complexity, Global Politics and National Security*, eds. David Alberts and Thomas Czerwinski (pp. 32–41). Washington, DC: Department of National Defense.

Ross, Marc Howard. 1993. *The Management of Conflict*. New Haven, CT: Yale University Press.

2002. "The Political Psychology of Competing Narratives: September 11 and Beyond" in *Understanding September 11*, eds. Craig Calhoun, Paul Price, and Ashley Timmer (pp. 303–320). New York: The New Press.

2007. *Cultural Contestation in Ethnic Conflict*. Cambridge: Cambridge University Press.

Rotberg, Robert. 2007. *Ibrahim Index of African Governance*. Boston: Mo Ibrahim Foundation.

Roy, Beth. 1994. *Some Trouble with Cows: Making Sense of Social Conflict*. Berkeley: University of California Press.

Rubbens, E. 1936. *Rapport sur l'Administration Belge du Ruanda-Urundi pendant l'Année 1935*. Brussels: Établissements Généraux d'Imprimerie.

Rutayisire, John. 2004. "Education for Social and Political Reconstruction – the Rwandan Experience from 1994 to 2004." Paper presented at the British Association for International and Comparative Education Conference at the University of Sussex, September 3–5.

Ryckmans, Pierre. 1931. *Dominer Pour Servir*. Brussels: Librarie Albert Dewit.

Salmi, Jamil. 2000. "Violence, Democracy, and Education: An Analytical Framework" in *Human Development Department LCSHD Paper Series*, 21. Washington, DC: The World Bank Latin America and the Caribbean Regional Office.

Salomon, Gavriel. 2002. "The Nature of Peace Education: Not All Programs Are Created Equal" in *Peace Education: The Concept, Principles, and Practices around the World*, eds. Gavriel Salomon and Baruch Nevo (pp. 3–13). London: Lawrence Erlbaum Associates.

Samoff, Joel. 1990. "'Modernizing' a Socialist Vision: Education in Tanzania" in *Education and Social Transition in the Third World*, eds. Martin Carnoy and Joel Samoff (pp. 209–273). Princeton, NJ: Princeton University Press.

Samuels, Shirley C. 1977. *Enhancing Self-Concept in Early Childhood: Theory and Practice*. New York: Human Sciences Press.

Samuelson, Beth, and Sarah Warshauer Freedman. 2010. "Language Policy, Multilingual Education and Power in Rwanda." *Language Policy*, 9(3): 191–215.

Sandrapt, Georges. 1939. *Cours de Droit Coutumier (Section des Candidats-Chefs)*. Astrida: Groupe Scolaire d'Astrida.

Savedoff, William D., Ruth Levine, and Nancy Birdsall. 2006. *When Will We Ever Learn? Improving Lives through Impact Evaluation*. Washington, DC: Center for Global Development.

Schabas, William A. 2008. "Post-Genocide Justice in Rwanda: A Spectrum of Options" in *After Genocide: Transitional Justice, Post-Conflict Reconstruction and Reconciliation in Rwanda and Beyond*, eds. Phil Clark and Zachary D. Kaufman (pp. 207–227). London: Hurst.

Schendel, Rebecca, Jolly Mazimhaka, and Chika Ezeanya. 2013. "Higher Education for Development in Rwanda." *International Higher Education*, 70: 19–21.

Scott, James. 1990. *Domination and the Arts of Resistance: Hidden Transcripts*. New Haven, CT: Yale University Press.

Scrase, Timothy J. 1993. *Image, Ideology and Inequality: Cultural Domination, Hegemony and Schooling in India*. New Delhi: SAGE Publications.

Sebahara, Pamphile. 1998. "La Construction du Clivage Ethnique au Rwanda." *Courrier ACP-UE*, 168: 86–87.

Sen, Amartya. 2006. *Identity and Violence: The Illusion of Destiny*. New York: W.W. Norton & Company.

Sherif, Muzafer. 1967. *Group Conflict and Co-Operation: Their Social Psychology*. London: Routledge.

Shyaka, Anasthase. Undated. *The Rwandan Conflict: Origin, Development, Exit Strategies*. Kigali: National Unity and Reconciliation Commission.

Simonsen, Sven Gunnar. 2005. "Addressing Ethnic Divisions in Post-Conflict Institution-Building: Lessons from Recent Cases." *Security Dialogue*, 36(3) : 297–318.

Simpenzwe, Gaspard. 1988. *Epitome de l'Enseignement Libre Subsidié au Rwanda*. Kigali: Régie de l'Imprimerie Scolaire.

Smith, Alan. 2001. "Segregation and the Emergence of Integrated Schools in Northern Ireland." *Oxford Review of Education*, 27(4): 559–575.

Smith, Alan, and Tony Vaux. 2003. *Education, Conflict and International Development*. London: UK Department for International Development.

Sommers, Marc. 2005. *Islands of Education: Schooling, Civil War, and the Southern Sudanese (1983–2004)*. Paris: International Institute for Educational Planning.

　　2012. *Stuck: Rwandan Youth and the Struggle for Adulthood*. Athens: University of Georgia Press.

Sommers, Marc, and Peter Buckland. 2005. "Negotiating Kosovo's Educational Minefield." *Forced Migration Review*, 22: 38–39.

Works Cited 197

Sowell, Thomas. 2004. *Affirmative Action around the World: An Empirical Study*. New Haven, CT: Yale University Press.

Spink, Jeaniene. 2005. "Education and Politics in Afghanistan: The Importance of an Education System in Peacebuilding and Reconstruction." *Journal of Peace Education*, 2(2): 195–207.

Stabback, Philip. 2004. "Curriculum Development, Diversity and Division in Bosnia and Herzegovina" in *Education, Conflict, and Social Cohesion*, eds. Sobhi Tawil and Alexandra Harley (pp. 37–83). Paris: UNESCO, IBE.

Stanton, Gregory H. 1998. *The Eight Stages of Genocide*. New Haven CT: Yale Center for International and Area Studies.

Starrett, Gregory, and Eleanor Abdella Doumato. 2007. "Textbook Islam, Nation Building, and the Question of Violence" in *Teaching Islam: Textbooks and Religion in the Middle East*, eds. Eleanor Abdella Doumato and Gregory Starrett (pp. 1–25). Boulder, CO: Lynne Rienner.

Staub, Ervin. 1989. *The Roots of Evil: The Psychological and Cultural Origins of Genocide and Other Forms of Group Violence*. Cambridge and New York: Cambridge University Press.

2003. *The Psychology of Good and Evil: Why Children, Adults, and Groups Help and Harm Others*. Cambridge and New York: Cambridge University Press.

Staub, Ervin, Laurie Anne Pearlman, Alexandra Gubin, and Athanase Hagengimana. 2005. "Healing, Reconciliation, Forgiving and the Prevention of Violence after Genocide." *Journal of Social and Clinical Psychology*, 24(3): 297–334.

Staub, Ervin, Laurie Anne Pearlman, and Vachel W. Miller. 2003. "Healing the Roots of Genocide in Rwanda." *Peace Review*, 15(3): 287–294.

Stephan, Walter. 1999. *Reducing Prejudice and Stereotyping in Schools*. New York: Teachers College Press.

Stewart, Frances. 2000. "Crisis Prevention: Tackling Horizontal Inequalities." *Oxford Development Studies*, 28(3): 245–262.

2002. "Horizontal Inequalities: A Neglected Dimension of Development" in *Queen Elizabeth House Working Paper Series*. Oxford: University of Oxford.

2007. "Conflict Prevention and Peaceful Development: Policies to Reduce Inequality and Exclusion." Oxford: Centre for Research on Inequality, Human Security and Ethnicity, Oxford University.

Stewart, Frances, and Graham Brown. 2007. "Motivations for Conflict: Groups and Individuals" in *Leashing the Dogs of War*, eds. Chester Crocker, Fen Hampson, and Pamela Aall (pp. 219–241). Washington, DC: United States Institute of Peace Press.

Straus, Scott. 2006. *The Order of Genocide: Race, Power, and War in Rwanda*. Ithaca, NY: Cornell University Press.

Suchenski, Micki. 2001. *A Comparative Look at Bilingual-Bicultural Education in Mexico and Guatemala*. Charlottesville: University of Virginia Press.

Sullivan, Daniel P. 2007. "Tinder, Spark, Oxygen, and Fuel: The Mysterious Rise of the Taliban." *Journal of Peace Research*, 44(1): 93–108.

Survivor's Fund (SURF). 2012. *FARG*. Available at: http://survivors-fund.org.uk/news/education/farg/

Swidler, Ann. 1986. "Culture in Action: Symbols and Strategies." *American Sociological Review*, 51(3): 273–286.

Tajfel, Henri. 1981. *Human Groups and Social Categories*. New York: Cambridge University Press.

1982. *Social Identity and Intergroup Relations*. New York: Cambridge University Press.

Tajfel, Henri, Michael Billig, R. P. Bundy, and Claude Flament. 1971. "Social Categorization and Intergroup Behaviour." *European Journal of Social Psychology*, 1(2): 149–178.

Tal-Or, Nurit, David Boninger, and Faith Gleicher. 2002. "Understanding the Conditions and Processes Necessary for Intergroup Contact to Reduce Prejudice" in *Peace Education: The Concept, Principles, and Practices around the World*, eds. Gavriel Salomon and Baruch Nevo (pp. 89–107). London: Lawrence Erlbaum Associates.

Tawil, Sobhi, and Alexandra Harley, eds. 2004. *Education, Conflict, and Social Cohesion*. Paris: UNESCO, IBE.

Tent, James F. 1982. *Mission on the Rhine: Reeducation and Denazification in American-Occupied Germany*. Chicago: University of Chicago Press.

Thomson, Susan. 2009. "'That Is Not What We Authorised You to Do ...': Access and Government Interference in Highly Politicised Research Environments" in *Surviving Field Research: Working in Violent and Difficult Situations*, eds. Chandra Lekha Sriram, John C. King, Julie A. Mertus, Olga Martin-Ortega, and Johanna Herman (pp. 108–123). London: Routledge.

Thyne, Clayton L. 2006. "ABC's, 123's, and the Golden Rule: The Pacifying Effect of Education on Civil War, 1980–1999." *International Studies Quarterly*, 50(4): 733–754.

Tiemessen, Alana. 2004. "After Arusha: Gacaca Justice in Post-Genocide Rwanda." *African Studies Quarterly*, 8(1): 57–76.

Tomlinson, Kathryn, and Pauline Benefield. 2005. *Education and Conflict: Research and Research Possibilities*. Berkshire: National Foundation for Educational Research.

Torney-Purta, Judith, Rainer Lehmann, Hans Oswald, and Wolfram Schulz. 2001. *Citizenship and Education in Twenty-Eight Countries: Civic Knowledge and Engagement at Age Fourteen*. Amsterdam: International Association for the Evaluation of Educational Achievement.

Torney-Purta, Judith, John Schwille, and Jo-Ann Amadeo. 1999. "Mapping the Distinctive and Common Features of Civic Education in Twenty-Four Countries" in *Civic Education across Countries: Twenty-Four National Case Studies from the IEA Civic Education Project*, eds. Judith Torney-Purta, John Schwille and Jo-Ann Amadeo (pp. 11–35). Amsterdam: International Association for the Evaluation of Educational Achievement.

Torsti, Pilvi, and Sirkka Ahonen. 2009. "Deliberative History Classes for a Post-Conflict Society: Theoretical Development and Practical Implication through International Education in United World College in Bosnia and Herzegovina" in *Peace Education in Conflict and Post-Conflict Societies: Comparative Perspectives*, eds. Claire McGlynn, Michalinos Zembylas, Zvi Bekerman, and Tony Gallgher (pp. 215–229). New York City: Palgrave Macmillan.

Turner, John C. 1975. "Social Comparison and Social Identity: Some Prospects for Intergroup Behaviour." *European Journal of Social Psychology*, 5(1): 5–34.

1999. "Some Current Issues in Research on Social Identity and Self-Categorization Theories" in *Social Identity*, eds. Naomi Ellemers, Russell Spears, and Bertjan Doosje (pp. 6–34). Oxford: Blackwell Publishers.

Ukiwo, Ukoha. 2007. "Education, Horizontal Inequalities and Ethnic Relations in Nigeria." *International Journal of Educational Development*, 27(3): 266–281.

Umutesi, Marie Béatrice. 2004. *Surviving the Slaughter: The Ordeal of a Rwandan Refugee in Zaire*. Madison: University of Wisconsin Press.

United States Agency for International Development (USAID). *Request for Proposals M/Op-03-Edu2 Revitalization of Iraqi Schools and Stabilization Education (Rise)*. Available at: http://www.usaid.gov/iraq/pdf/web_education.pdf.

United Nations Development Programme (UNDP). 1997. *Human Development Index 1997*. New York: United Nations Development Programme.

2007a. *Millennium Development Goals: 2007 Progress Chart*.

2007b. *Turning Vision 2020 into Reality: Addendum – Corrigendum*. Kigali: United Nations Development Programme.

2007c. *Turning Vision 2020 into Reality: From Recovery to Sustainable Human Development*. Kigali: United Nations Development Programme.

2011. "HDI Rankings." In *Human Development Report 2011*. New York: United Nations Development Programme.

United Nations Educational Scientific and Cultural Organization (UNESCO). 1990. *Jomtien Declaration: World Declaration on Education for All*. Jomtien: UNESCO.

2000. *Dakar Framework for Action*. Dakar: World Education Forum.

2003a. "Curriculum Change and Social Cohesion in Conflict-Affected Societies." In *Colloquium Report*. Geneva: IBE.

2003b. "Textbooks and Learning Materials Respecting Diversity: Components of Quality Education That Can Foster Peace, Human Rights, Mutual Understanding and Dialogue. An Overview of UNESCO's Role in the Revision and Review of Textbooks and Learning Materials." Paris: UNESCO.

2009. *Factsheet: Sub-Saharan Africa – Education for All Global Monitoring Report*. Paris: UNESCO.

2010a. *Education Profile – Rwanda*. Paris: UNESCO.

2010b. *Protecting Education from Attack*. Paris: UNESCO.

United Nations General Assembly. 2011. *Children and Armed Conflict, Report of the Secretary-General*. New York: United Nations.

United Nations High Commissioner for Refugees (UNHCR). 2010. *Democratic Republic of the Congo, 1993–2003*. New York: United Nations.

United Nations International Children's Emergency Fund (UNICEF). 2009. *The State of the World's Children*. New York: United Nations Childrens' Fund.

United Nations Security Council. 2012. *Letter dated 26 June 2012 from the Chair of the Security Council Committee established pursuant to resolution 1533 (2004) concerning the Democratic Republic of the Congo addressed to the President of the Security Council*. New York: United Nations.

Uvin, Peter. 1996. *Development, Aid and Conflict: Reflections from the Case of Rwanda*. Helsinki: UNU World Institute for Development Economics Research (UNU/WIDER).

1998. *Aiding Violence: The Development Enterprise in Rwanda*. Bloomfield, CT: Kumarian Press.

Van Evera, Stephen. 1994. "Hypotheses on Nationalism and War." *International Security*, 18(4) : 5–39.

Van Hove, J. 1953. "L'Oeuvre d'Éducation au Congo Belge et au Ruanda-Urundi" in *Encyclopédie du Congo Belge* (pp. 749–789). Brussels: Editions Bieleveld.

Vansina, Jan. 1962. *L'Évolution du Royaume Rwanda des Origines à 1900*. Brussels: Académie des Sciences d'Outre-Mer.

2004. *Antecedents to Modern Rwanda: The Nyiginya Kingdom*. Madison: University of Wisconsin Press.

Vidal, Claudine. 2001. "Les Commémorations du Génocide au Rwanda." *Les Temps Modernes*, 613: 1–46.

Vinck, Honoré. 1995. "The Influence of Colonial Ideology on Schoolbooks in the Belgian Congo." *Paedagogica Historica*, 23(2): 355–406.

Volkan, Vamik. 1997. *Blood Lines: From Ethnic Pride to Ethnic Terrorism*. Boulder, CO: Westview Press.

Wallach, John. 2000. *The Enemy Has a Face: The Seeds of Peace Experience*. Washington, DC: United States Institute of Peace Press.

Wegner, Gregory. 2002. *Anti-Semitism and Schooling under the Third Reich*. New York: RoutledgeFalmer.

Weiner, Myron. 1983. "The Political Consequences of Preferential Policies: A Comparative Perspective." *Comparative Politics*, 16(1): 35–52.

Weinstein, Harvey M. 2011." The Myth of Closure, the Illusion of Reconciliation: Final Thoughts on Five Years as Co-Editor-in-Chief." *International Journal of Transitional Justice*, 5(1): 1–10.

Weinstein, Harvey M., Sarah Warshauer Freedman, and Holly Hughson. 2007. "School Voices: Challenges Facing Education Systems after Identity-Based Conflicts." *Education, Citizenship and Social Justice*, 2(1): 41–71.

Weisskopf, Thomas E. 2004. *Affirmative Action in the United States and India: A Comparative Perspective*. London: Routledge.

Wigny, P. 1941. *Rapport Annuel du Ruanda-Urundi, 1940*. Brussels: Établissements Généraux d'Imprimérie.

Williams, James. 2004. "Civil Conflict, Education, and the Work of Schools: Twelve Propositions." *Conflict Resolution Quarterly*, 21(4): 471–481.

Williams, Sue, and Paul McGill. 2004. "Education: Part of the Problem, Essential for the Solution." *The New Courier (UNESCO)*, Special Issue: 26–28.

Wimmer, Andreas, Lars-Erik Cederman, and Brian Min. 2009. "Ethnic Politics and Armed Conflict: A Configurational Analysis of a New Global Data Set." *American Sociological Review*, 74(2): 316–337.

Windel, Aaron. 2009. "British Colonial Education in Africa: Policy and Practice in the Era of Trusteeship." *History Compass*, 7(1): 1–21.

Winthrop, Rebecca. 2010. *Punching Below Its Weight: The U.S. Government Approach to Education in the Developing World*. Washington, DC: Center for Universal Education at Brookings.

World Bank. 2005. *Reshaping the Future: Education and Post-Conflict Reconstruction*. Washington, DC: The World Bank.

Wurmser, Meyrav. 2003. "Reading, Writing and De-Baathification." *The Weekly Standard*, 8(34): 15–17.

Zasloff, Barbara, Adina Shapiro, and A. Heather Coyne. 2009. *An Education Track for the Israeli-Palestinian Peace Process*. Washington, DC: United States Institute of Peace Press.

Ziemer, Gregor Athalwin. 1972. *Education for Death, the Making of the Nazi*. New York: Octagon Books.

Zorbas, Eugenia. 2009. "What Does Reconciliation after Genocide Mean? Public Transcripts and Hidden Transcripts in Post-Genocide Rwanda." *Journal of Genocide Research*, 11(1): 127–147.

Index

2I2 *Index*